MIND ASSOCIATION OCC

This series is to consist of occasional volumes of original papers on predefined themes. The Mind Association will nominate an editor or editors for each collection, and may co-operate with other bodies in promoting conferences or other scholarly activities in connection with the preparation of particular volumes.

PUBLICATIONS COMMITTEE

J. D. Kenyon
M. A. Stewart
G. G. L. Stock

Perspectives on THOMAS HOBBES

Perspectives on THOMAS HOBBES

Edited by
G. A. J. Rogers and Alan Ryan

CLARENDON PRESS · OXFORD

Oxford University Press, Walton Street, Oxford OX2 6DP
Oxford New York Toronto
Delhi Bombay Calcutta Madras Karachi
Petaling Jaya Singapore Hong Kong Tokyo
Nairobi Dar es Salaam Cape Town
Melbourne Auckland
and associated companies in
Berlin Ibadan

Oxford is a trade mark of Oxford University Press

Published in the United States
by Oxford University Press, New York

First published 1988
First issued in paperback 1990

British Library Cataloguing in Publication Data
Perspectives on Thomas Hobbes.—(Mind Association occasional series)
1. English philosophy. Hobbes, Thomas, 1588–1679
I. Rogers, G.A.J. II. Ryan, Alan, 1940–
192
ISBN 0–19–823914–9

Library of Congress Cataloging in Publication Data
Perspectives on Thomas Hobbes/edited by G.A.J. Rogers and Alan Ryan.
p. cm.—(Mind Association occasional series)
A collection to mark the fourth centenary of Thomas Hobbes published in association with a fourth-centenary Hobbes conference arranged by the British Society for the History of Philosophy.
Includes index.
1. Hobbes, Thomas, 1588–1679.—I. Rogers, G.A.J. (Graham Alan John), 1938– . II. Ryan, Alan. III. Series.
B1247.P42 1988 192–dc19 88–23466
ISBN 0–19–823914–9

Phototypeset by Cotswold Typesetting Ltd., Gloucester
Printed and bound in
Great Britain by Courier International Ltd,
Tiptree, Essex

PREFACE

The collection published here brings together papers by scholars of several lands to mark the fourth centenary of the birth of Thomas Hobbes. It is published as the first volume in an occasional series sponsored by the Mind Association and in association with a fourth-centenary Hobbes conference arranged by the British Society for the History of Philosophy. It thus happily links the oldest and the newest of the national philosophy societies in the United Kingdom, something of which we can be sure Hobbes himself would have approved.

Although several of the papers included will have been given at the Hobbes conference, the volume is in no sense a conference proceedings. The editors particularly had in mind both to include only papers of high quality and also that the collection should appear in the centenary year, with a consequentially early deadline.

We have standardized references as far as it was both possible and desirable given the lack of critical editions of many of Hobbes's works, particularly *Leviathan* (something which the OUP is currently rectifying) and the method of reference used by some of the contributors. With regard to *Leviathan*, whilst no critical edition has been adopted most of the contributors have used that of C. B. Macpherson, Penguin Books, Harmondsworth, 1968, which very usefully includes the page numbers of the original 1651 edition in the text.

Our thanks are due not only to the contributors themselves, but to the Mind Association and the Oxford University Press for entering into this innovative and, we believe, fruitful arrangement for publication. We would in particular wish to thank Dr M. A. Stewart and Mrs Angela Blackburn for their very helpful advice at all stages of the production, and to Mrs Jo-Ann Rogers for preparing the Index.

G.A.J.R.
A.R.

Keele and Princeton
February 1988

CONTENTS

LIST OF CONTRIBUTORS

DAVID GAUTHIER is Distinguished Service Professor of Philosophy, University of Pittsburgh.

NOEL MALCOLM is Political Correspondent of *The Spectator*.

ARRIGO PACCHI was, until his tragically early death in 1989, Professor of Philosophy, University of Milan.

D. D. RAPHAEL is Emeritus Professor of Philosophy, Imperial College, University of London.

G. A. J. ROGERS is Reader and Head of the Department of Philosophy, University of Keele.

ALAN RYAN is Professor of Politics, Princeton University.

TOM SORELL is a Lecturer in Philosophy, the Open University.

FRANÇOIS TRICAUD is Professor of Philosophy, Université Jean Moulin Lyon III.

RICHARD TUCK is a Fellow of Jesus College, Cambridge.

ABBREVIATIONS

AntiWhite	Thomas Hobbes *Critique du 'De Mundo' de Thomas White,* Édition critique d'un texte inédit par Jean Jacquot et Harold Whitmore Jones (Paris, 1973) (the Latin text). English translation by Harold Whitmore Jones: *Thomas White's 'De-Mundo' Examined* (London, 1976)
BL	British Library
De Cive EV	*De Cive: The English Version.* A critical edition, by Howard Warrender (Oxford, 1983)
De Cive LV	*De Cive: The Latin Version.* A critical edition, by Howard Warrender (Oxford, 1983)
Elements	*The Elements of Law Natural and Political,* edited with a Preface and Critical Notes by Ferdinand Tönnies (London, 1889). Another edition, with different pagination was issued in Cambridge, 1928
EW	*The English Works of Thomas Hobbes* edited by Sir William Molesworth, 11 vols. (London, 1839–45)
LW	*Thomas Hobbes Malmesburiensis: Opera Philosophica quae Latine Scripsit,* collecta studio et labore Gulielmi Molesworth, 5 vols. (London, 1839–45)

Introduction

G. A. J. ROGERS

I

That a volume should be published to mark the fourth centenary of the birth of Thomas Hobbes needs no excuse. He remains perennially in the highest ranks of political theorists and a philosopher of great ability and considerable originality who coloured the thought of his and subsequent ages in a way uniquely his own. The essays published here testify to his continuing fascination for us today and to the relevance of his ideas to the late twentieth century.

Hobbes's birth is well known from his own account. He wrote of it in Latin verse in his brief autobiography. In less rewarding English prose, it has been rendered thus:

> Our Saviour, the man-God, had been born one thousand, five hundred, and eighty-eight years, and the famous enemy fleet, the Armada, soon destined to perish in our sea, was standing at anchor in the Spanish ports, and the fifth day of April was beginning, when, in the early spring, the little worm that is myself was born at Malmesbury. From my father, who was minister, I received baptism, and the name he gave me was his own.[1]

Later in the same poem he tells us famously that 'Fear and I were born twins! My mother, hearing that the Armada was bringing the day of doom to our race, gave birth to fear and myself together.'[2] Although the Armada was not to set sail for two months the words give us a little vignette of the impact the

[1] Hobbes wrote the autobiography when he was eighty-four. It was first published in 1681 in *Tracts of Thomas Hobb's*, published by W. Crooke. The translation published here is that of Benjamin Farrington as it appeared in the *Rationalist Annual*, 60 (1957), 22–31. It is of the first eight lines, to be found on p. 23.

[2] Modified from Farrington's translation, as above, pp. 23–24.

threat of the likely invasion was having on a small market town. Whether Hobbes was indeed of a markedly more fearful disposition than average is problematic. But there can be little doubt that when he wrote these lines in his eighty-fourth year he had a mind to reinforce a central claim in his political philosophy about human motivation.

Hobbes is one of the few English philosophers, and perhaps the only one of note, who has constructed what can be seen as a grand philosophical system. It is no doubt partly because of this that a high proportion of the best writing on him is by those educated in traditions of systematic philosophy more often associated with the continent of Europe than with Britain. Consequently it has been both easy and pleasurable to include in this volume examples of work on Hobbes by non-native English-speaking scholars.

Ever since Mersenne and Gassendi judged so well of him in the 1640s he has enjoyed a reputation throughout Europe to rank little below such other acknowledged English thinkers as Locke and Newton. Sorbière reports that when Gassendi was presented with a copy of *De Corpore Politico* he first kissed it and said, 'This treatise is indeed small in bulk, but in my judgement is the very marrow of science.'[3] It is not only his political thought which has received acknowledgement. He has, for example, been seen as the advocate of empiricism in a form more pure than that of either Bacon or Locke.[4] And Descartes himself, who, if we accept the argument in Richard Tuck's contribution to this volume, had a decisive intellectual impact on Hobbes, was prepared to admit some merit in his opponent's works, that he was at least 'a much greater master of Morality than of Metaphysics or Natural Philosophy . . .'.[5] If Hobbes's reputation in continental Europe remains high, the same may also be said of his contemporary standing in the English-speaking world. *Leviathan*, though it was not always so, is now regarded as a classic text and is on the syllabus of every major university.

[3] The story is reported in the Hobbes article in *Biographia Britannica* (London, 1758), 2599–622. The story can be found on p. 2605.

[4] Cf. Charles de Remusat, *Histoire de la Philosophie en Angleterre depuis Bacon jusqu'à Locke* (Paris, 1875), i. 325.

[5] On the basis of reading *De Cive*. Lettre au Pere? 1643? Descartes, *Correspondance, publiée avec une introduction et des notes par Charles-Adam et Gérard Milhaud* (Paris, 1956), vi. 88.

Hobbes, of course, has always been controversial. His personal search for peace was ever mixed with a willingness to engage in contention, and he did not always choose the right ground on which to fight.[6] Indeed much of the best philosophy produced in England in the second half of the seventeenth century, as well as much of the worst, may be seen as a critical response to Hobbes and to Hobbist ideas detected in others. In this regard he bears comparison with the enormous impact of Descartes in the same period.[7] It was not, however, easy to acknowledge debts to Hobbes, and much safer to attack him. To claim the 'Monster of Malmesbury' as an ally was to court danger. The unattractive Daniel Scargill, Fellow of Corpus Christi College, Cambridge, who had offered to defend positions extracted from *Leviathan*, was, in 1669 removed from the university, in part for his Hobbist beliefs.[8] In 1683 Oxford ordered the public burning of *Leviathan* and *De Cive*. Such responses had no doubt been encouraged by the decision of Parliament in 1666 to investigate both books. And all had been provoked by what was seen as a rising tide of Hobbists and atheists, a tide which, as Quentin Skinner has shown, had some basis in fact.[9] The hostility to all things Hobbist arose at a time when the name of Hobbes had been invoked to justify a style of life quite at odds with the public position of the university and the church, and quite different, too, from that lived by Hobbes himself. Well before the great man's death, to be a Hobbist was identified with atheism, loose-living, and self-centredness. It is

[6] Hobbes by his own admission would often argue for the sake of it. His most notable quarrel was the protracted and unnecessary dispute with Wallis of which Aubrey's comment that 'surely their Mercuries are in opposition' seems very apt. (Cf. *Brief Lives* (Harmondsworth, 1962), Hobbes article.)

[7] For some account of this in England see G. A. J. Rogers, 'Descartes and the English', in *The Light Nature: Essays in the History and Philosophy of Science presented to A. C. Crombie*, ed. J. D. North and J. J. Roche (Dordrecht, Boston, and Lancaster, 1985), 281–302.

[8] For an account of the event and its context see James L. Axtell, 'The Mechanics of Opposition: Restoration Cambridge v. Daniel Scargill', *Bulletin of the Institute of Historical Research*, 38 (1965), 102–11. Some accounts of this event appear to be given in order to display the university in a bad light, but Scargill was himself clearly of a very dubious character, and the charge of Hobbism was only one aspect of the issue. For a version which might be accused of the above see *Biographia Britannica*, ed. cit., p. 2611.

[9] Cf. Quentin Skinner, 'The Context of Hobbes's Theory of Political Obligation', in *Hobbes and Rousseau: A Collection of Critical Essays*, Maurice Cranston and Richard S. Peters (New York, 1972), 109–42.

hardly surprising that by the 1670s few would want to be so identified.

If there were few open Hobbists by the end of Hobbes's life, neither is there evidence of a secret school. Despite the fact that his influence on political thought is undoubtedly enormous, and that his materialist philosophy is perhaps as cogent a statement as that philosophy was to receive, few remained convinced of its ultimate acceptability. Indeed the run of British philosophy from the Cambridge Platonists, Locke, Berkeley, through to Hume, was marked by general rejection of, if not strong hostility to, any purely materialist ontology.

Yet the extent and depth of Hobbes's impact was always far greater than that measured by the number of conversions. The fact of the matter is that in a variety of ways Hobbes impinged on almost all aspects of philosophical thought to the extent that many topics would never be considered in quite the same way again. He had, first of all, offered a picture of the world with a single-substance ontology. Everything was either body or it was nothing. Or, as he himself expressed it, '. . . every part of the Universe, is Body, and that which is not Body, is no part of the Universe: And because the Universe is All, that which is no part of it is *Nothing*; and consequently *no where* . . .'.[10] The atheistical tendencies in such an ontology were quickly recognized, but, of course, denied by Hobbes as he took shelter behind an agnosticism about the nature of God which he chose to describe as 'Incomprehensible'.

It would, however, be unwise on this, or indeed on any basis, to follow too quickly Hobbes's seventeenth-century accusers with the charge of atheism. As Professor Pacchi well shows in his contribution, it is much easier to accuse Hobbes than to show that the charge is justified, and there is much argument on the other side. Whatever the final truth about his religious views, Hobbes's theory of the universe required from him a plausible account of the mental, the fact of human consciousness, compatible with his materialist ontology. If his account does not always carry conviction, we must remember that it is a task which modern materialist philosophers have also found difficult to accomplish, despite being able to build on a physics more

[10] *Leviathan*, 4. 46; in the Penguin ed. edited by C. B. Macpherson (Harmondsworth, 1968), p. 689.

sophisticated than the mechanistic system created in the seventeenth century. That earlier view had been constructed above all by Galileo, Descartes, Hobbes, and Gassendi.

Of these great figures of the seventeenth century, though, it was Hobbes alone who offered a one-substance theory. He linked it with a powerful model of human beings which not only was compatible with his version of materialism, but actually flowed from it since 'the cause of all things must be sought in the varieties and modes of motion'[11] of the bodies which make up the universe.

We should perhaps also note, at least in passing, that in Hobbes's scheme of things there was little room for the forces of magic and necromancy which had until this time played such a large part in the life and thought of the seventeenth century, and it may well be that Hobbes's alternative conception of things contributed some small part to their decline, as was evidently believed by John Sheffield, Duke of Buckingham, who in a poem on Hobbes and his writings wrote:

> While in dark Ignorance we lay afraid,
> Of Fancies, Ghosts, and ev'ry empty Shade;
> Great HOBBES appear'd, and by plain Reason's Light,
> Put such fantastic Forms to shameful Flight.[12]

Certainly the works of Hobbes contain a view of the world in which much of the trappings, if perhaps not the core, of what has traditionally been thought of as the religious conception of the world play no part.

As we have already noticed, Hobbes's reputation as a political theorist is now so well established it needs no words to support it. It was not always so clearly so, despite the fact that Hobbist elements, and especially Hobbist theories of obligation, can be detected in many tracts of the mid-century.[13] Some of the earlier doubts and hostility can no doubt be attributed to the novelty of

[11] From Hobbes's prose biography, quoted in the Introduction by Richard S. Peters to the collection of Hobbes's writings, *Body, Man, and Citizen* (London and New York, 1962), 7.

[12] The poem is given in full in *The Moral and Political Works of Thomas Hobbes of Malmesbury* (London, 1750, two vols.), i. vii–viii. Whether or not Buckingham followed Hobbes's materialism, we can suppose from his writings and behaviour sympathy for Hobbes's political analysis.

[13] Skinner, op. cit.

his ideas. They were so new and startling that many would not, or could not, allow full weight to his argument. Neither his premisses about human nature nor his conclusions about the power of sovereigns were acceptable, not to mention his account of the place of religion in society, and much else besides. As Samual Mintz has aptly remarked, 'The first task of a seventeenth-century divine would be to destroy *Leviathan*; the second might be to understand it.'[14] Although such sentiments are not wholly dead they are rightly much in decline. But the merit of Hobbes's argument has until quite recently too often been run together with the issue of his atheism. It is, however, doubtful that the secularization of society, and a playing down of the issue of Hobbes's supposed atheism, will in itself guarantee a lack of controversy in the interpretation of his thought. But it seems very unlikely that he would have minded that. Certainly, for all the interest in his other writings, his political philosophy remains his crowning glory. His uncompromising account of man and society remains not only a classic presentation of one view of the human condition, but his method of analysis and the synthesis that he accomplished is such that his own high estimate of his achievement, that it was he alone who founded civil philosophy as a science, looks as true today as it did to him in 1655.[15]

There is, however, one aspect of Hobbes on which there has always been agreement. He was a master of English prose. Indeed, for many it was just in the power of his language that the main threat lay. As Pepys testifies, everybody wanted to read *Leviathan*,[16] and even those who disliked the argument were ready to admit the merit of his style. Today his readers may still enjoy the latter, and find much merit in his argument beside. As John Stuart Mill remarked, over a century ago, Hobbes is indeed 'a great name in philosophy, on account both of the

[14] Samuel Mintz, *The Hunting of Leviathan* (Cambridge, 1962), 45.

[15] Cf. Hobbes, the Epistle Dedicatory to *The Elements of Philosophy: The First Section Concerning Body*, *EW* i. ix.

[16] '. . . and so to the Exchequer and several places, calling on several businesses, and particularly my bookseller's, among others, for Hobbs's *Leviathan*, which is now mightily called for; and what was heretofore sold for 8*s*. I now give 24*s*. at the second hand, and is sold for 30*s*., it being a book the Bishops will not let be printed again.' Entry for 3 Sept. 1668, *The Diary of Samuel Pepys*, ed. Robert Latham and William Matthews (London, 1976), ix. 298.

value of what he taught and the extraordinary impulse which he communicated to the spirit of free inquiry in Europe'.[17]

II

The papers in this collection represent current thought on a variety of topics which relate to Hobbes and his philosophy as seen from Europe and North America. All of them are published here for the first time, though a shorter version of one of them has appeared elsewhere. The first two illuminate important aspects of his intellectual development and his biography. There follow five papers on aspects of Hobbes's political thought, one on the nature of his religious commitments, and, finally, one on Hobbes's likely influence. The remainder of this Introduction provides some introductory remarks about each of these papers.

The relationship between Hobbes and Descartes has for some time raised problems for historians. Richard Tuck produces new answers to some of these, arguing that Hobbes's debts to Descartes are different and more substantial than is generally supposed. Hobbes's philosophy, he suggests, seems to have 'been developed as the next move in a game where Descartes was the previous player' (p. 28). As part of his case Tuck attributes the Short Tract not to Hobbes but to Payne, and he argues for a new dating of several of Hobbes's most important writings. Within the new framework so created he then offers an account of the place of Hobbes's materialist theory of perception within his thought, a theory which includes as a central tenet an early expression of the famous distinction between the primary and secondary qualities of objects. On Tuck's reading, Hobbes's account emerges as one important answer to the scepticism generated about perception by Descartes's hyperbolical doubt.

Why was Hobbes never elected to the Royal Society? This is the question Noel Malcolm addresses in the second paper. It is one that has in the past received a variety of replies. One argued in 1969 by Quentin Skinner, in contrast to earlier more ideologically based answers, was that Hobbes was strongly disliked by some of the founding Fellows. Malcolm agrees with

[17] 'Fragment on Mackintosh', p. 19, as quoted in *Cyclopaedia of Biography*, conducted by Charles Knight, in 6 vols. (London, 1858), iii. 441.

much of Skinner's paper but believes it leaves certain aspects of the wider issues open. Malcolm sees his explanation as falling somewhere between the 'old-fashioned, straightforward explanation in terms of Hobbes's unacceptable heterodoxy' and 'the new-fashioned sociology of knowledge propounded by Schaffer and Shapin' (p. 46). His answer includes the novel suggestion that some members of the Royal Society were keen to exclude Hobbes not because they opposed his (notorious) views but rather because they were too close to their own, something they were keen to play down.

The Royal Society is of course concerned with science, and Hobbes claimed, as we have seen, to be the founder of the science of politics. What exactly we are to understand by that claim, and how it relates to Hobbes as a supposed methodological individualist is the subject of Tom Sorell's paper. He suggests that we should not read Hobbes as deriving his politics from his physics and a mechanistic psychology, but rather that the politics stands on premisses which have an independent and more direct validation in our experience. Sorell also casts doubt on a favourite view of Hobbes, that his method was one of resolution and composition.

The issue of Hobbes's individualism is also addressed by Alan Ryan. He is strongly aware of the complexity of Hobbes's position and the different levels, epistemic, moral, and political, at which varieties of individualism arise. Thus, although there is no logical entailment between mechanical materialism and epistemological individualism, there is nevertheless a link through the belief that men are self-regulating automata. Ryan's analysis leads on to an exploration of an aspect of the vexed Hobbist issue of obligation, in particular the apparent conflict between Hobbes's claim that we are under an unconditional obligation to obey the law of nature and his insistence that only voluntary contracts are binding. Ryan suggests, as a solution to this tension, that the basis of our obligation to the law of nature lies in the special relationship between God and humans, namely that he is the author of our being. This contrasts with our relationship with an earthly sovereign, to whom we have voluntarily given our assent, and from whom we always retain the right to withdraw our commitment. Ryan also examines the connected issue of the implications which Hobbes's moral and epistemological individualism have for the economic basis of society. He argues that Hobbes's analysis, in contrast with the varying interpretations of Macpherson, Strauss, Arendt, and Wolin, implies no particular economic system nor a particular kind of role for the citizen. In that sense, Hobbes was a pluralist.

Did Hobbes have a fixed conception of the state of nature? Or was it a changing one, reflecting his own dissatisfaction with all his attempts to characterize it? François Tricaud, through an examination of the different wordings in the three classic formulations, detects important shifts in Hobbes's understanding of it, and problems which these varying positions generate both for Hobbes's theory and for our understanding of him. He throws light on whether we should treat Hobbes's account as one intended to be historically accurate or merely offered as an explanatory model. He also considers the idea of *war* in Hobbes's varying accounts, the conditions which give rise to it, and the meaning and role of *rights* in such a state. His examination of these matters leads him, surely correctly, to urge caution before assuming too easily that there is any simple logical key to the complexity of Hobbes's thought.

What exactly is the role played by the idea of a social contract in Hobbes's civil philosophy? If the matter was ever thought settled, Jean Hampton's recent book, *Hobbes and the Social Contract Tradition* (Cambridge University Press, 1986), has reopened the issue. Her argument is that Hobbes appeals not to a contract but to a self-interested agreement or convention. This interpretation has major implications for the nature of Hobbes's account of sovereignty, and it is to the Hampton thesis that David Gauthier's paper addresses itself. He defends 'the traditional account of a true contract in which the subjects alienate their rights to a ruler' (p. 125). In the course of his argument he does, however, depart from the position which he defended in *The Logic of Leviathan* (Oxford at the Clarendon Press, 1969). For now Gauthier argues that 'an alienation social contract theory is not . . . incompatible with limited sovereignty' (p. 151). The issues raised here are clearly central to Hobbes's whole position.

Hobbes prided himself on being a just man, and justice is an important concept in his political philosophy. But what exactly

Hobbes meant by justice remains a matter of dispute. For example, does he, as has been argued, have both a wider and a narrower conception of it? David Raphael argues not. But he does show that although conceived narrowly in terms of covenants made, Hobbes's concept of justice has wide scope, central to his ethical and political system, which in turn has important implications for his account of obligation. It is also closely connected with the role of the social contract in his theory (cf. Gauthier's paper), and this in its turn is connected with the fact that although physical power is necessary for a ruler to rule it is not enough (cf. p. 163). For any ruler to be effective he must command the *willing* obedience of his subjects most of the time. Raphael goes on to examine the connections between Hobbes's understanding of justice and such traditional distinctions as those of commutative and distributive justice, as well as its connections with punishment.

As we have seen, Hobbes has often been accused of atheism. But in recent years he has been defended against that charge in various ways. Professor Pacchi offers new and important insights into this issue in his paper 'Hobbes and the Problem of God'. He argues that a central text for reaching a proper understanding of Hobbes's position is his book-length manuscript, only published in 1973, *Thomas White's 'De Mundo' Examined*. Through a study of this text and other Hobbes writings Pacchi produces a very strong case indeed for regarding Hobbes not only as a theist, but as one whose argument for the material nature of the world, and whose account of liberty and necessity, both rest on that theism.

Our final paper brings us back to the issue touched on earlier in this introduction, the matter of Hobbes's influence on his contemporaries. I argue that the overt hostility almost universally expressed towards Hobbes in the second half of the seventeenth century masks the real impact that he had on his readers, who were reluctant to acknowledge any positive influence because each feared the accusation of being a Hobbist. It is, nevertheless, possible to chart such likely influence, and I suggest as two examples the Cambridge Platonist, Henry More, and the leading English philosopher of the later seventeenth century, John Locke.

I
Hobbes and Descartes

RICHARD TUCK

If Hobbes had died (as he almost did) in the summer of 1647, at the unremarkable age of 59, he would have left a curious intellectual legacy.[1] Apart from his early translation of Thucydides, he had published only one book, *De Cive* (April 1642, with a second, much more widely distributed edition in January 1647). In addition, in 1641 his objections to Descartes's *Meditations of First Philosophy* had been included anonymously with the other five sets collected by Descartes, and by Descartes's and Hobbes's mutual friend Marin Mersenne. Finally, a short essay on optics had appeared under his name in a collection edited by Mersenne (*Universae geometriae, mixtaque, synopsis*, 1644), and Mersenne's *Ballistica* of the same year had included a summary by Mersenne of Hobbes's general philosophy.[2] This was the sum total of what was publicly available of Hobbes's ideas.

And yet great things had been expected of Hobbes for many years by his friends; Mersenne tirelessly praised his work in correspondence with philosophers throughout Europe, while Sir Charles Cavendish (the brother of one of Hobbes's English patrons) also constantly urged him to write and publish. Their expectations were matched by those of Hobbes himself: in the preface to *De Cive* he claimed that he had been working for some years on a complete *summa* of the 'Elements of Philosopy', of which *De Cive* was merely the third section. The work indeed appeared under the title *Elementorum Philosophiae Sectio Tertia De Cive* (though the 1647 edition shortened this to *Elementa*

[1] For the details of his illness, see his letter to Sorbière, in Ferdinand Tönnies, 'Siebzehn Briefe des Thomas Hobbes an Samuel Sorbière', *Archiv für Geschichte der Philosophie*, 3 (1889–90), 207.

[2] Texts of these latter works can be found in *LW* v. 217–48 and 309–18.

Philosophica de Cive). During the last hundred years students of Hobbes's works have gradually come to see why he enjoyed such a reputation, for a remarkable series of manuscript treatises have come to light, most of which had circulated quite widely among his acquaintances. Molesworth in 1845 already knew about a Harleian manuscript on optics (in English) dating from 1645/6.[3] The next manuscript to be discovered (and in many ways the most impressive) was *The Elements of Law*, completed in 1640, which Tönnies printed in 1889. Tönnies also found a couple of manuscripts among Cavendish's papers in the Harleian collection of the British Museum which he printed at the same time; one was anonymous, but was attributed by Tönnies to Hobbes, and called by him 'A Short Tract on First Principles', while he gave to the other the title 'Tractatus Opticus'. (He printed only extracts from the 'Tractatus'.) Tönnies thought 'A Short Tract' was very early—probably *c.*1630—and he conjectured that the 'Tractatus' was written 1637–40, though most later writers have disagreed about this.[4]

During the twentieth century there have been further discoveries. In 1934 Cay von Brockdorff partially published a manuscript at Chatsworth which was clearly an early draft of *De Corpore*;[5] in 1943 Mario Rossi published notes by Lord Herbert of Cherbury on another early draft,[6] and in 1952 Jean Jacquot discovered some notes by Cavendish on yet another early version.[7] Finally, the most unexpected discovery of all occurred in the Bibliothèque Nationale the same year, when Cornelis de Waard noticed that an apparently anonymous manuscript critique of a cosmological work by Thomas White had 'Hobs' on the spine, and was clearly by Hobbes. This turned out to be a

[3] *EW* vii. 467–71. The MS is dated 1646, but was drafted in 1645. See the letter from Cavendish to Pell, in Mersenne, *Correspondance* (Paris, 1932–), xiii. 523, and also from Hobbes to Sorbière, Tönnies, op. cit. 69.

[4] Tönnies (ed.), *The Elements of Law* (London, 1889), xii–xiii, 193–226.

[5] 'Die Urform der "Computatio sive Logica" des Hobbes', *Veröffentlichungen des Hobbes Gesellschaft* (Kiel, 1934). The complete MS is printed in the Jean Jacquot and Harold Whitmore Jones edn., Hobbes, *Critique du 'De Mundo' de Thomas White* (Paris, 1973), 461–513.

[6] *Alle fonti del deismo e del materialismo moderno* (Florence, 1943), 104–19; cf. also Richard Aaron, 'A possible early draft of Hobbes's *De Corpore*', *Mind*, 54 (1945), 342–56, and Jacquot and Jones, ed. cit. 448–60.

[7] 'Un document inédit: les notes de Charles Cavendish sur la première version du *De corpore* de Hobbes', *Thales*, 8 (1952), 33–86 (only a partial publication; the full text is to be found in Jacquot and Jones, ed. cit. 461–513.

manuscript which Frithiof Brandt in 1928 had conjectured must have existed, and which had been composed largely between September 1642 and March 1643; it comprised 459 manuscript pages, and was therefore the most substantial unprinted Hobbesian work yet discovered.[8]

The printed works of Hobbes in 1647 were, therefore, only a small proportion of his total *œuvre*, and the non-political portions of his philosophy were particularly under-represented. Such a state of affairs, it should be said, was not uncommon for Renaissance scholars (nor, indeed, for those of a much later period): Descartes, too, wrote extensive manuscript treatises (one of which teetered on the edge of publication) long before anything of his appeared in print, while Pierre Gassendi drafted and redrafted his great commentary on Epicurus for two decades. Hugo Grotius displayed a similar pattern in his intellectual activity, with some of his major early works remaining in manuscript until the nineteenth century; one was discovered only two years ago.[9] There are some exceptions to this: John Selden, for example, seems quickly to have put into print almost everything that he wrote from the very beginning of his scholarly career. But the general discrepancy between what was written and what was printed was a state of affairs which was peculiarly liable to produce exaggerated claims about plagiarism and priority, and which tended to put an author's autobiographical assertions into the front line of philosophical debate. Almost all Hobbes's printed works carry prefaces locating the work in question in the circumstances of his life, while Descartes in 1637 put as the introduction to a set of three essays on philosophical subjects a 'discourse' which has become a classic of intellectual autobiography, the *Discours de la Méthode*.

It is against this background that we must consider the relationship between Hobbes and Descartes. The two men did not actually meet until the year after Hobbes's illness, but they had been acquainted with each other's work for some years.

[8] First notice of the MS appeared in Jean Jacquot, 'Notes on an unpublished work of Thomas Hobbes', *Notes and Records of the Royal Society of London*, 9 (1952), 188–95; the edition was by Jacquot and Jones, ed. cit., and Jones subsequently published an English translation (Bradford University Press, 1976). Brandt's remarks are to be found in his *Thomas Hobbes' Mechanical Conception of Nature* (Copenhagen and London, 1928), 168.

[9] This is his *Miletius*, recently discovered in the library of the Remonstrant Church at Amsterdam by Professor G. H. M. Posthumus Meyjes.

From 1628 until 1649 Descartes lived virtually in secret in the United Provinces (with only occasional visits to France), and most communication between him and the outside intellectual world was conducted through Mersenne. Hobbes probably met Mersenne for the first time while visiting France between the autumn of 1634 and October 1636, but they did not become close friends; though Mersenne knew by March 1640 that Hobbes had produced 'des choses bien particulières en Philosophie'.[10] Hobbes did not, for example, read Descartes's *Discours* or its accompanying essays in manuscript: in October 1637 he received a copy of the printed book from Sir Kenelm Digby with a covering letter which makes it clear that Hobbes knew very little about it.[11] But on 5 November 1640 Hobbes sent Mersenne a 56-page letter which apparently consisted largely of a critique of Descartes's *Discours* and *La Dioptrique* (which was one of the essays published with the *Discours*). Mersenne passed some extracts from this critique on to Descartes, who began to reply to them in January 1641. At the same time Mersenne, obviously impressed by Hobbes's critical acumen, decided to enlist him as one of the respondents to Descartes's *Meditations*. He sent Hobbes a manuscript of the *Meditations* on 18 November, and had received his comments by 23 December, remarkably quickly.[12]

The argument conducted by the two men, through Mersenne, about Descartes's optics lasted until April 1641, and is remarkable for its level of personal abuse and intellectual short-sightedness. Hobbes was particularly sensitive to the possibility that Descartes might claim that Hobbes had stolen from him his basic ideas about 'the nature and production of light and sound', and of all 'fantasies' or 'ideas'. He first made his concern about this known to Mersenne in a letter of March 1641, and insisted that he had explained his ideas to Charles Cavendish and his brother the Earl of Newcastle as early as 1630, and

[10] This is based on Mersenne's letter to Theodore Haak, 10 Mar. 1640 (*Correspondance*, xi, 404) in which Mersenne says 'Vous avez un certain Mr Hobbes parmy vous, que j'ay veu icy conducteur d'un Seigneur. Si vous le connoissiez, il a des choses bien particulières en Philosophie.' Hobbes had visited Paris as 'conducteur' of the young Earl of Devonshire in the latter part of 1634. The tone of Mersenne's letter does not suggest very close acquaintance with Hobbes.

[11] F. Tönnies, 'Contributions à l'Histoire de la Pensée de Hobbes', *Archive de philosophie*, 12 (1936), 89.

[12] Mersenne, *Correspondance*, x. 210–12.

therefore well before Descartes's first published work in 1637;[13] this was a claim which he continued to make for the rest of his life, though as far as I know neither of the Cavendish brothers ever commented on it. In the dedication of *The Elements of Law* to the Earl in May 1640, Hobbes said that his principles were 'those which I have heretofore acquainted your Lordship withal in private discourse',[14] but he did not say when. Informed of this claim by Mersenne, Descartes treated it with contempt, and though he did concede that Hobbes's philosophy resembled his own in so far as it was based solely on 'figures and movements', he insisted that the conclusions which Hobbes drew were so clearly faulty that the two doctrines could not be compared. He also drew attention in a suggestive way to Hobbes's reluctance to publish.[15]

What Descartes had been presented with *via* Mersenne was a set of critical notes, and (as he complained) he had very little idea of what the underlying philosophical position of his opponent was. Modern historians have also found some difficulty in assessing just how developed Hobbes's physics and metaphysics were at the time of his encounter with Descartes, and to what extent they had been elaborated precisely in response to the Frenchman. For G. C. Robertson (unfamiliar as he was with much of the manuscript material), it was clear that Hobbes had *no* developed non-political philosophy until after his political theory was written down in 1640–2, and although later writers (including notably J. W. N. Watkins) have sometimes argued the contrary on the basis of the so-called 'Short Tract', no one has (I think) yet claimed that Hobbes's general philosophy was as sophisticated as his civil philosophy by 1641. (Tom Sorell has recently treated all Hobbes's principal printed works as expressing a unified set of scientific ideas, but even he has not tried to argue that the ideas were actually formulated systematically before the appearance of *De Cive*.) The encounter with Descartes has been treated as the collision between an inchoate mechanistic theory on Hobbes's side and a fully formed mechanistic theory on Descartes's.[16]

[13] Ibid. 569. [14] *Elements of Law*, p. xv.

[15] Mersenne, *Correspondance*, x. 588.

[16] See G. C. Robertson, *Hobbes* (Edinburgh and London, 1886), 55; J. W. N. Watkins, *Hobbes's System of Ideas* (2nd edn., London, 1973), 12 ff.; Tom Sorell, *Hobbes* (London, 1986).

The conventional modern view in fact goes back to Brandt's great book on Hobbes of 1928, in which Brandt summarized his view as follows:

May we consequently not maintain that, provided Hobbes' evidence is reliable, to him the honour is due of having on his own account independently of Descartes, thought out the mechanical conception of nature? To us it would appear *that the answer is in the affirmative.* But it is scarcely necessary to add that here there is only a question of the fundamental features broadly speaking. It is precisely mechanism as a principle = the leading thought which is the point at issue. In the special elaboration, in the attempt to formulate the laws of motion and to apply these, Hobbes cannot reasonably bear comparison with Descartes . . .[17]

However, I want in this paper to argue that Brandt was wrong on both counts: there is no good evidence that Hobbes had any consistent natural philosophy before 1637, but there is some unacknowledged evidence that his natural philosophy was put in an elaborate and sophisticated form much earlier than is usually thought. In fact, I will claim what no one yet has claimed, that Hobbes had actually written up his general philosophy in almost as detailed a form as his civil philosophy by 1641. Having established a different chronology, I will then consider what that tells us about the confrontation between Descartes and Hobbes. What I shall argue is that what we can tell about the character of this early philosophical work by Hobbes suggests that it was developed very largely in response to the issues raised by Descartes in 1637, and that Hobbes's criticisms of Descartes in 1640–1 were fundamental to his own philosophy.

Brandt, and all subsequent writers, have relied for their belief that Hobbes had indeed put a philosophical position together before 1637, on one of Tönnies's discoveries, the 'Short Tract'. Tönnies conjectured that this tract dated from 1630, precisely on the strength of Hobbes's claim to Mersenne; Brandt, more cautiously, argued that it dated from before 1636. His reasoning was as follows. The tract contains an account of light as the *emanation of species*; we know from a letter which Hobbes wrote to the Earl of Newcastle in October 1636 that by that date he utterly rejected the emanation of species, and insisted on a mediumistic transmission of light, and this was the view which

[17] Brandt, op. cit. 142.

he took for the rest of his life; therefore the Short Tract must date from before 1636. But the Short Tract contains the fundamentals of Hobbes's philosophy, in particular the commitment to explain everything in terms of local motion and the denial that anything can move itself. So Hobbes was right to declare that his basic ideas were formed before he read Descartes.[18]

This has been an immensely powerful argument in forming the bases of the modern interpretation of Hobbes, since it selects as the starting-point of Hobbes's philosophy this commitment about mechanical explanation. Nothing else in the Short Tract is particularly Hobbesian; we can see this clearly in its theory of light. The traditional, Aristotelian theory of *species* held that they were not themselves bodies but were 'corporeal forms' which could propagate themselves through a medium; the idea was that a luminous body had the power to transform the adjacent part of a transparent medium into a likeness of itself, that this likeness in turn could produce another likeness of itself, and so on. Colours, and other visible properties, on this account, were real features of the parts of the medium, and resembled more or less exactly the real properties of the luminous body. The Short Tract proposed instead that species must be substances actually emanating from the light-source and passing through space to an observer. But visible properties, it acknowledged, were accidents of the species—that is, really inhering in it in some way. The account was thus an anti-Aristotelian modification of the traditional theory; but it was very different from Hobbes's later theory.

The crucial difference was not so much over the question of mediumistic transmission rather than emanation, as over the question of the *reality* of visible properties: Hobbes always insisted that (in the words of the 1636 letter) 'light and colour are but the effects of . . . motion in the brayne'. There is nothing *really* in the external world which in any way resembles what we think we perceive. I shall argue later that this was the crucial issue in the new philosophy, rather than the simple commitment to mechanical explanation, and I shall do so partly because there is actually no evidence whatsoever that the Short Tract is by Hobbes. It is among the papers of Sir Charles Cavendish, and it is anonymous; the handwriting of the manuscript closely

[18] *Elements of Law*, p. xii; Brandt, op. cit. 48–50, 85.

resembles that of Robert Payne.[19] Payne was chaplain to the Earl of Newcastle, and a close friend of both Hobbes and Cavendish; he was also regarded by Hobbes as possessing a philosophical gift of his own (as, of course, did Cavendish). Many different ideas were tried out in the Cavendishes' circle during the 1630s and 1640s, and Hobbes's philosophy was only one of the theories on offer. There is no reason to suppose that the Short Tract is not by Payne himself, or (possibly) by Cavendish, or by some other person; there is no special reason, other than Tönnies's enthusiasm, for attributing it to Hobbes.

If we forget about the Short Tract, then we are left with a group of letters from the mid-1630s as the first evidence of any philosophical activity by Hobbes. In January 1634 the Earl of Newcastle asked Hobbes to buy a copy of Galileo's *Dialogues* in London; during the first part of that year Hobbes discussed optics with an old associate of Newcastle and his brother, Walter Warner, and on his trip to France in that year Hobbes got in touch with a friend of Charles Cavendish, the mathematician Claude Mydorge (as well as with Mersenne). Hobbes was clearly hard at work on both natural philosophy and political theory during that journey (he studied Selden's *Mare Clausum*, for example), and his letters to Newcastle in 1636 reveal a considerable philosophical sophistication and confidence.[20]

But if this was all we had, Brandt would have been right in supposing that Hobbes's general philosophy was undeveloped until the mid-1640s. There is, however, a text which very plausibly comes from an early stage in Hobbes's development, but which shows great maturity; this is the so-called 'Tractatus Opticus', parts of which Tönnies printed in 1889. The dating and character of this manuscript have been the occasion of some debate among Hobbes scholars, but Brandt at least recognized its great importance in the history of Hobbes's philosophy.[21] The

[19] See for example Payne's letters to Sheldon (many of them about Hobbes) in BL Additional MS 4162.

[20] Historical Manuscripts Commission, *13th Report Part II, Manuscripts of the Duke of Portland* (1893), 124, 126, 128; J. Halliwell, *A Collection of Letters Illustrative of the Progress of Science* (London, 1841), 65; *EW* vii. 454.

[21] See his remarks, op. cit. 9. Brandt's discussion of the date and character of the MS is on pp. 86–99; it is followed broadly by the most systematic recent writer on these matters Arrigo Pacchi in his *Convenzione e ipotesi nella formazione della filosofia naturale di Thomas Hobbes* (Florence, 1965), 177.

title 'Tractatus Opticus' was given to it by Tönnies (unfortunately, since that is also the name of the 1644 essay on optics printed by Mersenne); it consists of 273 folios now bound into Harleian MS 6796, and presumably (like the rest of that manuscript) was once part of Charles Cavendish's papers.[22] The work is divided into four chapters (*capita*—as we shall see, the precise terms for the divisions are important); *Caput primum* is 'De luce, illuminatione et diaphano' (147), *Caput secundum* 'De natura reflectionis et refractionis' (159), *Caput tertium* 'De varietate reflexarum a figuris, convexis et concavis sphaericis' (173), and *Caput quartum* 'De visione per medium simplex et directum' (199). Each chapter consists of elaborate and sophisticated arguments about optics, usually directed against Descartes's *Dioptrique*. But the work was not intended to be entirely free-standing; some of its arguments depend on conclusions about motion apparently already established 'in sectione antecedente' or 'sectione prima' (148).

As Tönnies, but really only Tönnies, realized,[23] these remarks about the earlier *sectio* are of great interest. In 1642 Hobbes, as we have seen, published *De Cive* under the title *Elementorum Philosophiae Sectio Tertia*. Its Preface explained that (in the words of my own translation: the English version usually cited is here particularly misleading):

I was working at Philosophy out of interest, and was collecting together and organizing the basic Elements of a universal philosophy, and gradually writing them up in three Sections; the first dealing with matter and its general properties, the second with man and his peculiar faculties and emotions, and the third with the State and citizens' duties. So Section One contains Metaphysics [*Philosophia prima*] and some elements of Physics: it sums up the principles of Time, Place, Cause, Power, Relation, Proportion, Quantity, Figure, and Motion. Section Two deals with imagination, memory, intellect, reasoning, appetite, will, Good, Evil, Honest and Dishonest, and other things of that kind. What Section Three deals with, I have already said. But while I was finishing this work, arranging it and slowly and with depression sorting it out [*or possibly even 'copying it out'—conscribo. This would account for the depression*] (for I do not indulge in controversy, I

[22] The MS was published in a cursory edition by F. Alessio, *Rivista critica di storia della filosofia*, 18 (1963), 147–288; my references to it are to the page numbers of the Alessio edition.

[23] Tönnies, *Hobbes: Leben und Lehre* (2nd edn., Leipzig, 1912), 85; Brandt, op. cit. 194.

simply reason), it so happened that my country, a few years before the Civil War broke out, began to burn with questions of Sovereignty and the due obedience of citizens—the forerunners of an approaching war.[24]

The English version says '. . . having digested them into three Sections by degrees, I thought to have written them so as in the first I *would* have treated [etc.] . . . Wherefore the first Section *would* have contained [etc.]' (my italics).[25] It thus obscures the fact that in 1642 Hobbes spoke about the other *sectiones* as already existing 'a few years before the Civil War'.

Hobbes always used the term *sectio* with care (again, if we discount the Short Tract). He reserved it for the three great divisions of his universal philosophy, known from their final titles (which were clearly adumbrated in 1642) as *De Corpore, De Homine*, and *De Cive*. In many of his works (including *The Elements of Law, De Corpore, De Cive*, and *Leviathan*) he subdivided his text; but he never referred to those subdivisions as *sectiones*. In *De Corpore, The Elements*, and *Leviathan* they are *partes* or *parts*, in *De Cive* they are simply given specific titles. Moreover, in all his works (except for *The Elements*), even where subdivisions are employed, the chapters run in a continuous numerical sequence from the beginning to the end of the work.

In the light of this, it is hard not to believe that the 'Tractatus Opticus' is in fact an early draft of *Sectio Secunda, De Homine*. Tönnies recognized that *sectio prima* must have referred to *De Corpore*, but he shied away both from drawing the conclusion that *De Corpore* must have been very early (on his dating of the Tractatus), and from seeing the Tractatus as a draft of *De Homine*. That the Tractatus does not simply refer to *sectio prima* but is itself a *sectio* is clear from the remark quoted above about *sectione antecedente*. Accordingly, for the rest of this paper I will refer to the Tractatus by the less misleading name of *Sectio Secunda*.

How, then, does it compare with the final *De Homine*, and what might its date be? *De Homine* appeared in 1658, after an immensely long gestation period. It was considerably shorter than the other two *sectiones*, and consisted of fifteen chapters.

[24] Howard Warrender, ed., *De Cive LV* 82.

[25] *De Cive EV* 35. For the evidence that it is not by Hobbes, see pp. 4–6, supplemented by my 'Warrender's *De Cive*', *Political Studies*, 33 (1985), 310–12.

'Of the apparent place of the object by Reflexion in plaine glasses' and chapter 5 'Of the same in glasses sphaerically convex'). Many of the turns of phrase are also identical.[28] But the nine chapters of *The Optiques* are approximately 40,000 words long, while the eight chapters of *De Homine* are 20,000 words—so even allowing for the greater terseness of Latin, it is clear that Hobbes had to shorten the English text to make it fit *De Homine* (and even then, of course, it bulks absurdly large in the final work). In the dedication of *The Optiques* to the Marquis of Newcastle, Hobbes promised to make his draft 'perfect' later in Latin, and what he envisaged was presumably that both parts of the English optics would find their way into *De Corpore* and *De Homine*. For some reason, the first part of *The Optiques* did not get translated into *De Corpore*, though that work does contain discussions of the nature of light along broadly similar (but much more succinct) lines.

While *The Optiques* is thus a very straightforward precursor of the published *De Homine, Sectio Secunda* is very different indeed from these chapters, so much so that it immediately looks like a *much* earlier draft. The one point of resemblance is that it too contains material which Hobbes finally divided up between *De Corpore* and *De Homine*, but the actual contents of its four chapters are very different from the material which was common to *The Optiques* and *De Homine*.

If Tönnies was right in dating it to 1637–40, this would clearly fit the great difference between it and the later drafts. But his dating was called into question by two later writers, Max Kohler in 1903 and Brandt in 1928, whose alternative views have on the whole prevailed with subsequent scholars (with the honourable exception of Jacquot).[29] Tönnies dated it as he did simply because of the extensive critique of Descartes embedded in it, which he thought would have been inappropriate much after 1637. But his critics produced arguments based on more specific features of the theory put forward in the manuscript;

[28] See e.g. fo. 77 of the MS, 'that which wee have now said, will serve to render up reason of two phaenomena, or two experiments which most men have observed and every man may' compared with p. 9 of *De Homine, Opera Philosophica* (Amsterdam, 1668), 'His cognitis . . .'.

[29] M. Kohler, 'Studien zur Naturphilosophie des Th. Hobbes', *Archiv für Geschichte der Philosophie*, 16 (1903), 73; Brandt, op. cit. 88–91, 201–4; Jacquot and Jones, op. cit. 16–17.

The first was on the origin of the human race and on physiological mechanisms for human survival and reprod tion. The next eight were on optics, including some very prec and technical discussions (e.g. chapter 6 is on reflecti chapter 7 on refraction, and chapter 9 on the shape of lenses telescopes). Chapter 10 was *De Sermone*, 11 *De Appetitu & Fu* 12 *De Affectibus sive Perturbationibus Animi*, 13 *De Ingeniis Moribus*, 14 *De Religione*, 15 *De Homine fictitio, sive de Persona.* can be seen from this, the book is very oddly constructed, an consists essentially of two parts, one on technical optics and th other on human faculties more generally considered. Hobbe acknowledged this division in the preface; moreover, in th preface to *De Corpore* three years earlier he had remarked tha 'there now only remains Section Two *De Homine*. I have the par which deals with Optics written out in eight chapters, and with the designs for the diagrams accompanying each chapter engraved and ready more than six years ago' (i.e. in 1649). This is confirmed by a letter from Hobbes to Sorbière in June 1649 in which he speaks of the plates for the diagrams being ready, and the first and more difficult part of the work being almost finished.[26]

But in fact, the basic ideas and structure of these chapters were achieved even earlier, in the English manuscript on optics (also in the Harleian collection—MS 3360) which Molesworth partly published. This manuscript is entitled *A Minute or First Draught of the Optiques* and is dated 1646. It was written as a connected and complete work on optics (and is the only complete work of Hobbes still unpublished). It is divided into two parts, the first of which deals with such topics as the nature of light, of transparency, and of reflection, while the second consists of nine chapters on vision. These last nine chapters (as G. C. Robertson realized, though his observation has been widely ignored, particularly by Brandt[27]) are identical in content to the eight optical chapters of *De Homine* (the reason for the different number is that chapter 5 of *De Homine*, 'De Loco Objecti Apparente in Speculis planis & Convexis per Reflectionem', is divided into two chapters in *The Optiques*—chapter 4

[26] Hobbes, *Opera Philosophica* (Amsterdam, 1668), sig. Aaa3^{v}; Tönnies, 'Siebzehn Briefe', p. 208.

[27] Brandt, op. cit. 175–6, 393; G. C. Robertson, op. cit. 59 n, 75.

unfortunately, in each instance their case was vitiated by the subsequent discovery of the *Critique* of Thomas White, as well as by various other considerations.[30]

The strength of something like Tönnies's original argument about the manuscript's date rests both on the closeness of the English *Optiques* to the printed *De Homine*, and the distance from both of them of *Sectio Secunda*, and on the fact that the critique of Descartes to be found in *Sectio Secunda* is very close to what we know about the critique which Hobbes sent to Mersenne in 1640, and that this is not true of any other known work of Hobbes. Brandt conjectured that the Mersenne 'Tractatus' was

[30] Kohler's argument was as follows: he observed that in *Sectio Secunda* the process of vision was described by Hobbes as a motion down the optic nerve to the brain *and thence to the heart*, and a corresponding reaction from the heart back to the eye (Alessio edn., p. 206). He then asserted that in both *The Elements of Law* and the short *Tractatus Opticus* published by Mersenne in 1644, the reaction which constitutes vision is said to begin or terminate *in the brain*; only in works published later (the first being *Leviathan* itself) did Hobbes talk about the heart playing a role in the process. Unfortunately for Kohler's argument the *Critique* (of 1643) also incorporates the heart into the mechanism of vision. Moreover, it is not clear that the theory of vision even in *The Elements* is so different from the later account. The point of incorporating the heart into the system of perception was to ensure that every act of perception had an emotional effect—there could be no emotionally neutral perceptions, and hence no emotionally neutral thoughts. Our passions are intimately and necessarily involved in all our dealings with the world. But this is said in *The Elements* also: 'Conceptions or apparitions are nothing really, but motion in some internal substance of the head; which motion not stopping there, but proceeding to the heart, of necessity must there either help or hinder that motion which is called vital; when it helpeth, it is called DELIGHT . . . but when such motion weakeneth or hindereth the vital motion, then it is called PAIN . . . [A]ll conceptions we have immediately by the sense, are delight, or pain . . .' (pp. 28–9). The physiology is not as clear in *The Elements* as in the other works, but the general theory seems to be on the same lines.

Brandt was cautious about Kohler's argument, since, while he did not know about the *Critique* either, he was aware that the preface to Mersenne's *Ballistica* of 1644 (which was in fact derived by Mersenne from the *Critique*) talked about the heart as well as the brain (Brandt, op. cit. 91). Instead, he developed his own argument about the date of the manuscript, which went as follows. *Sectio Secunda* explains light as a pulse from an illuminating body—that is, a wave or pumping action, which Hobbes analysed by analogy with the diastolic and systolic motion of the heart. Hobbes attributed this motion to the Sun; but he also talked about another motion, which he termed *motus cribrationis*—a movement which he compared to the sifting of objects in a sieve or the manual drawing of a circle without a compass, and which he described as 'simple' motion (Alessio edn., pp. 152–3). What Hobbes meant by this was that if a planet is in a circular orbit round the Sun and turns continually on its own axis so that its diameter remains always in the same alignment, every point on the surface of the planet will complete the orbit at the same speed (which would not be the case if the planet did not rotate about its own axis—the points nearer to the Sun would travel round the orbit more slowly than those further away). The analogy with the manual drawing of a circle is clearest: the artist moves the pencil in such a way that his hand is always in the same

[cont. on p. 24]

part of that critique,[31] and it is certainly true that much of what is said in the 'Tractatus' is referred to in the correspondence between Descartes and Hobbes in 1641; but all of the issues which Brandt pointed to were also discussed in *Sectio Secunda*. Moreover, one of the central issues in the debate between Descartes and Hobbes in 1641 was not mentioned in the 'Tractatus', nor in any other work by Hobbes, but plays a key role in *Sectio Secunda*: this was Descartes's use of the term *determination*. In his discussions of reflection and refraction in the *Dioptrique*, which were based on an analogy with a tennis ball struck by a racquet, Descartes distinguished between 'the power . . . which causes the ball to continue moving' and 'that which determines it to move in one direction rather than another'.[32]

position relative to his body, since otherwise he would have to turn his wrist right round in order to draw the circle. Hobbes expressly denied that such a movement could cause the sensation of light, but he used it to explain the observed path of the Earth round the Sun.

Brandt claimed that the *motus cribrationis* does not feature in any of Hobbes's other works until *De Corpore*, where (not under that name, but simply under the name of *motus simplex*—though a sieve is still an analogy for it, as is the manual circle) it becomes the explanation for light as well—the diastolic/systolic action disappears. Brandt concluded that *Sectio Secunda* must therefore date from the later 1640s, after even the English optical treatise of 1646 (which does not mention *motus cribrationis*) (Brandt, op. cit. 203, 393). He was not familiar with the contents of the English treatise, however, and quite gratuitously cast doubt on the perfectly reasonable observation by Robertson that it resembled *De Homine* (ibid. 183, 393). Moreover, Brandt's theory too was vitiated by the discovery of the *Critique*, for on fo. 36[v] it has a discussion of 'simple motion' which makes exactly the same points as *Sectio Secunda*, though it uses only the drawing of a circle as its analogy and not the sieve. The *Critique* also uses diastolic/systolic motion as an explanation for light, so that its physics is virtually identical with that of *Sectio Secunda*. As it happens, the English treatise does not employ diastolic/systolic motion either, replacing it with the idea of a continous pressure from the Sun which is continuously resisted by the nervous system—so that we can say reasonably safely that the physics of the *Critique* and *Sectio Secunda* disappeared between 1644 (when Hobbes allowed the *Tractatus Opticus* to be printed with a theory of light based on the diastolic/systolic motion) and 1646.

There is one other argument which has been advanced, albeit indirectly, as the basis for a late dating of *Sectio Secunda*. This was by A. E. Shapiro in 1973, who accepted Brandt's dating, but also pointed out that in *Sectio Secunda* Hobbes expressly introduces as a novel term the word *radiatio* to replace the more usual *radius* or *ray* (of light) (Alession edn., p. 160; Shapiro, 'Kinematic Optics: A Study of the Wave Theory of Light in the Seventeenth Century', *Archive for the History of the Exact Sciences*, 11 (1973), 134–266, p. 151, and that this term does not appear in the Mersenne-published short *Tractatus*. But it does not appear in *any* of Hobbes's printed works, including *De Corpore* and *De Homine*, both of which use the term *radius* (*De Corpore*, 27. 13–14, *De Homine*, 5. 1, etc.). So nothing can be deduced from this.

[31] Brandt, op. cit. 94–6.

[32] Descartes, *Philosophical Writings*, trans. J. Cottingham, R. Stoothoff, and D. Murdoch (Cambridge, 1985), i. 157.

In *Sectio Secunda* Hobbes was highly critical of this distinction, claiming that Descartes confused 'determination' and 'determinate motion' (p. 164). Descartes argued that a moving body could be 'determined' to move simultaneously in two different directions, and that when the body struck a plane surface or entered a medium of different density one or other of these 'determinations' could be affected without the other being similarly altered, at least to the same degree. Hobbes objected that it made little sense to talk about a 'determination' having *degrees*, or being something which could be measured: the only thing which could be quantified was *velocity*, and one should say instead that a moving body in a two-dimensional plane had a compound velocity, consisting of a determinate speed in one dimension and a determinate speed in the other dimension. (Without directly addressing Descartes, he used the same idea in *The Optiques*, talking of motion 'compounded of two motions (as if it were caused by two winds)' (fo. 10^{v}).) Just this point was clearly made in Hobbes's letter of November 1640 to Mersenne, and Descartes responded to it on 21 January 1641 with a comment calling into question Hobbes's technique of adding velocities.[33] This became the central point of the subsequent correspondence. As Pierre Costabel has pointed out, Hobbes was indeed on rather shaky ground here, something Hobbes himself was forced to acknowledge at one point;[34] and though (e.g. in *De Corpore*, chapter 24) he continued to analyse motion in substantially this way, he never again referred directly to Descartes in this context.

Indeed, it is a striking fact that in 1646, in the English optical treatise, Hobbes referred in warmer terms to Descartes than he ever employed elsewhere. At one point he said that the attempts by earlier writers to explain the differences in apparent magnitude and position of objects had failed since

> all of them (except onely Monsieur des Cartes now of late) supposed light and colour, that is to say the appearance of objects which is nothing butt our fancy to bee some accident in the object it selfe, and so have sought the place of that which hath no place, for nothing hath a place but bodie, and if improperlie wee assigne place to accidents, wee cannot assigne them any other then the place of the body whose

[33] Mersenne, *Correspondance*, x. 427.

[34] Ibid. 432–3, 575.

accidents they are . . . And seeing Monsr: des Cartes who only hath sett forth the true principles of this doctrine, namely that the Images of objects are in the fancie, and that they fly not through the aire, under the empty name of *Species intentionales* but are made in the braine by the operation of the objects themselves, and hath not pursued the seeming figure, greatnesse and distance in the Speciall and particular cases, I have therefore endeavord as farre as I can to doe that . . . (fos. 74–5)

There is one further, slight but suggestive, indication about the date of *Sectio Secunda.* It is of course written in Latin, but it includes several quotations *in extenso* from the *Dioptrique* (e.g. p. 164). The *Dioptrique* was published in French, but a Latin translation approved by Descartes himself appeared in 1644, and was certainly read in the Mersenne circle (Mersenne recommended it to the Italian philosopher Torricelli, who had no French). The quotations from the *Dioptrique* in *Sectio Secunda* are however not from that translation, and are presumably Hobbes's own translations of key passages. It is unlikely that a serious critic would not quote his opponent in the form his opponent approved, unless the appropriate text was not yet available; though it is not *impossible*, and this argument cannot therefore be used to clinch the dating of the manuscript. However, added to what we have already seen, it does help to make an early date very plausible.

If this is accepted, then we have a new picture of Hobbes's early work and one which makes much better sense of many things that should always have seemed more puzzling. Both the *Elements of Law* and the *Critique of Thomas White* marshall extremely sophisticated physical and metaphysical arguments, which very often closely resemble those of Hobbes's later systematic works. Neither is itself a work of constructive natural philosophy: the *Elements* uses certain general epistemological premisses to mount a political argument, while the *Critique* is a point-by-point criticism of White's *De Mundo.* That such works could have appeared in 1640 and 1643 without a substantial and properly worked-out body of material already in existence and available for Hobbes to draw on, should have seemed fantastic to every student of the subject. But if Hobbes was literally correct in the preface to *De Cive*—that is, if all three *sectiones* of the great work were drafted by 1640—then the *Elements* and the *Critique* straightforwardly drew on an easily accessible source of ideas and arguments. It should also have seemed unlikely that Mersenne (whose part in the publication of *De Cive* is clear[35]) would have countenanced its appearance as *Sectio Tertia* unless he had been confident that his friend could produce *Sectiones Prima* and *Secunda* reasonably quickly. But if Mersenne had seen a manuscript based on those sections (particularly a manuscript as impressive as *Sectio Secunda*), then he would have had every reason for confidence.

One further biographical point is worth considering before I turn to consider the philosophical implications of this new chronology. It is the puzzle of why Hobbes took so long to complete his general project. This was a puzzle for his friends also, who by 1646 were beginning to ask what had happened to the *Elementa*. Hobbes answered Sorbière's question about this in June of that year as follows:

> Part of the reason why I am taking so long over the first section of my *Elements* is simply laziness; but more importantly I am not satisfied with how I have explained my meaning. For I am trying to repeat in Metaphysics and Physics what I hope I have done in moral philosophy—that is, leave no foothold for a critic to stand on.[36]

Both of the reasons which Hobbes gave seem plausible. By his own standards of astonishingly quick and copious production, the first years of his exile in France were marked by 'laziness'; but they were also marked by a much fuller acquaintance with modern French philosophy than he had hitherto enjoyed. He clearly did come to have a keener sense of the criticisms which might be made of his work than he had possessed in 1640 (and his burgeoning friendship with Pierre Gassendi may be very important in explaining Hobbes's desire to rewrite and modify his early work). However, most subsequent readers of Hobbes have regretted that he took so long: both *De Corpore* and *De Homine* are unsatisfactory works in many respects, and lack the freshness and clarity of his early productions.

I now want to consider what difference this new chronology makes to our understanding of Hobbes's philosophical enterprise. This first point to make is one which I have already made:

[35] *De Cive LV* 6–7; my 'Warrender's Hobbes', *Political Studies*, 33 (1985), 309.
[36] Tönnies, 'Siebzehn Briefe', p. 69.

if we discount the *Short Treatise*, there is no evidence that Hobbes was seriously interested in modern philosophy until about the time of his visit to France in 1635–6. What the actual genesis of his interest was, is hard to say; though it seems initially to have arisen through acting as an agent for the Earl of Newcastle and his brother, who were both already concerned with optics and mathematics (largely, no doubt, because of the *military* implications of both sciences—the Cavendish brothers were heavily involved in military matters). But in the course of meeting English and French mathematicians connected with the Cavendishes (such as Walter Warner in England and Claude Mydorge in France), Hobbes seems to have evolved a distinctive philosophical position of his own.

The second point to make is that the development of that philosophical position seems to have been very heavily influenced by a critical reading of Descartes. The two earliest extensive works we possess by Hobbes (if my chronological argument is correct) are the *Elements of Law* and *Sectio Secunda*. The latter is virtually designed as a critique of Descartes, while even in the former (as we shall see presently) there are extensive traces of an hostility to Descartes. Hobbes's philosophy gives the impression of having been developed as the next move in a game where Descartes was the previous player.

The essential character of that game is clear enough from Hobbes's own testimony. He twice insisted that his original idea, which (he alleged) he had discussed with the Cavendishes in 1630, was (as he put it in 1646) 'that light is a fancy in the minde, caused by motion in the braine, which motion againe is caused by the motion of the parts of such bodies as we call *lucid*', or as he said in his letter to Newcastle of October 1636, 'whereas I use the phrases, the light passes, or the colour passes or diffuseth itselfe, my meaning is that the motion is onely in the medium, and light and colour are but the effects of that motion in the brayne'.[37] It was on this issue above all that Hobbes wished to claim priority over other philosophers.

What was at stake here was nothing less than the invention of modern philosophy. To understand what was involved, we have to remember that the group of philosophers round Mersenne

[37] *EW* vii. 468, HMC 13th Rep., ii. 130.

were distinguished by two things: first, they accepted the sceptical arguments against Aristotelianism (in all its forms) which had been advanced during the previous fifty years by men such as Montaigne and Pierre Charron, and which reproduced the scepticism of antiquity; and second, they were not content simply to remain sceptics. A post-sceptical science was their goal, which would be immune to the kind of arguments brought against Aristotle. At the heart of this enterprise, at least as far as metaphysics or physics was concerned, was the problem of perception. The Aristotelians claimed that, by and large, how things looked to an observer was how they *really* were; Aristotle himself in the *De Anima* had remarked that what appears white to a normal observer under normal conditions must actually *be* white (*De Anima*, 418^{a}11–16). The sceptics in turn ridiculed this claim, and insisted that human perception of the world was irremediably faulty: the pervasiveness of optical illusion and the variety of different perceptions of the same thing ruled out any science based on experience. Human beings could have no true knowledge of the external world.

But what neither the ancient nor the Renaissance sceptics ever claimed was that one *could* have true knowledge of an *internal* world, of one's perceptions *themselves*. As Miles Burnyeat has stressed, the idea that sense-impressions could themselves be objects of knowledge—objects perceived by an observer in a necessarily veridical way—was one which never occurred to any ancient philosopher.[38] The one figure of antiquity who came close to having the idea was not a sceptic, but Epicurus, who is recorded as having said something to the effect that 'every *phantasia* is true' (*phantasia* being the Greek word which is nowadays translated as 'presentation' and which means essentially the direct object of thought or perception). However, the current view is that this remark (in the words of C. C. W. Taylor) 'is not the familiar empiricist axiom that we have complete and incorrigible acquaintance with our sense-contents', but the claim that there must be some real, material explanation for all perceptions.[39] This is a claim which (in the

[38] M. F. Burnyeat, 'Idealism and Greek Philosophy: What Descartes Saw and Berkeley Missed', in *Idealism Past and Present*, ed. G. Vesey (Cambridge, 1982), 19–50.

[39] C. C. W. Taylor, 'All Perceptions Are True', in *Doubt and Dogmatism*, ed. M. Schofield, M. Burnyeat, and J. Barnes (Oxford, 1980), 119.

modern empiricist tradition) is usually associated with the axiom of incorrigible acquaintance, but it is not identical to it. Nevertheless, it is not surprising that Gassendi was to turn to Epicurus as the closest ancient analogue to a modern philosopher.

This clear sense which modern scholars have now come to possess, that ancient scepticism did not advance to the modern position on perception, is of fundamental importance in understanding seventeenth-century post-sceptical writers, for it explains their sense of great novelty, and their rush to claim priority for the basic idea that we have immediate and veridical knowledge of our sense-impressions and *only* our sense-impressions—there can be no comparable knowledge of the external world. The three principal figures in the 'Mersenne group', Descartes, Gassendi, and Hobbes, in fact all have some claim to be the first person to have the idea, though all three wished to develop it in different ways. All three, it should be said, also came on the idea some years after Galileo in *Il Saggiatore* of 1623 had published a long discussion of heat and other tactile properties as unreal or non-inherent in material objects, but instead as purely internal events. Galileo expressly disclaimed any intention of pursuing this idea into the realm of *sight*, but there is no doubt that the credit for the essential anti-Aristotelian move should in fact be his.[40] It is curious, however, that neither Descartes nor Hobbes ever admitted that both of them had been pre-empted by Galileo, and it may be that it was the development of the *optical* applications of the idea which seemed to them of crucial importance.

The first one of the 'Mersenne' three to have had the idea may in fact have been Gassendi. In 1624 he published the first book of his *Exercitationes paradoxicae adversus Aristoteleos*, in which the kind of critique which Renaissance sceptics had levelled at Aristotle was restated, and in which he promised seven more books to expand the argument. The second (and only other) book did not however appear until 1649, in an avowedly incomplete form; the original manuscript of this second book was rediscovered in

[40] Galileo, *Opere*, Edizione nazionale, ed. A. Favaro, 20 vols. (Florence, 1890–1909), vi. 347 ff.; Brandt, op. cit. 79 ff. provides a full translation and discussion of the relevant passage.

1959 and securely dated to 1624/5.[41] It was in this book that he observed for the first time that though (in the words of one chapter-heading) 'there is no science, especially of an Aristotelian kind', we can nevertheless be said to have secure knowledge of our own perceptions—'we can preserve a science which can be called the science of experience or appearance'.[42] The nature of this science is merely hinted at or promulgated in the *Exercitationes*, but Gassendi had undoubtedly made a tentative move *beyond* scepticism.

Mersenne welcomed Gassendi's *Exercitationes*, no doubt because they expressed with greater clarity and elegance something which he had himself been groping after in his own *La vérité des sciences contre les sceptiques ou pyrrhoniens* of 1625. *La vérité* was a work designed to refute both modern scepticism and the post-Aristotelian sciences such as alchemy by a variety of arguments (the most significant of them being that we could give a good account of the workings of our senses, for example through the theory of refraction, and thereby correct illusions). Mersenne did not, however, state clearly in this work the proposition that we have no direct or immediate knowledge of anything other than our *phantasiae*. But he encouraged Gassendi to proceed with his philosophy, and Gassendi became increasingly interested in the ideas which seemed to underlie Epicurus' stray remarks about perception. During the 1630s he worked away at a massive *summa* of what he alleged to be Epicureanism, though it was only loosely based on the authentic accounts of Epicurus; the work was finally published after various false starts in 1649. Hobbes had read it by October 1644 and commented that 'it is as big as Aristotle's philosophie, but much truer and excellent Latin'.[43] In its final form, it included full discussions of epistemology, physics, and ethics; unfortunately we do not yet fully understand the genesis of the work, though it is probable that the epistemological and physical sections were substantially completed by 1642.

At the centre of his version of Epicureanism was the argument that science depends on an analysis of *signs*—that is, observations or sense-perceptions are the signs of the real natural events,

[41] Gassendi, *Dissertations en forme de paradoxes contre les Aristotéliciens* . . ., ed. B. Rochot (Paris, 1959), xi ff.
[42] Ibid. 499; Gassendi, *Opera*, iii (Lyons, 1658), 260.
[43] Mersenne, *Correspondance*, xiii. 250.

standing in the same relationship to them as the conventional sign for a word stands for the word, or as words themselves may signify objects. They are not the same as the event, nor do they *represent* the event in the way in which a picture might represent reality: nothing about the actual properties of reality can be read off straightforwardly from the sign. Signs are however *caused* by the events. In essence, as we shall see, this attack on a literally representational theory of perception was common to Mersenne, Descartes, and Hobbes as well as Gassendi.

But because both this work on Epicurus and Gassendi's second book of *Exercitationes* were still unpublished in the mid-1630s, the field was wide open for other people to put forward the central idea as their own. It was in fact to be Descartes who both put the idea forward in print for the first time, and also added a major new twist to it. But he too made a claim about when the idea came to him which is difficult to substantiate, and which has led to the chronology of his philosophical development becoming a treacherous and confusing subject.

In the *Discours* of 1637, Descartes alleged in a striking passage that the fundamental idea about how to refute scepticism came to him while in winter quarters on service with the army of Maurice of Nassau in 1619. One of the problems about this allegation is that in Descartes's earliest sustained piece of philosophical writing, the *Rules for the direction of the mind*, which he seems to have composed at intervals between 1619 and 1628, there is no trace of any great interest in scepticism. Conventional scholasticism was a target, but in general Descartes endorsed mathematics as the model of an absolutely certain science, and also endorsed the view that such a science could be founded on a set of intuitively obvious principles. Moreover, the account of sense-perception which we find in the *Rules* is that

> sense-perception occurs in the same way in which wax takes on an impression from a seal. It should not be thought that I have a mere analogy in mind here: we must think of the external shape of the sentient body as being really changed by the object in exactly the same way as the shape of the surface of the wax is altered by the seal. This is the case, we must admit, not only when we feel some body as having a shape, as being hard or rough to the touch etc., but also when we have a tactile perception of heat or cold and the like . . .[44]

[44] Descartes, *Philosophical Writings*, i. 40.

This is identical to the account which Aristotle gave of perception in the *De Anima*, in which the simile of a piece of wax being impressed (sense-*impression*) was also utilized.

The *Discours*, on the other hand, takes scepticism about all these claims as its starting-point. The first work in which he clearly stated his mature view about the relationship between internal perceptive states and the external world was in fact *The world or treatise on light*, which he composed between 1629 and 1635. He was apparently on the point of publishing it when he heard about the condemnation of Galileo by the Inquisition, and he thereupon decided to abandon the whole of it rather than cut out the section which endorsed a Galilean cosmology. It was published posthumously in 1664. As its title reveals, it was the first full-scale attempt by Descartes to take light and vision as the central examples of the mechanism of perception, an attempt which was continued in his *Optics* of 1637. In *The world*, he remarked

> Of all our senses, touch is the one considered the least deceptive and most certain. Thus, if I show you that even touch makes us conceive many ideas which bear no resemblance to the objects which produce them, I do not think you should find it strange if I say that sight can do likewise. Now, everyone knows that the ideas of tickling and of pain, which are formed in our mind on the occasion of our being touched by external bodies, bear no resemblance to these bodies. Suppose we pass a feather gently over the lips of a child who is falling asleep, and he feels himself being tickled. Do you think the idea of tickling which he conceives resembles anything present in the feather? . . . Now, I see no reason which compels us to believe that what it is in objects that gives rise to the sensation of light is any more like this sensation than the . . . [action] of a feather . . . [is] like a tickling sensation.[45]

This was the first of the two crucial moves which Descartes was to make, and it meant that he had now (so to speak) drawn level with Gassendi. Both men had repudiated the idea that what we perceive *resembles* the actual world in any simple way. At the beginning of *The world* Descartes indeed made precisely the same point which Gassendi was making at about the same time, that perceptions can be taken as non-representational *signs* of an external reality.

[45] Ibid. i. 82. This is precisely Galileo's point in *Il Saggiatore*.

Words, as you well know, bear no resemblance to the things they signify, and yet they make us think of these things, frequently even without our paying attention to the sound of the words or to their syllables. Thus it may happen that we hear an utterance whose meaning we understand perfectly well, but afterwards we cannot say in what language it was spoken. Now if words, which signify nothing except by human convention, suffice to make us think of things to which they bear no resemblance, then why could nature not also have established some sign which would make us have the sensation of light, even if the sign contained nothing in itself which is similar to this sensation? . . .[46]

It was between 1633 and 1637 that he made the second of the two moves. The *Discours* takes the form of a clear statement of scepticism in a Montaigne- or Charron-like form, and proposes as a provisional way of living, given this sceptical view, the characteristic sceptical solution, namely a willingness to abide by the laws and customs of one's country. But it then adds a new element to classical scepticism which was clearly derived from Descartes's recent study of the implications of a non-representational theory of perception. If our sense-impressions merely *signify* an external world and are *caused* in some inscrutable way by it, how can we know anything at all about its properties? How, indeed, do we even know that it *exists*, since, after all, apparently significant perceptions occur to us in dreams which presumably have no real correlates? This so-called 'hyperbolical' doubt is a relatively simple problem to raise in the course of an enquiry into non-representational theories of perception, but (as Burnyeat has stressed) it had never been raised in its Cartesian form before (the only hint of anything like it occurs in the context of a very different kind of discussion in Plato's *Parmenides*).

The reason for its novelty is presumably that there had never before been a generation of philosophers to whom non-representational theories of perception seemed so plausible, and who were therefore concerned to explore their deepest implications. Earlier sceptics had argued that the representation of reality in our sense-perceptions goes wrong in various ways and is unreliable: we do not know whose view of reality is the correct one. But this does not lead to Cartesian hyperbolical doubt any

[46] Ibid. i. 81.

more than it necessarily leads to the idea that we have veridical knowledge of our perceptions (a colour-blind man is still seeing *something*). But if seeing is non-representational, then the world may in reality be quite other than it appears to *anyone*, and it may not even be *there*. Again, we can take the analogy with language seriously: some words (namely, proper names) signify material objects, but most do not, and some signify apparently material objects that do not or could not exist, such as chimeras. In general one might say that quite a lot of the new philosophical view espoused by Gassendi, Descartes, and Hobbes can be captured by viewing it as the application to *perception* of a long-standing set of concerns with the fit between *language* and the world.

After 1637, the sceptical challenge to the new philosophy was not Montaigne or Charron but the hyperbolical doubt. Descartes's own answer is famous, but famously contentious: it was in essence a combination of the *cogito* argument with the proof of God's existence. The *cogito* argument is that a thinking being must be certain at least of its own existence, and it must be certain that it perceives correctly the immediate object of its acquaintance, the *phantasia*. 'Even if I were to suppose that I was dreaming and that whatever I saw or imagined was false, yet I could not deny that the ideas were truly in my mind.'[47] The proof of God's existence (a version of the ontological argument) then acts as a guarantee that the ideas in our minds correspond more or less to an external reality, since a God of the orthodox kind would not play tricks on his creatures or lead them into comprehensive error.

It should be stressed that this solution to scepticism, though Descartes proclaimed it in the *Discours* as the foundation of all sciences including ethics, is (even if a valid one) a solution only to the *epistemological* side of scepticism. In the *Discours*, Descartes presented himself initially as an adherent of sceptical moral relativism as well as epistemic uncertainty; but to establish the existence of a material world more or less corresponding to the general perception we have of it, is not going to solve the moral relativist's problem—his doubts arise precisely from the generally perceived absence of a consensus among men about the

[47] Ibid. i. 128.

fundamentals of morality. Descartes's subsequent intellectual career illustrates this, for he never produced a major work on ethics (being virtually the only great philosopher never to do so—the other obvious and revealing instance being Wittgenstein). When in the 1640s he corresponded with Princess Elizabeth of Bohemia on ethical and political matters, it was Machiavellism, the political language most appealing to the sceptic, which in general furnished him with his vocabulary.

When the Mersenne circle read the *Discours*, it was the proof of God's existence on which in general their criticism focused. When Gassendi joined the other philosophers (including Hobbes) recruited by Mersenne to answer Descartes's *Meditations*, he directed much of his fire against this aspect of the argument. In Gassendi's view, it was unreasonable to expect certainty of *that* kind in anything, and therefore there was no need to employ the elaborate and dubious apparatus of the proof in order to provide it. Strikingly, however, Gassendi avoided tackling the hyperbolical doubt directly: all he could find to say about it at first was that 'whatever you say, no one will believe that you have really convinced yourself that not one thing you formerly knew is true, or that your senses, or God, or an evil demon, have managed to deceive you all the time.[48] (The evil demon was the new twist which Descartes had added to the doubt—perhaps all our perceptions are brought about by the operations of a malevolent demon who wishes to deceive us.) Later, Gassendi added lamely,

> since during our lives we are alternately awake or dreaming, a dream may give rise to deception because things may appear to be present when they are not present. But we do not dream all the time, and for as long as we are really awake we cannot doubt whether we are awake or dreaming.[49]

Descartes ridiculed Gassendi's refusal to take the hyperbolical doubt seriously, and to an extent he was right to do so, as it was intended to be a sceptical critique of precisely the kind of non-representational theory of perception which Gassendi had begun to advance in the 1620s.

Hobbes, however, had a much more robust answer, and

[48] Ibid. ii. 180.
[49] Ibid. ii. 231.

indeed his importance within the Mersenne circle consisted in the fact that he was able to take on board the hyperbolical doubt without having to turn to the proof of God's existence as a solution to it. It may be that he developed his original idea independently of both Gassendi and Descartes; certainly, his letters of 1636 contain the essentials of the theory. In addition to the claim that colour is not *really* in the object of vision, but is a property solely of the sense-impression itself, Hobbes was already clear about the consequent impossibility of having comparably secure knowledge of the external world—thus he observed in August that

> in thinges that are not demonstrable, of which kind is the greatest part of naturall philosophy, as dependinge upon the motion of bodies so subtile as they are invisible, such as are ayre and spirits, the most that can be atteyned unto, is to have such opinions, as no certaine experience can confute, and from which can be deduced by lawfull argumentation, no absurdity.[50]

(This is a passage which appears in almost the same form—though in Latin—in *Sectio Secunda* (Alessio edn., p. 147), another indication of an early date for that MS.)

Upon this basis, Hobbes developed an alternative to Descartes which is outlined clearly in the *Elements of Law* and in *Sectio Secunda*. He argued in the *Elements* as follows (page references to the Tönnies 1889 edition). First, conventional Aristotelian accounts of perception are indeed false, something Hobbes established using familiar sceptical arguments—'every man hath so much experience as to have seen the sun and other visible objects by reflection in the water and in glasses, and this alone is sufficient for this conclusion: that colour and image may be there where the thing seen is not' (p. 4). Instead, Hobbes repeated the fundamental claims of the new philosophers:

(1) That the subject wherein colour and image are inherent, is not the object or thing seen.
(2) That that is nothing without us really which we call an image or colour.
(3) That the said image or colour is but an apparition unto us of that motion, agitation, or alteration, which the object worketh in the brain or spirits, or some internal substance of the head.

[50] HMC 13th Rep., ii. 128.

(4) That as in conception by vision, so also in the conceptions that arise from other senses, the subject of their inherence is not the object, but the sentient (p. 4).

Gassendi would have agreed with all this, as would Descartes to an extent—after all, in his *Dioptrique* he wrote that 'I would have you consider the light in bodies we call "luminous" to be nothing other than a certain movement, or very rapid and lively action, which passes to our eyes through the medium of the air and other transparent bodies',[51] though the particular account of the relevant motion which Hobbes proposed differed from that of Descartes. Hobbes, as we have seen, suggested a pumping action, like the heart circulating blood; Descartes suggested a *tendency* to move, a *conatus*, by the luminous object in the plenum between it and the observer.

However, Hobbes made it clear in *Sectio Secunda* that the question of what the *actual* motions are which produce perception is ultimately undecidable, in the passage which developed his remarks in one of his 1636 letters.

The natural sciences differ greatly from the other sciences. In the latter, nothing is needed nor admitted as a foundation or primary principle of demonstration other than the definition of terms, by which ambiguity is excluded. They are first truths; every definition is a true and primary proposition because we make it true ourselves by defining it, that is, by agreeing about the meaning of the words. Thus if it pleases us to call this a Triangle, then it is true, that this figure △ is a Triangle. But in the explanation of natural phenomena, another kind of procedure must be followed, which is termed Hypothesis or supposition. Suppose a question is raised about the efficient cause of any event which is obvious to the senses, the sort of thing which we usually term a Phenomenon. Any answer will standardly consist in the designation or description of some motion, to which the Phenomenon is necessarily consequent; and since it is not impossible for dissimilar motions to produce the same Phenomenon, it is possible for the effect to be correctly demonstrated using the hypothetical motion, even though the hypothesis may be untrue. Nothing further is required in Physics, therefore, than that the motions we suppose or imagine are conceivable, that the necessity of the Phenomenon can be demonstrated from them, and that nothing false can be derived from them (Alessio edn. p. 147).

[51] Descartes, *Philosophical Writings*, i. 153.

All one could say with certainty, was that (in the language of the *Elements*)

> whatsoever accidents or qualities our senses make us think there be in the world, they are not there, but are seemings and apparitions only. The things that really are in the world without us, are those motions by which these seemings are caused (p. 7).

The reason for Hobbes's confidence in the 'real' existence of these motions is suggested in *Sectio Secunda*: 'it is not conceivable that there could be vision without action nor action without motion' (Alessio edn., p. 150). The point is that we have direct acquaintance with our percepts, and we cannot deny that they exhibit change; change is only conceivable as caused by the action of one material body moving against another. The lost draft of *Sectio Prima* referred to in *Sectio Secunda* contained a demonstration that 'all action is local motion in the agent' (Alessio edn., p. 148), and Hobbes stuck to this principle throughout his life. Moreover, we cannot conceive of self-moving objects, and we cannot conceive of any cause of movement other than another object impinging on the moving object in question (the *Elements* refers to this assumption in a discussion of the impossibility of incorporeal spirits and the nature of a first cause, in chapter 11). So we can have confidence in the validity of the *form* which our science should take (namely something like ballistics), but we cannot have comparable confidence in the validity of any *particular* explanation—that must remain essentially hypothetical.

With this theory, Hobbes was completely untroubled by the Cartesian doubt. As he said in the *Elements*, it is not

> impossible for a man to be so far deceived, as when his dream is past, to think it real: for if he dream of such things as are ordinarily in his mind, and in such order as he useth to do waking, and withal that he laid him down to sleep in the place where he findeth himself when he awaketh (all which may happen) [,] I know no *κριτήριον* or mark by which he can discern whether it were a dream or not, and do therefore the less wonder to hear a man sometimes to tell his dream for a truth, or to take it for a vision (p. 12).

Hobbes was untroubled because, unlike Gassendi, he stuck in a clear-headed fashion to the argument that whatever we experience, whether in sleep or waking, or at the hands of a malicious demon, has been caused by some material object or objects impinging upon us. We cannot know what that object is *really* like, but the Cartesian doubt does not matter: our inability to conceive of change without cause and cause without moving material objects is sufficient to establish the real existence of *something*. Nevertheless, Hobbes proposed a partial distinction between perceptions, hinted at in the above passage. The sequence of percepts or conceptions can take various forms; it can be 'casual and incoherent, as in dreams for the most part', or it can be orderly. The explanation of disordered thought could be word-association, or more or less any psychological process; ordered thought, on the other hand, involves such things as consciously working out means to an end, or methodically resurrecting a lost memory.

Hobbes's response to Descartes thus freed him from any need to take the Cartesian proof of God's existence seriously. In chapter 11 of the *Elements* he outlined his own theology, stressing that the only conception of God that was possible was of a first cause, and that to attribute any other properties to him (such as knowing or loving) is pointless and meaningless. When he replied to Descartes's *Meditations*, he stressed that God is (so to speak) a 'dummy' term, and ridiculed the description of him as 'supremely intelligent'—'what, may I ask, is the idea which enables M. Descartes to understand the operation of God's understanding?'[52]

By 1640 Hobbes with these arguments had side-stepped modern scepticism. It is true that our perceptions do not give us a veridical picture of the world, and it is true that we cannot even know whether we are awake or asleep. But these facts are compatible with true science, or at least science which takes the form of explanations which meet the necessary criteria for good scientific explanation. Descartes had argued the same, but only on the basis of a wholly unpersuasive theory about God's existence; Hobbes thus seemed (at least to himself) to have put forward the only convincing post-sceptical metaphysics. But it was a metaphysics which, in its developed form, was partly designed to meet Descartes's hyperbolical doubt, and thus to rescue the basic idea of the modern philosophy from the

[52] Descartes, *Philosophical Writings*, ii. 131.

sceptical attack which Descartes had launched upon it from within the movement. As Hobbes said in 1646, about his fundamental theory of perception,

> the same doctrine having since been published by another, I might bee challenged for building on another man's ground. Yett philosophical ground I take to be of such a nature, that any man may build upon it that will, especially if the owner himselfe will nott.[53]

From the point of view of many modern readers, the structure which Hobbes erected on this ground is much more to their taste, and houses more fittingly their ontological assumptions, than the one which Descartes built.

[53] *EW* vii. 468.

2

Hobbes and the Royal Society

NOEL MALCOLM

Why was Thomas Hobbes never elected a Fellow of the Royal Society? This is a question which has often been asked. I agree with many of the details of the answers which have been given to it; but I believe that, in putting those and other details together, it is possible to arrive at a rather different overall conclusion. In the process it may also be possible to add something to our knowledge of Hobbes—and perhaps even to our knowledge of the Royal Society.

Our first witness, as always, must be John Aubrey, FRS. As any biographer of Hobbes quickly comes to realize, Aubrey had an extraordinarily accurate memory for the details of Hobbes's life; this may be true in general of those subjects of *Brief Lives* who were personally known to Aubrey. But that does not mean that Aubrey had no concerns of his own to bring to bear on the interpretation and presentation of Hobbes's biography. His friendship and sympathy for Hobbes was itself one of the strongest of these moulding influences. He was keen to show that hostilities to his old friend were in the main personal, local, specific, and petty affairs. And in addition Aubrey was himself an active and enthusiastic member of the Royal Society—not a maggoty-headed antiquary but a thoroughly modern scientist, as Michael Hunter has amply shown—many of whose closest friends were also Fellows of the Society. So it is not surprising that his comments on this question in his 'Life of Hobbes' are, as Simon Schaffer and Steven Shapin have recently said, an act of posthumous reconciliation.[1]

In the middle of a list of Hobbes's friends and admirers which includes eight Fellows of the Royal Society, Aubrey inserted the following passage:

[1] *Leviathan and the Air-Pump* (Princeton, 1985), 132.

> To conclude, he had a high esteeme for the Royall Societie, having sayd (vide Behemoth pag. 242 . . .) that 'Naturall Philosophy was removed from the Universities to Gresham Colledge', meaning the Royall Societie that meets there; and the Royall Societie (generally) had the like for him: and he would long since have been ascribed a member there, but for the sake of one or two persons, whom he tooke to be his enemies. In their meeting at Gresham Colledge is his picture, drawen by the life . . . which they much esteeme . . .[2]

This account is reconciliatory to the point of being disingenuous. The picture was one commissioned by Aubrey himself, and presented by him to the Royal Society in 1670.[3] The passage quoted from *Behemoth* consisted, in its original context, not of praise for the Society but of vituperation against the Universities, from which, Hobbes was claiming, science had fled. More difficult to judge is Aubrey's comment on Hobbes's relations with Henry Stubbe, 'whom he much esteemed for his great learning and parts, but at the latter end Mr. Hobbs differ'd with him for that he wrote against the lord chancellor Bacon and the Royall Societie'.[4] Here I suspect that what Hobbes objected to was not the fact that Stubbe wrote against the Royal Society, but rather the nature of the arguments on which he based those attacks: his defence of Aristotelian and Galenist medical theory, his qualified defence of scholastic philosophy, and his argument that the new philosophy was an engine to unhinge Protestant Christendom, by encouraging religious heterodoxy and allowing the scholastic weapons of controversial theology to rust away.

Aubrey's attempts at reconciliation had begun during Hobbes's lifetime. In 1675 he wrote to Hobbes, informing him of Robert Hooke's desire that if Hobbes had any mathematical or scientific papers to be printed, he would send them to Hooke to have them published by the Royal Society.[5] Here again it is difficult to avoid the conclusion that this conciliatory gesture had been prompted by Aubrey himself. Hooke, so far as we know, only met Hobbes twice; his account of the impression

[2] *Brief Lives, chiefly of Contemporaries*, ed. A. Clark, 2 vols. (Oxford, 1898), i. 371–2.

[3] *Ibid.* i. 354; Shapin and Schaffer, *Leviathan and the Air-Pump*, p. 132.

[4] Aubrey, *Brief Lives*, i. 371.

[5] Aubrey's letter does not survive, but its contents are made clear by Hobbes's reply: see n. 7, below.

Hobbes made on him is not favourable, and the only sporadic references to Hobbes in Hooke's private writings are not complimentary either.[6] But we do know that at this period Hooke was feeling increasingly resentful towards Hobbes's arch-enemy Wallis, whom he suspected of stealing his ideas, and it is likely that Aubrey wanted to make use of this common hostility to draw Hobbes and Hooke together. Hobbes's reply harped on this theme: 'does Mr. Hooke think it fit that any thing of mine should passe through the hands of Dr. Wallis . . .?' The general tenor of Hobbes's answer was that he had no objections to the nature of the Society as such, but that he could not yet forgive them for having publicly sanctioned insulting attacks on him by some of their members—meaning, above all, Boyle and Wallis. If he had anything new to publish, Hobbes wrote,

> I could be content it should be published by the society much rather then any other, provided that they that continually attend the businesse, and are of the society upon no other account then of their Learning, either had forborn to do me injury or made me reparation afterwards . . . As for the members, I have amongst them for the most part sufficient reputation . . . but that is nothing to the body of the Society, by whose authority the evill words and disgraces put upon me by Dr. Wallis are still countenanced, without any publique Act of the Society to do me Right. . . .[7]

This does at least furnish some solid evidence of Hobbes's view of the matter, and it is on such evidence as this that Quentin Skinner built his account of the whole affair in his important article of 1969. 'The truth', he wrote, 'seems to be simply that Hobbes first of all raised the enmity of three of the founding Fellows, who managed to keep him out, and that he eventually came to feel sufficiently slighted by this treatment to insist on holding aloof'.[8] The true explanation, in other words, should be in terms of the particular, the commonsensical, and the all-too-human, as opposed to large-scale explanation in terms of fundamental ideological or religious issues dividing Hobbes

[6] For a valuable summary of the evidence see Shapin and Schaffer, *Leviathan and the Air-Pump*, p. 133 n. For Hooke's account of his first encounter see n. 20, below.

[7] 24 Feb. 1674/5; F. Tönnies, 'Hobbes-Analekten I', *Archiv für Geschichte der Philosophie*, NS 17 (1904), 291–317 (here pp. 313–14), from the copy of the letter in Bodleian MS Aubrey 12, fos. 166–7.

[8] 'Thomas Hobbes and the Nature of the Early Royal Society', *Historical Journal*, 12 (1969), 217–39 (here p. 220).

from the Society. I would want to agree very strongly on the importance of these human contingencies; but I shall try to argue that such an explanation still leaves something unaccounted for, and that we must have some recourse to the large-scale categories of what may be loosely called ideology. And I shall also try to argue that a proper understanding of those wider issues does not involve falling back into the old-fashioned, straightforward explanation in terms of Hobbes's unacceptable heterodoxy; nor does it involve falling forwards, so to speak, into the new-fashioned sociology of knowledge propounded by Schaffer and Shapin.

A good starting-point might be the letter just quoted, in which Hobbes complained that although many individual members had a good opinion of him, 'the body of the Society', as a corporate person, seemed content for some reason to let itself be publicly associated with attacks on Hobbes by writers such as Wallis. When Professor Skinner writes that a handful of Fellows managed to keep Hobbes out, we want to know why this was such an apparently easy thing to do, given that Hobbes had more than a handful of friends and admirers in the Society. And quite properly he supplies an answer to this question. The reason why the Society as a whole endorsed in this way the hostility of a few of its members was a very simple one: Hobbes was a club bore.

One reason for saying this is to point out that we should think of the Royal Society as a club, rather than thinking of it as a modern professional institution operating strict criteria of admission. Some significant scientists in this period never became Fellows (particularly, as Michael Hunter's geographical analysis has shown, those living away from London); and conversely some Fellows—bishops and noblemen above all—were sleeping partners with little real interest in science.[9] This is a salutary point to make; but it may become misleading. The Royal Society was not just a club; although some of its members were appointed for largely honorific reasons, it was essentially intended as a club *of scientists*. Rather than say that they were not strictly applying the criteria of what counted as doing science, we should say that for the most part they were applying the

[9] See the 'Introduction' to M. Hunter, *The Royal Society and its Fellows 1660–1700*, BSHS Monographs, no. 4 (Chalfont St Giles, 1982), esp. pp. 7–8, 25–7.

criteria or standards of their day, standards which may seem very wide or vague in our eyes. And those criteria were certainly broad enough to include Hobbes. Hobbes was a scientist by anybody's standards; his major work on physics, *De Corpore* (1655), is a description of the system of nature on a par with similar works by Descartes, Gassendi, or Digby; and if Walter Charlton could become a Fellow on the strength of similar, but derivative, exercises in system-building, it seems clear that Hobbes, *a fortiori*, could have been elected as a scientist.

Nor were Hobbes's scientific achievements confined to system-building. He had done intensive work on optics, analysing problems such as that of the place of the image in a parabolic reflector, and he had been the first person to give the correct dynamic explanation of the sine-law of refraction.[10] He was far from refusing to dirty his hands in practical science. When Descartes in his *Dioptrics* compared refracted light to a bullet fired at an angle into a solid surface, it was Hobbes who, as his Latin Optical Manuscript shows, performed experiments with an airgun to test the theory.[11] In Paris in the 1640s he took a course in chemistry in the Jardin des Plantes; he also studied Vesalius and performed dissections with William Petty.[12] It also seems likely that he had dissected deer with William Harvey.[13] He read widely in contemporary physics and astronomy; and in 1648 he bought the Marquess of Newcastle's collection of telescopes and microscopes, which included two telescopes by Torricelli and four by Eustachio Divino, of which the largest, 'Eustatio Divino, his Greate Glass', was 29 feet long.[14] This monster was probably left behind in France; of the two microscopes, Hobbes gave one to his friend Sorbière before he left the country, and the other he had already given to Petty, who proudly told Benjamin Worsley in 1648 that he valued it at

[10] BL MS Harl. 3360, pp. 73–81; on Hobbes's optical work see A. Shapiro, 'Kinematic Optics: A Study of the Wave Theory of Light in the Seventeenth Century', *Archive for the History of the Exact Sciences*, 11 (1973), 134–266 (esp. pp. 154–5), and J. Bernhardt, 'Hobbes et le mouvement de la lumière', *Revue d'histoire des sciences*, 30 (1977), 3–24.

[11] Hobbes, 'Tractatus Opticus', ed. F. Alessio, *Rivista critica di storia della filosofia*, 18 (1963), 147–228 (here p. 164).

[12] Aubrey, *Brief Lives*, i. 336–7.

[13] G. Keynes, *The Life of William Harvey* (Oxford, 1978), 388.

[14] Portland MSS, Nottingham University Library, MS Pw. 1. 668.

'£3 sterling'.[15] When Hobbes rejoined his patron the Earl of Devonshire in England in the 1650s he seems to have given him the taste for astronomy or optics: the Earl's accounts show that he bought a 'perspective glass' from the famous instrument-maker, Richard Reeve, in 1656.[16] (It was in Reeve's shop in 1663 that Hooke first encountered Hobbes, together with the Earl of Devonshire.)[17] In 1659 the Earl had bought Hobbes's entire collection of 'prospective glasses' for the huge sum of £80.[18]

Hobbes was, then, enough of a scientist to qualify for admission to any scientists' club. But was he a club bore? The evidence here is rather contradictory. Hostile sources suggest that he was generally overbearing and irascible. Walter Pope, for example, in the course of trying to show how opposed Seth Ward was to Hobbes (for reasons which will become clear later), wrote: 'if any one objected to his [sc. Hobbes's] Dictates, he would leave the Company in a passion, saying, his business was to Teach, not Dispute.' (Pope adds: 'He had entertained an aversion to Dr. *Ward*, for having written something against him . . . and before he would enter into the Assembly, he would enquire if Dr. *Ward* was there, and if he [were he] came not in . . .'.)[19] Robert Hooke's description of his first meeting paints a similar picture, though we should not forget that it occurs in a letter Hooke sent to Boyle shortly after the latter's public controversy with Hobbes: 'I found him to lard and seale every asseveration with a round othe, to undervalue all other men's opinions and judgments, to defend to the utmost what he asserted though never so absurd . . .'.[20] This was certainly a popular view of Hobbes. It was insinuated, for example, into the English translation of Sorbière's account of his visit to England in 1663. When Sorbière talked to Charles II they both agreed that if Hobbes had been a little less dogmatic ('s'il eust esté un

[15] S. Sorbière, *Lettres et discours sur divers matières curieuses* (Paris, 1660), 436; Sheffield University Library, MS Hartlib 8/27, fo. 2^r: 'copy of Mr Worsley's letter 22 June 1648'.

[16] Chatsworth, MS Hardwick 14, entries for Oct. 1656.

[17] See below, n. 20.

[18] Chatsworth, MS Hardwick 33, entries for Apr. 1659.

[19] *The Life of the Right Reverend Father in God Seth, Lord Bishop of Salisbury* (London, 1697), 118.

[20] BL Additional MS 6193, fos. 68^v–69^r; printed in R. Boyle, *Works*, ed. T. Birch, 5 vols. (London, 1744), v. 533.

peu moins dogmatique'), he would have been very useful to the Royal Society. The English version subtly traduced Sorbière's meaning: 'it was agreed on all Hands, that if Mr. *Hobbs* were not so very Dogmatical, he would be very Useful and Necessary to the Royal-Society . . .'.[21]

Sorbière's own characterization of Hobbes, however, was rather different. In print he portrayed him as an amusing, thoughtful, and kindly man, and in a letter to Hobbes written after his return to France he exclaimed: 'you are a good friend, a good courtier, and of the best temperament in the world. I remember our walk together at Tilbourne, and the gaiety of all your conversations last year, which I shall always remember as one of the happiest times of my life.'[22] Aubrey, who was also Hobbes's familiar friend, wrote that '(though he was ready and happy in repartying in *drollery*) he did not care to give a present answer *to a question*, unless he had thoroughly considered it before: for he was against "too hasty concluding" . . .'.[23] And Hobbes himself replied to his critics on this point in *Mr. Hobbes Considered*:

> Then for his morosity and peevishness, with which some asperse him, all that know him familiarly, know the contrary. 'Tis true that when vain and ignorant young scholars, unknowne to him before, come to him on purpose to argue with him, and fall into undiscreet and uncivill expressions, and he then appeare not well contented, 'twas not his morosity, but their vanity, which should be blamed.[24]

This passage rings true, it may be said, precisely because it does carry the rather lofty tone of Hobbes's easily wounded pride. But we can appeal to Hobbes's deeds as well as to his words. As he pointed out parenthetically in his attacks on Boyle, one of the most important proto-scientific societies of the period had been the regular gathering of philosophers and scientists in Mersenne's rooms in the convent of Minim friars in Paris. Hobbes had attended these meetings frequently throughout the 1640s,

[21] *Relation d'un voyage en Angleterre* (Paris, 1664), 97; *A Voyage to England* (London, 1709), 40.

[22] Chatsworth, Hobbes MSS, Letters from foreign correspondents, letter no. 60 (1 July 1664). I am most grateful to the Trustees of the Chatsworth Settlement for permission to cite this ms., and to the Librarian, Mr Peter Day, for his help.

[23] Aubrey, *Brief Lives*, i. 356.

[24] Cited by Aubrey, *ibid.* i. 336; Hobbes, *EW* iv. 439.

and had formed a warm friendship with Mersenne, Gassendi, Roberval, and other leading figures with whom he disputed there. This is not the record of an unclubbable man.

The conflicting testimonies to Hobbes's character can after all be reconciled, if we assume that he was pleasant and tractable with those whom he regarded as his friends, and intolerant only in company which he felt was predisposed to hostility towards him. And Hobbes *did* feel that the Royal Society as a whole was hostile to him. Hooke's account of his first encounter with Hobbes begins by saying that he did not know who this old man was, and wondered why he was staring at him in a strange way without saying anything; but his surprise at this ceased when he learned that the old man was Hobbes, 'supposing', Hooke wrote, 'he had been inform'd to whom I belong'd'.[25] The fact that Hooke was an employee of the Society was sufficient to explain Hobbes's baleful glare. When in the following year the Danish scholar Ole Borch visited Sorbière in Paris, he noted in his journal what Sorbière had told him about his latest correspondence with Hobbes. Hobbes has tried to show, he wrote, 'that he has solved the problem of the duplication of the cube. There is however someone else who thinks his reasoning is faulty. But to him Hobbes has already replied that he is not a Fellow of the Royal Society, and that he (Hobbes) is arming himself against that society'.[26] ('Arming himself' here translates 'se armare', with its nicely balanced implication of defensive hostility.) And in the dedicatory epistle to the 1668 edition of the *Dialogus Physicus* (the attack on Boyle) Hobbes wrote: 'Many political writers and clerics contend with me on the subject of the sovereign's right. A new sort of mathematicians contend with me about geometry . . . Those Fellows of the Royal Society who have most credit and are as it were the masters of the rest, contend with me about physics . . . All these people are inimical towards me.'[27] This passage was, admittedly, not present in the original edition of 1661. But the whole tone of the book, which gratuitously extended its criticism of Boyle's book into a

[25] BL Additional MS 6193, fo. 69^{r}.

[26] *Olai Borrichii Itinerarium 1660–1665*, ed. H. Scheperlern, 4 vols. (Copenhagen/London, 1983), iii. 192. The term Borch uses for the Royal Society is 'Collegium Naturae': cf. iii. 70. The 'someone else' was Slusius.

[27] Hobbes, *LW* iv. 236–7.

criticism of the whole Society, had already expressed his feeling that the Society was influenced by what he openly referred to (in 1661) as 'hatred of Hobbes'.[28] He felt that he was, and would remain, an unwelcome outsider.

If the Society had been simply a club, it would be difficult to see why Hobbes's friends at least (who did not find him a bore) should not have made some attempt to elect him. Unlike most clubs, the Royal Society had a qualified majority-vote system of election, with no provision for blackballing. But the attempt was never made—this despite the fact that Hobbes was on good terms with the King, whose patronage the Fellows were keen to secure and strengthen, and despite the fact that Hobbes was perhaps the only living scientist (with the possible exception of the mathematician Richard White) who had direct personal relations with Bacon, the Society's patron saint and arch-bestower of intellectual respectability. Nor did Hobbes lack friends in the Society. Out of the 56 Fellows to join the Society before March 1661, no fewer than 15 are known to have been friends of Hobbes, or members of his circle of patrons, or admirers of his works.[29] And if we look back over the previous dozen years or so at the pattern of Hobbes's friendships and acquaintances, we find that he had belonged (and to some extent still did belong) to some of the main groupings of writers, philosophers, and practising scientists among whom the origins of the Royal Society are usually identified.

It is worth going back, then, to 1650 or before, to consider what patterns of acceptance and rejection Hobbes underwent in the intervening years. The striking thing that emerges, if we look at attitudes to Hobbes in the late 1640s, is that he was thought of by many people principally as a scientist, and that his reputation stood extremely high, on the basis of very little published work (a brief treatise on optics, and a few other pages on epistemology, physics, and in particular telescopes, in compilations published by Mersenne in 1644).[30] In England

[28] *Ibid.* iv. 273.

[29] Petty, Pell, Matthew Wren, Digby, Austen, the Earl of Devonshire, Ent, Brereton, Oldenburg, Lord Cavendish, Evelyn, Scarborough, Waller, the Marquess of Dorchester, Lord Bruce.

[30] Mersenne, *Cogitata Physico-Mathematica* (Paris, 1644), section of preface to 'Ballistica' and part of proposition 24 (pp. 74–82); *Universae Geometriae Synopsis* (Paris, 1644), 'Optica', Bk. 7 ('Tractatus Opticus') and a fragment on telescopes (pp. 473–5).

news and expectations of his current work were spread by letter-writers, either corresponding directly with him like his old friend Robert Payne, or learning about his work from men such as Sir Charles Cavendish on the continent. And in Europe there was the corresponding network of Mersenne himself, supplemented by the assiduous efforts of admirers such as Sorbière and Martel. Sorbière knew that Hobbes had written at least one more optical treatise in manuscript, and that he was preparing a major work on physics. And of course everyone who had seen one of the rare 1642 copies of *De Cive* knew from its title (*Elementorum Philosophiae, Sectio Tertia De Cive*) that the two prior sections of Hobbes's complete system of philosophy were to be expected from the press. When Sorbière went to the trouble of arranging the printing of a second edition of *De Cive* in Holland in 1646–7, his real motive was to stimulate Hobbes into producing the rest of his scientific works for Elzevier as well. (He wrote to Bartholin in 1647: 'I have organised the edition of *De Cive* in order to elicit from that admirable man what he has promised to send on the subject of *nature*.')[31]

Others in England had the same appetite for Hobbes's scientific works. In February 1650 a book appeared which many readers thought was the long-awaited second section of Hobbes's system, *De Homine*. The deception was probably deliberate: Robert Payne wrote in March to Sheldon that the book was 'printed lately by Fr. Bowman, out of a MS. Copy of Mr Lockey's, who persuaded Bowman to publish it as the second part of Mr Hobbes's intended Work'.[32] (Four months later Payne was telling Sheldon of his recent correspondence with Hobbes: 'As for ye other workes, not yet published . . . I have sollicited him to hasten their edition.')[33] The publication of 1650 was in fact simply the first half of Hobbes's *Elements of Law*, which had been available in numerous manuscript copies in England since 1640. But the title given to it in 1650 was designed to appeal to all those who were eagerly awaiting Hobbes's scientific analysis of human psychology: *Humane Nature, Or, the*

[31] F. Tönnies, 'Siebzehn Briefe des Thomas Hobbes an Samuel Sorbière, nebst Briefen Sorbière's, Mersenne's . . .', *Archiv für Geschichte der Philosophie*, 3 (1889–90), 58–71, 192–232 (here p. 198), from a copy of Sorbière's letter in the Bibliothèque Nationale, Paris, MS fonds latin 10352, vol. 1, fo. 112.

[32] BL MS Birch 4162, fo. 112r (26 Mar. 1650).

[33] BL MS Lansdowne 841, fo. 174r (16 July 1650).

fundamental Elements of Policie, Being a Discoverie Of the Faculties, Acts, and Passions of the Soul of Man, from their original causes; According to such Philosophical Principles as are not commonly known or asserted. The prefatory material to this book included a letter to the reader which was almost certainly by Seth Ward, commending Hobbes's philosophy as constructed 'upon such principles and in such order as are used by men conversant in demonstration'.[34] In the eyes of Seth Ward, then, Professor of Astronomy and a leading figure in the Oxford experimental club, Hobbes was definitely 'one of us'.

To the same volume, Ward's friend and fellow-scientist Ralph Bathurst contributed an elegant and hyperbolic poem in praise of Hobbes, comparing him to Archimedes. Hobbes was touched by this and sent Bathurst two complimentary copies of *Leviathan* when it appeared a year later (one of which was perhaps intended for Ward); in reply Bathurst wrote to him that 'I hope your learned booke of Optickes, and that other *de corpore*, if it be yet finished, may no longer lie concealed: especially since now the best wits, as well here as in other countries, are so greedy to listen after workes of that nature, and to vindicate themselves from the superficiall doctrines of the schools . . .'.[35] Bathurst had probably heard about Hobbes's 'learned book of Optickes' from another active member of the Oxford experimental club; for the book in question was none other than the English Optical Treatise of which William Petty had produced the fair copy for Hobbes in Paris in late 1645 and early 1646.[36] Petty was to remain a lifelong friend and admirer of Hobbes. So here we have three central figures in what is often presented as the main forerunner of the Royal Society, all with high opinions of Hobbes's importance as a exponent of the new philosophy. Most of the other members' attitudes to Hobbes at this stage are unknown. Aubrey lists Rooke as a friend of Hobbes, though on what evidence we do not know.[37] But even John Wilkins, when he came to criticize Hobbes in the *Vindiciae Academiarum* four years later, described him as 'a person of good ability and solid parts', and in order to deflate Hobbes's claims of novelty

[34] Hobbes, *EW* iv, *Human Nature*, 'To the Reader'.

[35] T. Warton, *The Life and Literary Remains of Ralph Bathurst* (London, 1761), 49 n.

[36] BL MS Harl. 3360.

[37] Aubrey, *Brief Lives*, i. 366.

emphasized that many of Hobbes's principles were already held by 'many men' who worked on science in Oxford.[38]

In these men's eyes Hobbes was a man of the present—and, where his works were concerned, of the future. But he was also a figure to be respected because he represented the older generation of English scientists and mathematicians, men such as Walter Warner or William Oughtred. Remnants of the intellectual world of Great Tew and Oxford in the 1630s lingered on in Oxford and elsewhere, and added depth to Hobbes's reputation: Hobbes's friend Payne (who was a friend of Bathurst) was one of them, the almost obscure Mr Lockey (later Bodley's Librarian) was another, and George Morley, whose scientific interests are strongly witnessed by his library catalogue, was a third.[39] History has turned Ward, Wilkins, and their colleagues into the impregnably central figures, beside whom even in this period Hobbes may seem like an upstart and an outsider. So it is worth remembering that in 1650 they looked up to Hobbes, both as a Grand Old Man and as an innovator of whom much was to be expected.

Hobbes's admirers had to wait a long time for the promised completion of his system. *De Corpore* appeared in 1655, *De Homine* (which incorporated part of the English Optical Treatise) in 1658. Perhaps it is true that the physical explanations they offered disappointed some of their readers; that is certainly true of the mathematical excursions in *De Corpore*; and perhaps some of the admirers already mentioned had developed a stronger taste for experimentalist science in the intervening years. But worse things than that had happened in the meanwhile. In 1654 Wilkins and Ward had attacked Hobbes in their *Vindiciae Academiarum* because of his criticism of the Universities in *Leviathan*. This was suddenly a serious issue, after a proposal had been made in the Barebones Parliament to abolish the Universities altogether. It was precisely *because* Hobbes still appeared in 1654 as an authoritative speaker on behalf of the new science that Wilkins and Ward took such trouble to attack him. And having taken this step (which involved trying to marginalize Hobbes by making him appear

[38] *Vindiciae Academiarum* (Oxford, 1654), 6–7.

[39] See J. C. Hayward, 'The *Mores* of Great Tew: Literary, Philosophical and Political Idealism in Falkland's Circle', Cambridge University Ph.D. dissertation, 1983, p. 174.

dogmatic, magisterial, ignorant, unoriginal, and out of date), Ward went further and attacked his theology in one of the first major theological critiques of *Leviathan*, entitled *In Thomae Hobbii Philosophia Exercitatio Epistolica*. Meanwhile Hobbes had foolishly taken up the challenge to demonstrate his superiority in geometry to the Oxford Professors of Mathematics, and was engaged in an increasingly bitter war of words with John Wallis. The real bitterness on Hobbes's side came from the fact that he regarded Wallis as a representative of the Presbyterian party. So with these two steps the argument had shifted into the realms of theology and church government.

What ideological significance should we accord to either or both of these steps? Ward's attack on Hobbes's theology sets a significant precedent. Hobbes's reputation for heterodoxy was growing gradually during this period; Ward could see which way the wind was blowing, and decided that attack was the best form of dissociation; and he needed to dissociate the new science from Hobbes precisely because Hobbes was such a major spokesman of it. Ward's attack on Hobbes was self-protective, diversionary, and pre-emptive.

In the case of church government, J. R. Jacob has suggested that this argument had a profounder significance at the level of metaphysics. The Oxford group, he argues, was deeply opposed to Hobbes's metaphysics because his attack on the notion of incorporeal spirits was an attack on their priestly powers to manipulate the world of spirits, and hence an attack on the claims of the clergy to exercise power over the people.[40] There is an argument of this sort in Part 4 of *Leviathan*; but that argument was directed against scholastic Aristotelianism, and there is no reason why Wilkins or Ward should have felt affected by it—except in so far as it was generally anticlerical in tone. The best disproof of Jacob's interpretation lies in Stubbe's letters to Hobbes during this period, in which the young Oxford scholar explained that Wallis was isolated on this issue: most of the other leading figures in Oxford were in fact quite close to Hobbes on the question of church government, and Wallis was the odd man out in a ruling alliance consisting mainly of Independents and pragmatic Anglicans. 'Wilkins of Wadham', Stubbe told

[40] *Henry Stubbe, Radical Protestantism and the early Enlightenment* (Cambridge, 1983), 16–17.

Hobbes in 1656, 'maintained in his colledge yt no forme of Church-gouernemt is *jure diuino*.'[41] There is a revealing comment in Bathurst's letter to Hobbes of 1651, a comment which Warton partly omitted from the printed version of the letter. After reading *Leviathan*, Bathurst begs Hobbes to publish his other works. 'And', he adds, 'thus much am I the rather bold to suggest to you, because if by your other workes already published, you have gained so high an esteeme, even when almost a whole order of men thought it concern'd them to cry downe your opinions, how much more shall those be received with honour, in whose argument no man's *Diana* will be call'd in question'.[42] The whole order of men here must surely be the priests or presbyters who claimed rights and powers over men's actions in the state.

Jacob's attempt to read a deep metaphysical significance into the division between Hobbes and men such as Wilkins on the issue of clericalism in the state fails, I believe, beause there was in fact little division between them; compared with high-church sacerdotalists or doctrinaire Presbyterians, Wilkins and Hobbes were in the same camp. J. G. A. Pocock has written, in a very suggestive phrase, that 'it is tempting to define the politics of the Oxford scientists at this time as conservative and empirical, authoritarian and latitudinarian'.[43] The general nature of their position was one of pragmatic acceptance of the need for authority. Wilkins's interest in the maintenance of the Cromwellian regime became a more personal one when he married Cromwell's sister in 1656. Not surprisingly, he favoured a monarchist, authoritarian system of government—authoritarian in the sense that it should be based on the authority of an individual rather than on the inherent rationality of a republican constitution. In 1657 he commissioned Matthew Wren (another scientist and future FRS) to write a defence of monarchy in answer to Harrington's *Oceana*. Wren's arguments

[41] BL Additional MS 32, 553, fo. 24ʳ.

[42] The MS of this letter has not been found, but a copy of Warton's book (see n. 35 above) in the Old Library, Trinity College, Oxford, has annotations by someone (perhaps James Ingram) who was able to compare the original MS with Warton's partial transcription of it. I am most grateful to Dr Dennis Burden, the Librarian, for this information.

[43] Harrington, *The Political Works*, ed. J. G. A. Pocock (Cambridge, 1977); 'Introduction', p. 84.

in this work (*Considerations on Mr. Harrington's Commonwealth of Oceana*) often take on an explicitly Hobbesian tone. When Harrington contrasts the Empire of Laws with the Empire of Men, Wren replies: 'I do not thinke my self bound to undertake all Challenges that are sent to Mr. *Hobs*: but the easinesse of the Defence in this Particular that Men Govern and not Laws, tempts me to be his second . . .'.[44] Wren was strongly influenced by Hobbes, and it was a singular piece of bad judgement that Sir Edward Hyde should have urged him in 1659 to write a refutation of *Leviathan*. (Wren toned down his support for Hobbes in his next book, *Monarchy Asserted*, but he could not resist surreptitiously waving a Hobbist flag by quoting Thucydides on the state of nature in Hobbes's translation.)[45]

When Harrington treated Wren as a representative of 'the Virtuosi' or 'the University Wits', this was not strictly accurate; but he was representative of some of the most prominent among them, whose views can be ascertained on the subject of government or church-government. When Seth Ward preached a sermon *Against Resistance of Lawful Powers* to the King in 1661 he put in some obligatory jibes against the Hobbist doctrine. But some of his own arguments have a distinct congruence with Hobbes, and help to explain Ward's pragmatic acceptance of authority for the sake of peace during the Interregnum. For example, commenting on 'the Power of the Magistrate in Matters of Religion', he writes: 'If none have Power to order Matters of Religion, there must be Confusion; if any other beside the supream Magistrate, there will be Division.'[46]

Looking back on Hobbes's disputes with Ward, Wilkins, and Wallis in the 1650s, one is struck at first by the contingency of it all; if only the Universities had not felt politically threatened in 1653–4, one feels, Hobbes would never have become embroiled in these disputes, and would never have suffered the running sore of his mathematical controversy with Wallis—which did in the end damage his reputation as a scientist. But, on the other hand, one is struck by the way that religious or political issues arose in which, the more disreputable Hobbes became, the more

[44] *Considerations* (London, 1657), 8.

[45] C. Wren, *Parentalia: or, Memoirs of the Family of the Wrens* (London, 1750), 53–4; M. Wren, *Monarchy Asserted* (Oxford, 1659), 35.

[46] *Against Resistance of Lawful Powers* (London, n.d.), 12–13.

necessary it was for the other scientists to dissociate themselves from him by attacking him, precisely because he was in some ways embarrassingly close to their own position. The political issues did not greatly embarrass them till after the Restoration; the association between a mechanistic world-view and religious heterodoxy had begun to trouble them in the 1650s and would continue to do so after the formation of the Royal Society.

Before turning to some of those issues in the 1660s, it is necessary to look briefly at Hobbes's other contacts with future Fellows in the previous decade. Hobbes was based in London for much of each year from 1652 onwards; the evidence for his activities is fragmentary, but we do know that he was on good terms with a number of future Fellows—beginning with Brereton, who probably negotiated on his behalf with the Council of State to sanction his return to England.[47] We know that in the early 1650s Hobbes moved in the circles of Selden and Harvey; Selden's friend John Vaughan, lawyer, amateur mathematician, and future FRS, became a great admirer of Hobbes, and it was probably through Harvey that Hobbes met John Aubrey.[48] He already knew Edmund Waller and John Evelyn, and he gained some acquaintance with Henry Oldenburg through the latter's employment under the Earl of Devonshire.[49] We also know that he was moving in the rather more free-thinking circles of Thomas White, the Catholic philosopher, his brother Richard White (astronomer and future FRS), John Davies, the translator of Naudé on witchcraft and the man who published Hobbes's *On Liberty and Necessity* with a fiercely anticlerical preface, and John Hall of Durham, the

[47] On Brereton's friendship with Hobbes see his letter to Pell, 5 Mar. 1652, in R. Vaughan (ed.), *The Protectorate of Oliver Cromwell*, 2 vols. (London, 1838), ii. 384; and his letter to Huygens, 29 Mar. 1652, in C. Huygens, *Œuvres complètes*, 22 vols. (The Hague, 1888–1950), i. 176.

[48] Selden and Vaughan: Aubrey, *Brief Lives*, i. 369; on the 'triumvirate' of Selden, Harvey, and Hobbes, see Keynes, *Life of Harvey*, pp. 386–90. Aubrey's personal acquaintance with Hobbes seems to date from the early 1650s; Aubrey had become a friend of Harvey in 1651 (*ibid.* 383).

[49] Evelyn: see his *Diary and Correspondence*, ed. W. Bray, 4 vols. (London, 1859), i. 280, 327 (7 Sept. 1651, 14 Dec. 1655). Waller: see Aubrey, *Brief Lives*, i. 369, 372; P. Wikelund, ' "Thus I passe my time in this place": An Unpublished Letter of Thomas Hobbes', *English Language Notes*, 6 (1969), 263–8; P. Hardacre, 'A Letter from Edmund Waller to Thomas Hobbes', *Huntington Library Quarterly*, 11 (1948), 431–3, Oldenburg: see his *Correspondence*, ed. A. Hall and M. Hall, 13 vols., (Madison, 1965–87), i. 74, letter 32.

educational reformer, friend of Hartlib, and apologist for Cromwell.[50] Thomas White was an intermediary between Hobbes's old friend Kenelm Digby and the Oxford mathematicians.[51] But perhaps the most important friend of Hobbes for our purposes was the physician and mathematician Charles Scarborough, whose house Walter Pope described as 'the Rendezvous of most of the Learned Men about London'.[52] (This was the 'Assembly' which, according to Pope, Hobbes would not enter when Seth Ward was there.) Scarborough was an admirer of Hobbes (he had a picture of him hanging in his chamber), and a central figure in those gatherings of scientists in London at the end of the decade which led to the formation of the Royal Society.[53]

It is in this context that I should like to offer a very speculative interpretation of a very slender piece of evidence. On 1 February 1659 Sorbière wrote to Hobbes from Paris, giving him further news of Montmor's academy, the group of French scientists who gathered at Montmor's house and had recently adopted a formal constitution (drawn up by Sorbière and another friend of Hobbes, du Prat). In this letter Sorbière sent Hobbes the complete list of rules for the academy, with the comment: 'I send them to you because you ask for them; and I do not mind if they are seen by everybody' (*& ie seray bien aisé qu'ils soient veus de tout le*

[50] T. White: see Hobbes, *AntiWhite,* 'Introduction', pp. 24–5. R. White: Aubrey, *Brief Lives*, i. 369. Davies: see J. Tucker, 'John Davies of Kidwelly (1627?–1693), Translator from the French', *Papers of the Bibliographical Society of America*, 44 (1950), 119–51; Naudé, *The History of Magick* (London, 1657). Hall: see the 'Account' of his life by Davies, prefixed to Hall's *Hierocles upon the Golden Verses of Pythagoras* (London, 1657), which mentions that he knew Thomas White and was known by Hobbes (sigs. b7r–A1r). Hall refers obliquely to Hobbes in his *Confusion Confounded* (London, 1654), sig. C1v.

[51] See the letters from Digby to Wallis (and Brouncker) in J. Wallis, *Commercium Epistolicum de Quaestionibus quibusdam Mathematicis* (Oxford, 1658).

[52] Pope, *Life of Seth [Ward]*, p. 117.

[53] See Pope's account (cited above); J. Wallis, *A Defence of the Royal Society* (London, 1678), p. 7, includes Scarborough in his list of London scientists in the mid-1640s (but cf. M. Purver, *The Royal Society: Concept and Creation* (Cambridge, Mass., 1967), 161–82); see also the letter from Anthony Thompson to Pell, 22 Nov. 1658, inviting him to a 'meeting . . . of some mathematicall freinds' in London, which would be attended by Rooke, Wren, Brouncker, Neile, Goddard, and Scarborough: J. Halliwell (ed.), *A Collection of Letters Illustrative of the Progress of Science* (London, 1841), 95–6. It is clear, I think, that Sprat's claim that the Oxford club removed to London in 1658 implies too sudden and definite a transition; there was a gradual process of osmosis during the 1650s, in which established scientists in London, such as Scarborough, acted as important focuses of association. (On the portrait see Aubrey, *Brief Lives*, i. 369.)

monde).[54] The phrasing of this suggests, perhaps, that Hobbes had asked for permission to show these rules to other people; and the most likely people to show them to would be men such as Scarborough, who had held similar meetings in his own house. It would be a rich irony if Hobbes had in this way contributed to the setting up of a formally constituted society at the end of the following year; and it would help to explain his deep resentment at being excluded from it.

The underlying reasons why that exclusion was bound to continue have already been hinted at. Hobbes was becoming an increasingly disreputable figure, both politically and theologically; and the people who felt that it was most in their interests to blacken his reputation further were the ones who were vulnerable to embarrassing comparisons between his position and their own. Most modern descriptions of the early years of the Royal Society still fail to give a sufficient sense of just how nervous of criticism the publicists of the Society were.[55] The whole of Part III of Sprat's *History*, for example, is taken up with arguing that the Society is not a danger to government, manners, education, or religion; Sprat's words are so convincingly soothing that we may tend to forget that there *was* a great mass of hostile opinion that needed to be soothed. Critics associated the new science with Epicureanism and atheism, and these were not just the hysterical fears of the ignorant outsiders: this problem deeply exercised the minds of Fellows such as More and Boyle. Critics attacked the Latitudinarianism of some of the principal publicists of the Royal Society, seeing a link between their claims on behalf of reason in natural knowledge, and the rationalism of their religious views, which demoted doctrinal differences and questions of divinely ordained church-government in favour of moral virtues, peace, and comprehension. And critics insinuated that just as their views implied an 'indifferency' in questions of church-government, so too they implied an 'indifferency' in politics.

On each of these overlapping issues there was a risk of being compared to Hobbes. As late as 1682 we can catch a revealing glimpse of this problem in Boyle's correspondence, which shows

[54] Sorbière, *Lettres et Discours*, p. 632.

[55] For an important exception to this rule, see M. Hunter, 'The Debate over Science', in J. R. Jones (ed.), *The Restored Monarchy 1660–1688* (London, 1979), 176–95.

a sudden flurry of concern over the publication under the Society's aegis of John Houghton's *Collection of Letters for the Improvement of Husbandry and Trade*. At a late stage it was noticed that the work included a sort of proto-Mandevillian argument, which appeared to recommend luxury and prodigality on economic grounds. Boyle's correspondent, John Beale, expressed fears of the criticisms this would unleash, and suggested that the Royal Society should reprint the public recantation of the penitent Hobbist Daniel Scargill.[56]

There is not space to discuss properly each of the areas of criticism and dissociation which have been briefly outlined. So the last part of this paper will concentrate on one of them, that of Latitudinarianism and rational religion, because although the comparisons with Hobbes were dangerously close to the mark in this area, it was here that the publicists of the Royal Society found their most useful weapons of anti-Hobbesian rhetoric.

Histories of English religious thought in this period are still dominated by the feeling that the rational or liberal theologians were making claims which were just obviously right, true, and reasonable, and that they can only have been opposed by obscurantists, reactionaries, or fanatics. We have swallowed, in other words, the Latitude-men's own account of their role. It is, I believe, impossible to understand the true nature of the movement in the 1650s and 1660s unless we realize that they were a campaigning minority (though rapidly gaining power through the hierarchy of the Church in the 1660s), and that their views were widely and correctly regarded as going against what had been the orthodox theology of the Church. Their emphasis on the reasonableness of religion and the reasonableness of God involved subverting the central tenet of anti-Tridentine Protestantism, the belief that man was saved by imputed righteousness only, not by any growth in his own intrinsic righteousness as a moral agent. In Mark Pattison's words, 'They spoke not of sin, but of vice . . . They had adopted the language of the moralists.'[57] It would be unreasonable of God, they felt, to damn those who tried hard, or to require of

[56] Boyle, *Works*, v. 508–10.

[57] *Essays*, ed. H. Nettleship, 2 vols. (Oxford, 1889); ii. 64. For the theological background to this change, see C. F. Allison, *The Rise of Moralism: The Proclamation of the Gospel from Hooker to Baxter* (London, 1966).

them anything more than they were naturally capable of: moral virtue and rational belief. A great deal of dogmatic theology was thus cast aside as irrelevant; this is echoed in the complaints of Stubbe, Barlow, Casaubon, and others that the New Learning encouraged neglect of the weapons of Protestant controversial theology. In the Restoration period the rational theologians were criticized on both sides: by high Anglicans such as Beaumont and by sectarian writers such as Bunyan. In each case the critics were trying to reassert the importance of getting one's doctrinal theology right. It is important to recognize, in other words, that when the Latitude-men loftily declared that they were above or outside theoretical controversies, this declaration was itself a way of taking sides in one of the most fundamental controversies of contemporary theology.

One of the strongest arguments they were able to use in this controversy after the Restoration was the myth of religious fanaticism and anarchy in the 1640s and 1650s. (By calling it a myth I do not mean to suggest that there was no truth in it, but rather to indicate the way it functioned talismanically in argument.) They could use this to suggest that the old Protestant theology led unacceptably to Antinomianism, and to imply that their moralizing version of religion was a necessary protection against the forces of enthusiasm and social disruption. And they could also suggest that any uncompromising attachment to particular details of doctrinal theology was a sign of fanaticism and—to use the key word—dogmatizing. In the rhetoric of the Latitude-men, their liberal theology offered a safe *via media* between two opposite dangers: atheism on the one hand, and dogmatism or fanaticism on the other. Against atheism they offered rational belief; and against dogmatism they offered a programme of moral virtues which emphasized charitableness, moderation, and a devotion to peace.

It was, I think, Joseph Glanvill who realized just how neatly this structure of argument could be turned to the defence of the new science. He was able to present the Royal Society as pursuing a virtuous *via media*, which could be described in terms of two interlocking sets of polarities. There was the polarity of Pyrrhonist scepticism on the one hand and dogmatism on the other: here Hobbes was an arch-dogmatist. But it was the dogmatic, a priori metaphysical theories of mechanistic Nature which were popularly regarded as leading to atheism; so on the religious pole, Hobbes was associated with the polarity of atheism, and the Royal Society was presented as treading the middle path of calm, rational belief between the atheists on one side and the fanatics and enthusiasts on the other.

The fullest expression of this pattern of argument comes in Glanvill's *Philosophia Pia; or, a Discourse of the Religious Temper, and Tendencies of the Experimental Philosophy, Which is profest By the Royal Society* (1671). 'It is the perverse opinion', Glanvill writes, 'of hasty, inconsiderate Men, that the study of Nature is prejudicial to the interests of *Religion*; And those that are *very* zealous, and *little* wise, endeavour to render the *Naturalist* suspected of holding secret correspondence with the *Atheist* . . .'[58] Not so, Glanvill explains—the study of Nature disproves the Atheist, and is a psychological corrective to fanaticism and 'the humour of disputing'. When Glanvill turns to attacking religious superstition, his arguments begin to seem uncomfortably close to those of Hobbes. But Hobbes is cleverly linked to enthusiasm through an anecdote about a madwoman in Warwickshire who made 'odde fetches of discourse . . . that look'd like scraps taken out of *Hobbes*, and *Epicurus*'; and then the display of hostility to Hobbes is taken further with an attack on 'men of the Epicurean sort' who 'have left *God*, and *Providence* out of their accounts . . .'. Here Glanvill hastens to explain that 'the late Restorers of the *Corpuscularian Hypothesis*, hate and despise that vile doctrine . . .'. Their version of mechanistic science, he insists, 'doth not in the least grate upon any *Principle* of *Religion*. Thus far I dare say I may undertake for most of the *Corpuscularian Philosophers* of our times, excepting *those* of Mr. *Hobb*'s way.'[59]

Glanvill's favourite theme was 'the humour of disputing', which he had already turned into a key element of the debate with his *The Vanity of Dogmatizing* (published in 1661; rewritten as *Scepsis Scientifica* and published in 1665 with a dedication to the Royal Society). It was probably from him that Sprat had derived the idea of obliquely presenting Hobbes as a 'Modern dogmatist'.[60] And it is on this issue that the underlying or

[58] *Philosophia Pia*, p. 1.
[59] *Ibid.* 16, 62–3, 106–9.
[60] T. Sprat, *The History of the Royal Society* (London, 1667), 33.

parallel argument in defence of rational religion comes most visibly to the surface. When Glanvill speaks about the value of empirical and practical knowledge, what I hear is not the voice of modified scepticism arising from a concern with problems of certainty in a Protestant–Catholic debate; nor is it a Puritan exaltation of practical activity. What I hear is the voice of the Latitude-man defending himself against the doctrinal theology of the old orthodoxy:

> The *Real* experimental Philosophy [teaches] that the most *valuable* knowledge is the *practical*; By which means they will find themselves disposed to more *indifferency* towards those *petty notions* in which they were before apt to place a great deal of Religion; and so to reckon, that *that* which will signifie lies in the *few, certain, operative* principles of the Gospel, and a *life* suitable to such a *Faith*.[61]

It was Sprat who announced that 'The universal Disposition of this *Age* is bent upon a *rational Religion*.'[62]

Hobbes too had offered a sort of rational religion in the second half of *Leviathan*; Sprat's version of the argument is significant because it shows just how far the rational theologians could go in resembling Hobbes while at the same time posing as defenders of true religion against the 'threat' of Hobbism. If anyone pointed out the similarities, the only response was to raise the stakes by expressing yet more disapproval of Hobbes, and presenting him as more of a danger in those terms (dogmatist, atheist, and so on) which enabled them to present their own position as a necessary defence and corrective. And the similarities could, as Meric Casaubon noticed, be striking indeed. 'Religion ought not to be the subject of *Disputations*', Sprat wrote; 'it should in this be like the Temporal Laws of all Countries.'[63] The Church should 'derive its *Doctrine* from the plain and unquestion'd parts of the *Word of God*, and . . . keep itself in a due subjection to the Civil Magistrate'.[64] When Sprat wrote that 'most of our religious controversies, may be . . . decided by plain reason', Meric Casaubon exploded: 'this I do not understand. The sense is obvious enough; but a sense so amazing, that it is not credible'. He compared it to Herbert's *De Veritate*, 'the end and drift

[61] *Philosophia Pia*, p. 44.
[62] *History*, p. 374.
[63] *Ibid.* 354–5.
[64] *Ibid.* p. 370.

whereof was, out of the Religions of mankind to extract a religion that should need no Christ.' Then, with a transparent reference to Hobbes, Casaubon added: 'Since him it is well known, that some body hath taken some pains to attemperate Christianity to the laws of every Countrey, and commands of Supreme Powers: and this he doth ground, or endeavour to ground, upon divers passages of Scripture. What can this import, in ordinary construction, but a new Religion?'[65]

There is not space here to enter into the complex question of just how far Hobbes's rational religion did resemble that of the Latitudinarian theologians—though it is a question worth investigating, now that some Hobbes scholars are beginning to treat him as a perfectly typical liberal Anglican from Great Tew.[66] Suffice it to say that there were some strong similarities on the surface, just as there were similarities in their attitudes to politics and church-government, and similarities between Hobbes and many of the Fellows of the Royal Society in their assumptions about the mechanistic nature of the physical universe. Significant differences can also be found in most cases, but it is the similarities that mattered—forcing the Royal Society to dissociate itself from Hobbes, and in the process to fuel the fires of criticism against him. Individuals may have known and befriended him; but it was the public image of the Society that was at stake, an image the management of which had been taken over by the publicists of rational religion.

Finally, a short and rather negative methodological post-script. Nowhere in this paper has the claim been made that there *was* an intrinsic connection between being a proponent of rational religion and being a scientist of the sort found in the Royal Society. If one happened to be both of these, one might well want to make some connections between them, and use the same sorts of argument to defend them both—particularly if those arguments were such very successful ones. If there is some truth in the impression that the more significant members of this group of scientists did have this type of religious attitude, then it

[65] *A Letter . . . to P. du Moulin . . . concerning Natural Experimental Philosophie, and some Books lately set out about it* (Cambridge, 1669), 17.

[66] For example, P. Johnson, 'Hobbes's Anglican Doctrine of Salvation', in R. Ross, H. Schneider, and T. Waldman (eds.), *Thomas Hobbes in his Time* (Minneapolis, 1974), 102–25. I put forward a rather different view of Hobbes's underlying theological position in my *Hobbes and Voluntarism* (Cambridge University Press, forthcoming).

is reasonable enough to seek an explanation of that fact. But it is simply not necessary to suppose that when we find that explanation it will also be the 'explanation' of the scientific beliefs they held. A statistical prevalence of liberal Jews among psychiatrists would not necessarily mean that the principles of psychiatry are derived from the doctrines of liberal Judaism.

The search for unifying explanations, located in different underlying categories of belief or action, may often be misleading. When a seventeenth-century scientist says that searching into nature is an inducement to greater piety towards God, the creator of nature, this does not necessarily mean that his fundamental reasons for doing science are deeply religious. When he says that useful applications can be derived from scientific research, this does not necessarily mean that his fundamental reasons for doing science are deeply social. Such statements might mean these things; but they might just mean that the speaker wanted to defend his activity and had a reasonable command of current platitudes. So I should like to offer just one possible reason for doing science in this period which is perhaps so obvious that one would not expect to find it mentioned by any modern historian of science: curiosity.

3
*The Science in Hobbes's Politics**

TOM SORELL

In the Epistle Dedicatory to *De Corpore* Hobbes remarked on the immaturity of science or philosophy as he knew it. Writing in 1655 he observed that natural philosophy was then 'but young', being no older than the researches of Copernicus, Kepler, Galileo, and Harvey. As for civil philosophy, it was still younger. Hobbes claimed that the subject had not existed before the appearance of his *De Cive* in 1642. He meant that no genuine *science* of morals and politics had existed. There had been a large pre-scientific literature, stretching back to the Romans and Greeks and even earlier writers. But this was comparable to work in celestial and terrestrial physics before Copernicus and Galileo: it was uncertain, unclear, and unprofitable. Only a new kind of political philosophy could instruct men in their civil duties, and only a new kind of natural philosophy could identify the causes of phantasms.

Hobbes was not the last philosopher to distinguish between the scientific and the non-scientific study of politics, and his claims about his own civil philosophy sometimes interest people because they seem to look forward to the claims of later writers. For example, Mill said that 'the backward state of the Moral Sciences can only be remedied by applying to them the methods of Physical Science, duly extended and generalized',[1] and it is possible to think of Hobbes as applying to the backward ethics and politics of his day the methods implemented so successfully

* Earlier versions of this paper were read in the spring and autumn of 1987 to a conference on the history of the social sciences at the City University of London and to a meeting of the Philosophical Society at Oxford University. On the latter occasion I had the benefit of a sympathetic reply from Noel Malcolm. References throughout are by volume and page of the Molesworth edition of Hobbes's English Works, and to the Tönnies edition of *The Elements of Law*.

[1] A System of Logic, Bk. 6.

by his heroes among the Continental physicists. On this sort of interpretation Hobbes anticipates Mill. He might also be understood to anticipate Comte and Saint-Simon. Or again, Hobbes can be identified as a precursor of such twentieth-century positivist philosophers as Carnap and Hempel. Like them he believes in the unity of science. Like them he puts forward a philosophy of science unencumbered by commitments to higher substances or to the existence of God.

Other elements of Hobbes's thought also link him with modern doctrine. For example, in describing the method he employs in philosophy, Hobbes often speaks of analysing wholes into more intelligible parts. Readers sometimes take him to be advertising the application of this method to bodies politic or commonwealths when, in the Introduction to *Leviathan*, he develops the metaphor of the artificial man and suggests that a task of the book is to identify the working parts of the commonwealth that correspond to the moving components of the man. These and other remarks concerning wholes and parts in his writings are sometimes considered to express methodological individualism, the doctrine that truths about societies either reduce to, or are wholly explained by, truths about particular individuals. Taken as the father of methodological individualism Hobbes is easily inserted into controversies that became heated in the nineteenth and twentieth centuries.

In relating Hobbes's ideas to the recent history of social studies, all of the interpretations I have mentioned take seriously the scientific pretensions of his morals and politics. They take seriously these pretensions but misidentify the sort of science Hobbes had in mind. As a result they misidentify the intellectual trends foreshadowed in *Leviathan* and *De Cive*. Properly understood Hobbes's civil science has less in common with scientific social studies in the nineteenth and twentieth centuries than with a certain strain of modern moral rhetoric. The interpretations I have mentioned are not wrong to look beyond seventeenth-century revolutionary England for echoes of Hobbes's ideas. Nor are they wrong to suggest links with relatively recent thought. The trouble with them is that they fasten on to the wrong kind of recent thought. Or so I shall argue. After indicating how Hobbes's civil science is usually understood and why this understanding is mistaken, I shall offer what I believe to be a more accurate account. Then I shall identify some modern counterparts of the sort of theory Hobbes put forward.

I

I begin, then, with the standard and (as I believe) distorted account of the science of politics Hobbes presented. According to this account Hobbes's politics is scientific either because it is straightforwardly a part of natural science, a 'subdepartment of physics',[2] or because it extends to bodies politic a scientific method whose primary application is to natural bodies or natural phenomena,[3] or because it is somehow 'deducible' from the more basic natural sciences of psychology, physics, and mechanics.[4] The shared theme of these suggestions, and the substance of what I shall be calling the 'standard interpretation', is that for Hobbes social studies owe their scientific status to their links with the natural sciences. They have no independent claim to be sciences, no method of their own that qualifies them for scientific status.

The standard interpretation is reasonable, but it seems to me to be mistaken. It is a reasonable interpretation of *Leviathan*, for example, because chapters in Part 1 of the book do contain some physics and psychology. They contain a little physics and a lot of mechanistic psychology. Part 1 of *Leviathan*, moreover, is supposed to prepare the ground for the twelve chapters on Commonwealth in Part 2, which contain the bulk of Hobbes's science of politics. Again, Hobbes sometimes suggests that there is a deductive relation between Part 1 and Part 2. All of these points support talk of one Hobbesian science being rooted in

[2] Alan Ryan, *The Philosophy of the Social Sciences* (London, 1970), 15.

[3] J. W. N. Watkins, *Hobbes's System of Ideas* (London, 1965), chs. 3 and 4, pp. 47–81. A broadly similar interpretation was put forward in M. M. Goldsmith, *Hobbes's Science of Politics* (New York, 1966). A more recent study under the influence of Watkins's interpretation is W. von Leyden's *Hobbes and Locke*: The Politics of Freedom and Obligation (London, 1981), 23 f.

[4] See R. Peters, *Hobbes* (Harmondsworth, 1956), 87; C. B. Macpherson, *The Political Theory of Possessive Individualism* (Oxford, 1962), 10; D. Gauthier, *The Logic of Leviathan: The Moral and Political Theory of Thomas Hobbes* (Oxford, 1969). Among more recent exponents of this view is G. Kavka. See his *Hobbesian Moral and Political Theory* (Princeton, 1986), 7–8. Kavka thinks that while Hobbes aimed at such a deduction, he did not succeed in providing one.

another. All of these points support a version of the standard interpretation, the version according to which Hobbes's politics is scientific because of its deductive links with the natural sciences of psychology, physiology, and physics.

Other pieces of textual evidence, however, go decisively against the standard interpretation. So that the force of these pieces of evidence is appreciated, it is important to remember that *Leviathan* was not the only, or the first, or even the official and authorized, statement of Hobbes's political science. When Hobbes named himself the inventor of civil philosophy it was on the strength of having published *De Cive* in 1642, not *Leviathan* in 1651. Now *De Cive* was written as the third of a three-part account of the elements of philosophy or science as a whole. It was intended to round off a trilogy on body, man, and citizen. As things turned out, *De Cive* was the first instalment of the trilogy to appear. In the edition of 1647 Hobbes explained why it didn't matter that *De Cive* appeared first. It didn't matter because *De Cive* could be understood on its own. As it was 'grounded on its own principles sufficiently known by experience, it would not stand in need of the former sections' (*EW* ii. xx), that is, the sections of the trilogy on man and body. So we have in *De Cive* the official version of the science of politics and we are told that it is a self-contained science. It is a self-contained science because it stands on its own principles. Do these principles belong to mechanistic psychology? In other words, does *De Cive* contain material corresponding to the part of *Leviathan* that matters crucially to the standard interpretation?

It does not.[5] Scientific psychology is supposed to have been got out of the way in part two of the trilogy, the part on man. It is not brought into the third part of the trilogy, and, as we have seen, it is not supposed to be necessary for understanding that part. On the contrary, the science of politics is supposed to be intelligible on its own. Now passages confirming that Hobbes believed in the autonomy of his science of politics can be found in writings that appeared after 1647, for example in chapter 6 of *De Corpore* (*EW* i. 74) and in chapter 31 of *Leviathan* (*EW* iii. 357). The upshot of these passages is briefly stated. Just as there is a science of politics in *De Cive* in the absence of parts one and

[5] Scientific psychology plays no part, but an anecdotal, even gossipy common-sense psychology *is* appealed to in the opening chapter of *De Cive*.

two of the trilogy, so there is a science of politics left in *Leviathan* if the first thirteen chapters of that book are subtracted.

The evidence against the standard interpretation does not stop there. Not only did Hobbes suppose that civil philosophy was autonomous of such prior sciences as psychology and physics: there are also passages which suggest that far from trying to make the scientific status of physics rub off on his civil philosophy, he regarded civil philosophy as *more* of a science than physics. At the beginning of this paper I mentioned Hobbes's view that natural philosophy was immature: his views about the relative standing of physics and politics as sciences are of a piece with this. In Hobbes's view the science *par excellence* was geometry, not physics. Geometry was fully demonstrable and perfectly certain, whereas physics depended on hypotheses that could be controverted (*EW* vii. 183–4). Underlying this difference, Hobbes believed, was a difference in the relation to our wills of the subject-matter of each science. The figures of geometry are things of our own construction, and the properties of the figures are due to motions made by ourselves. We are the makers of the figures and have a maker's knowledge of their properties, that is to say, an ideal knowledge (ibid.). In the case of the things studied by physics, on the other hand, the motions that create the properties are God's, and we can only say what these might have been (*EW* vii. 3, 88). More certain explanations are ruled out by the fact that there is no effect an omnipotent God could not have produced in more than one way. Since physics can at best second-guess God's activity while geometry is perfectly informed about the human activities that produce *its* effects, geometry is the surer science. And, Hobbes adds, civil philosophy is like geometry. For the things that civil philosophy studies, namely bodies politic, are likewise our own artefacts, and so of their properties we can have a maker's knowledge as well.

The standard interpretation is thus wrong about the scientific status physics is supposed to have in Hobbes's system. At least one version of the standard interpretation is also wrong in assuming that physics deals in laws or that it is concerned with prediction. One of the oddities of Hobbes's philosophy of science, when viewed from the twentieth century, is that it seems to *detach* the ability to do science from the ability to frame categorical laws and from the abilities of predicting and retrodicting. This is clear from the Epistle Dedicatory to *Seven Philosophical Problems* and from *Leviathan*, chapter 7 (*EW* iii. 52). Against this background it is hard to accept Alan Ryan's estimate of the strengths of Hobbes's picture of a social science rooted in natural science. Ryan says that

> there is a plausibility about Hobbes's picture that persists in spite of its many crudenesses and logical deficiencies. Its basic tenet is that the outcome in any physical system is in principle open to prediction, because it is causally determined; physical determinism holds everywhere, for the laws governing physical matter are universal laws.[6]

The 'basic tenet' Ryan speaks of may indeed belong to a picture provided by philosophers working long after Hobbes. It is not to be found in Hobbes himself.

II

Before trying to improve on the standard account, I want briefly to take up another interpretation that is much better grounded in the texts than the standard one, and which is sometimes combined with the standard one, but that is *also* mistaken. This is one of the interpretations that is used to identify Hobbes as the founder of methodological individualism, and so it is worth considering.

The interpretation that I have in mind is partly inspired by Hobbes's remarks concerning scientific understanding in chapter 6 of *De Corpore*. Scientific understanding, Hobbes says, is understanding of causes, and 'the cause of the whole is compounded of the causes of the parts'. In his article 'Methodological Individualism Reconsidered',[7] Stephen Lukes takes Hobbes's remark about scientific understanding to apply to societies, and he suggests that for Hobbes the causes of the social compound reside in its parts, namely individual men. But when Hobbes says that the cause of the whole is compounded of the causes of the parts, he immediately adds:

[6] Ryan, op. cit. 103.

[7] *British Journal of Sociology*, 19 (1968), 119–29. Reprinted in A. Ryan ed., *The Philosophy of Social Explanation* (Oxford, 1973).

Now by parts, I do not here mean parts of the thing itself, but parts of its nature; as, by parts of man, I do not understand his head, his shoulders, his arms etc. but his figure, quantity, motion, sense, reason and the like, which accidents being compounded or put together, constitute the whole nature of man, not the man himself (*EW* i. 67).

Applying these remarks to what Lukes calls 'social compounds', the idea would be that the causes of the compound are the causes of the parts of the nature of the compound, not parts of the compound itself. So the parts of the compound would not be individual people but would perhaps be the various functions of government and the roles played by the governed. This guess about the parts of the nature of the social compound fits in with what is said in the Introduction to *Leviathan*. But it is hard to be sure what would count as a part of the nature of the social compound or what it would be to build up the compound from the causes of the parts: Hobbes does not consider the case of social compounds when he considers compounding wholes out of the causes of their parts in *De Corpore*.

Though he is routinely interpreted as holding that civil philosophy resolves commonwealths into their parts, there is only slight support for this reading in Hobbes's explicit remarks about method and even less in his actual practice as a civil philosopher. As far as I know only a single passage about method in Hobbes's writings supports the view that his civil philosophy is concerned with analysing or resolving social compounds and reconstructing them out of the causes of their parts. This is a famous passage from the Preface to the Reader of *De Cive*. Since commentators make so much of it, it is worth quoting at length:

Concerning my method I thought it not sufficient to use a plain and evident style in what I had to deliver, except I took my beginning from the very matter of civil government, and thence proceeded to its generation and form, and the first beginning of justice. For everything is best understood by its constitutive causes. For as in a watch, or some such small engine, the matter, figure and motion of the wheels cannot be well known, except it be taken insunder and viewed in parts; so to make a more curious search into the rights of states and duties of subjects, it is necessary, I say, not to take then insunder, but yet that they may be so considered as if they were dissolved; that is, that one rightly understand what the quality of human nature is, in what matters it is, and in what not, fit to make up a civil government, and how men must be agreed amongst themselves that intend to grow up into a well-grounded state (*EW* ii. xiv).

The first thing to say about this passage is that it does not compare watches with bodies politic but with the rights of states and the duties of subjects.[8] And in saying what has to be done to understand the working of the watch on the one hand and the nature of the rights and duties on the other, Hobbes in fact draws attention to differences between the two cases. First, the watch has to be physically disassembled; the rights and duties are only to be operated on in thought. Next, while the watch is supposed to be disassembled into its working parts, the rights and duties are to be considered *dissolved*, that is, considered as entirely absent. Hobbes does not begin his study of the rights and duties by considering their component parts. That is, he does not begin with an unresolved conception of the rights of states and then divide it up into conceptions of judicature, punishment, levying taxes, making wars, and so on. He is not proposing to show, either, how there are certain corresponding duties on the part of subjects. Instead, he plans to imagine away the rights and duties altogether and consider men as if they had no ties of justice to one another, no obligations from covenants. In other words, he intends to lay bare the social relations that human beings are suited for by nature. This is his starting-point. Only after describing how a well-founded state could be conjured up from this situation does he consider the component rights of sovereign authority and the component obligations of citizenly duty.

Instead of analysing bodies politic and compounding them of the causes of their parts, instead of applying a method of resolution and composition, Hobbes applies a method of *dissolution and innovation* to rights and duties.[9] He first imagines that no rights and duties exist and then lays down the ones that ought to exist if creatures with our nature are to live in lasting commonwealths. The rights and duties that ought to exist are

[8] The Latin original does compare watches with bodies politic: it has tended to be ignored by countless commentators (myself included, see *Hobbes* (London, 1987), ch. 2), who have assumed mistakenly that Hobbes was the translator of the text in *English Works*, vol. ii. Noel Malcolm, who drew my attention to the Latin, agrees with me that Hobbes does not use the method of resolution and composition usually attributed to him.

[9] Similar to the procedure of 'imitating the creation' urged on the reader at the beginning of *De Corpore* (*EW* i. xiii).

not necessarily the rights and duties that do exist. On the contrary, Hobbes says in chapter 20 of *Leviathan* that the rights and duties appropriate to the well-grounded state have never been acknowledged (*EW* iii. 195). Hence my claim that in his civil philosophy dissolution leads to innovation. It leads to the proposal of an unheard-of distribution of rights and duties, a novel constitution for a state. Individualism does not come into it except in the sense that in the absence of rights and duties, in the state of nature, men are assumed to pursue personal conceptions of the good, and are assumed to have an interest in the purpose of the well-grounded state, namely security, whatever the content of these personal conceptions is. The assumption that people pursue the good individualistically falls short of methodological individualism, however, which asserts that all facts about social compounds reduce to facts about individuals. Hobbes is not dealing, except indirectly, in facts about social compounds, only in precepts for constructing them as they ought to be constructed. He does not reduce the properties of the ideal state to properties of individuals but only shows that states can have those ideal properties while human nature is individualistic.

All of this is easier to see if the passage I have been discussing is taken in context. In the paragraph that precedes the passage, Hobbes is describing the kind of doctrine he is going to put forward in *De Cive*. The doctrine is supposed to refute a number of false opinions about the grounds for deposing kings and the grounds for being obedient to a king's commands. To refute these opinions Hobbes develops a theory of the basis of kingly power and civil obedience. He needed to detach this theory from disputes that were current at the time he was writing, disputes about whether, for example, Charles I deserved to be deposed or disobeyed. So he started from the hypothetical situation—the state of nature—in which no rights of kings and no duties of subjects existed at all. This enabled him to ask whether it would be necessary to invent such rights, and if so, which.

Hobbes's use of the device of the state of nature is sometimes misunderstood. For example, Nozick has suggested that in Hobbes and Locke the device is particularly well suited to what he calls 'explanatory political theory', the sort of theory that specifies in non-political terms how the political realm could have been generated, though it was not actually generated that way.[10] It seems, however, that in Hobbes the device is *not* used for the purpose of explaining how the political realm was generated. Instead, it contributes to a venture in rhetoric broadly conceived.[11] Hobbes wanted to persuade an audience of malcontents that remaining obedient to a *de facto* protective power was for the best. In order to win his readers over he thought he had to overcome the operation of strong passions, notably avarice and ambition, which inclined them to opportunistic rebellion. The strong passions arose in his readers from their experience of political arrangements in an actual state. To induce detachment from this experience and blunt the effects of the associated passions Hobbes tried to conjure up a vivid conception of anarchy or statelessness, the ingredients of which are present in human nature. The conception of anarchy or statelessness is calculated to bring into operation passions favourable to obedience, namely fear of death and hope of attaining a moderately scaled good life. These passions were supposed to motivate his readers to look for and implement means of avoiding statelessness. The means are the precepts Hobbes calls the laws of nature. His science of politics consists partly of a deduction of these laws and partly of an application of them in arguments against seditious opinions, notably those current in England in the 1640s.[12]

III

What, then, are the laws of nature? In Hobbes's writings they are understood as precepts enjoining 'good manners', that is, settled patterns of behaviour that are good in a public and well-defined sense of the term. In *The Elements of Law*, *De Cive*, and *Leviathan*, the statement of the laws of nature assumes the form of

[10] *Anarchy, State and Utopia* (Oxford, 1974), ch. 1.

[11] In his recent *The Rhetoric of* Leviathan (Princeton, 1986), David Johnston claims that *Leviathan* is a self-consciously rhetorical statement of Hobbes's politics, very different from the 'scientific' account put forward in *The Elements of Law*. Though it is too large an issue to argue out here, I think that Johnston overdraws the tension between science and rhetoric and therefore exaggerates the difference between the early *Elements of Law* and the later *Leviathan*. It seems to me that even in 1640 Hobbes believed that science and a persuasive politics were compatible, but it took some time for him to develop a philosophy of science that bore out this belief. My own position is outlined in 'Hobbes's Persuasive Civil Science', forthcoming in a volume on rhetoric and philosophy edited by Jonathan Rée.

[12] See the final chapter of my *Hobbes* (above, n. 8).

a deduction, which is what makes the statement of the laws into a science. The first law is supposed to be plausible in the light of certain reasonable conclusions about pre-political human behaviour. If people were not under government, if they existed in the state of nature, then they would be driven by their passions into a violent and ultimately fatal competition for scarce goods. In other words, they would be driven to open war. Hobbes thinks that this is revealed not only by a scientific account of the passions but by candid self-observation. Rational reflection would dictate to each person caught up in the conflict that it would be desirable to end the conflict if doing so were not too dangerous. Thus the first law of nature: that whoever can safely do so seek peace and keep it (*EW* iii. 117). The second law of nature calls for behaviour calculated to secure peace: the right of each person in the state of nature to do and take what he likes is to be laid down by each in return for a similar laying down of right by every other person (*EW* iii. 118). The medium of this laying down of right is a covenant of each person in the state of nature with every other. Each agrees by entering the covenant to vest responsibility for his security and well-being in a designated man or body of men, the man or body of men thereby becoming a government enpowered to declare and enforce laws. By entering the covenant people become subject to those laws and are morally obliged to observe them by what binds them to the covenant, namely the third law of nature. This identifies justice with the keeping of covenants. There are at least a further fifteen or sixteen such laws. All of them, Hobbes claims, are implicit in the maxim, 'Do not do that to another, which thou woudst not have done to thyself.' And he thinks that as he states them the laws of nature call for behaviour that his readers would anyway have regarded as virtuous. Equity, justice, a willingness to be accommodating—all of these things he assumed his readers would call 'good' in advance (cf. *EW* ii. 48).

Hobbes's civil science does not only consist of the deduction of the laws of nature. It also contains methods for giving those laws weight in one's practical deliberation and for bringing the laws to bear on one's hearing or reading of rhetoric. In particular, Hobbes thinks civil science can function as an antidote to seditious opinions spread by writers or orators. In this capacity civil science acts against one of the principal causes of the dissolution of the state, for Hobbes identifies erroneous opinions about citizenly duty as important causes of anarchy, and he thought that orations, either in the form of church sermons or secular ranting, were an important source of these opinions.

One such erroneous opinion was that political arrangements were unjust and worthy of opposition when they failed to decentralize or spread authority (*EW* ii. 150). Hobbes distrusts any organization of government that multiplies authorities, divides obedience, and waters down the sovereign power. In *De Cive*, for example, he considers an arrangement vesting the power of making war in a monarch and the power of raising taxes in an independent authority. He claims that this arrangement is muddled: since only those who can raise the money can wage wars, the monarch is, contrary to assumption, not really in a position to decide about military campaigns after all. Hobbes objects on similar grounds to the detachment of legislative from executive powers. No one could really own all of the powers of sovereignty *except* that of law-making, for the legislature could restrict or outlaw the exercise of the powers that remained, at their pleasure. The legislature would thus be sovereign (*Elements of Law*, 2. 8. 7). In the same vein Hobbes says that people who believe in a separation of government powers are guilty of misunderstanding the nature of a body politic: a body politic is no loose association of individuals, but a whole entity with the unity of a person (ibid).

The list of seditious opinions that Hobbes deals with could be extended, but the examples before us suffice to show how he goes about rebutting them. In each case he takes something with initial plausibility that might be said to justify rebellion; he then translates what is plausibly said into the well-defined terms of his theory of sovereignty and subjection. In the process of translation some of the plausible contentions are reduced to incoherence, while others are shown to be doubtful or to need further defence.

IV

On the interpretation that I favour, Hobbes's civil science contains far more advocacy than explanation, far more moralizing than decomposition of bodies politic into their working parts. Hobbes unfolds a series of prescriptions and prohibitions which we must abide by in order to keep the peace, and he provides a method of applying these in practical deliberation as well as a method of testing rhetoric against them.

I promised at the beginning to indicate some counterparts of this sort of approach in much later writing, and I am going to conclude by mentioning one or two names from this century and the last. First John Stuart Mill. In invoking this name I am not taking back the objection to the interpretation mentioned at the beginning, for I would link Hobbes's political theory not with the 'moral sciences' in Mill's sense but with what he describes as the 'art' corresponding to the sciences of human nature and policy, namely the art of morality and policy. According to the last chapter of the *System of Logic*, the purpose of this art is to suggest, in the form of principles in the imperative mood, ends to be pursued. Mill envisages a hierarchy of such principles, the greatest happiness principle subsuming a number of secondary principles. The form of this Art is reminiscent of the form of Hobbes's doctrine of the laws of nature. And like Hobbes, Mill applies the principles of his Art in some well-known pieces of moral rhetoric, notably his speech in favour of the retention of capital punishment. Of course, the parallel between Mill and Hobbes is not perfect, since, for one thing, Mill's own exercises in persuasion have to be seen against the background of his liberal defence of the free expression of opinion and the maximum use of persuasion in preference to coercion. Hobbes put a low value on freedom of speech in comparison with peace, and he thought that the pursuit of peace often justified restrictions on the expression of opinion. Another difference is that Mill rests far less of his case on definitions than Hobbes does.

In our own century, apart from R. G. Collingwood[13] and Carl Schmitt,[14] who in very different ways adapted Hobbes's theory to an account of European but especially German social disorders between the wars, I can only mention writers whose approach resembles Hobbes's in this or that important respect. If one considers that the point of Hobbes's rhetoric is often to deflate the worth of liberty by a revisionary definition of liberty

[13] *The New Leviathan* (Oxford, 1942).

[14] In his *Leviathan* of 1938.

in terms of the state of nature, then Hobbes's work is broadly comparable to that of writers who in the twentieth century have sought to defuse appeals to social justice by deflationary definitions of that concept. I have in mind such writers as Milton Friedman and von Hayek. In a different vein there is the moral rhetoric produced in the last thirty years by English Catholic writers, such as Elizabeth Anscombe and Michael Dummett. These writers not only address some of the very topics Hobbes addressed—one of Anscombe's political essays is called 'On the Source of the Authority of the State'[15]—they seem to be at home with the law-ethics tradition to which Hobbes belongs. Then, more vaguely, Hobbes's philosophically informed rhetoric corresponds with some of the writing to be found within the recently founded applied ethics journals. It has far less in common with work that seeks, by its use of quantitative methods, or by arguments from a Realist philosophy of science, to show that social studies significantly resemble physics.

[15] *Ratio*, 20 (1978). Reprinted in vol. iii of Anscombe's *Collected Philosophical Papers* (Oxford, 1981), 130–55.

4
Hobbes and Individualism

ALAN RYAN

That Hobbes was one of the begetters of modern individualism is widely asserted. Quite what it was that he thus begat is equally widely disputed. Here I try to show that Hobbes espoused a consistent (though not in all respects persuasive) form of individualism in intellectual, moral, and political matters. I draw on two earlier essays of mine, though I do so in order to advance beyond them, not to rest on them.[1] One problem is gestured at by my title: what kind of an individualist was Hobbes? Was he the 'economic' individualist and booster for capitalism that C. B. Macpherson described?[2] Was he perhaps less a 'market-oriented' individualist than the advocate of the self-centred but self-abnegating bourgeois moral style depicted in Leo Strauss's famous account, or of the 'privatized' individualism described in Sheldon Wolin's *Politics and Vision*?[3] I suggest at the end of this essay that Hobbes's individualism was moral and intellectual, not economic, a doctrine of moral and intellectual autonomy—in essence, the individualism of the 'modern' character described in Michael Oakeshott's essay *On Human Conduct*.[4]

However, Hobbes was a systematic thinker, and his conviction that he had created a *science* of man and society raises

[1] 'The Nature of Human Nature in Hobbes and Rousseau', in Jeremy Benthall, *The Limits of Human Nature* (London, 1974); 'Hobbes, Toleration and the Inner Life', in David Miller and L. A. Siedentop (eds.), *The Nature of Political Theory* (Oxford, 1981). This present essay is a companion to 'A More Tolerant Hobbes?', in Susan Mendus (ed.), *Essays on Toleration* (Cambridge, 1988).

[2] C. B. Macpherson, 'Hobbes's Bourgeois Man', in Keith Brown (ed.), *Hobbes Studies* (Oxford, 1965), 169–83; *The Political Theory of Possessive Individualism* (Oxford, 1962); 'Introduction' to Thomas Hobbes, *Leviathan* (Harmondsworth, 1968).

[3] Leo Strauss, *The Political Philosophy of Hobbes* (Oxford, 1936); Sheldon Wolin, *Political and Vision* (Boston, 1961).

[4] Michael Oakeshott, *Hobbes on Civil Association* (Oxford, 1975).

intriguing questions about the connections between his epistemological and his moral commitments. How does Hobbesian individualism relate to the atomism of Hobbes's mechanical materialism? Is there a logical tie, a conceptual affinity, or no relationship at all?[5] I shall argue that there is a conceptual affinity between his atomism and his intellectual individualism, but something closer to a logical tie between his intellectual individualism and his political individualism.

That Hobbes was in several senses an epistemological individualist is hardly disputable. One of those senses is given by his contempt for intellectual authority. 'Goliath defied the host of Israel, and Mr Hobbs defyeth the whole host of learned men', complained Alexander Ross, and he was echoed by most other critics.[6] Yet, Hobbes defended the absolute and arbitrary authority of the sovereign, and one might suppose that in a system as tightly constructed as his, all forms of authority must stand or fall together; Hobbes plainly thought not. Were his views at odds with each other or as consistent as he supposed? I try to show their consistency.

In part, my case is that Hobbes was impressed by the self-sufficiency of most individuals in everything other than mere self-preservation. Self-indulgent pride, intellectual or political, was deplorable; self-confidence was not. But this picture is methodologically individualist in implying that all modern, politically governed communities are sustained by individual commitment to the terms of co-operation, and it gives rise to an awkwardness (to put it no more strongly) that I have to defuse in the second section of what follows. Within Hobbes's political theory, in the narrow sense, there is a tension between his insistence that a man is obligated to obey the sovereign only by some positive act of his own and the utilitarian flavour of his account of the sovereign's powers and duties. The first is individualistic in asking the question, 'why am *I* obliged to obey?', the second less so in asking, 'what overall good is achieved when there exists a sovereign whom everyone obeys?' Within the more individualist construction, there is also a

[5] On which see Maurice Goldsmith, *Hobbes's Science of Politics* (New York, 1968) and J. W. N. Watkins, *Hobbes's System of Ideas*, 2nd edn. (London, 1973), both of them at odds with Strauss, op. cit.

[6] Alexander Ross, *Leviathan Drawn Out With A Hook* (London, 1653), p. A5.

tension between his insistence that we renounce *all* our rights in favour of the sovereign and his insistence that it is up to the individual to decide when he would do better to flee or resist rather than obey and submit.

I cannot promise a conclusive resolution of these anxieties, but I hope to provide the apparatus needed for the purpose. It comes in three parts. First, a treatment of Hobbes's epistemological anti-authoritarianism and individualism; second, a discussion of Hobbes's theory of obligation and its moral basis; last, a defence of the view that Hobbesian individualism is neither quietist nor capitalist nor 'bourgeois'.

EPISTEMOLOGICAL INDIVIDUALISM

'He was wont to say that if he had read as much as other men, he should have knowne no more then other men.'[7] Aubrey's tribute to Hobbes's confidence in the resources of his own mind and his conviction of the absurdity of claims to intellectual authority is echoed by hostile critics: 'Mr Hobbes consulted too few Authors and made use of too few Books.'[8] They found it hard to believe in Hobbes's wholesale contempt for Aristotle, for tradition, or the pretensions of any body of men to lay down the truth about the world; they set it down to brazen pride and a taste for novelties. Yet Hobbes's position was plain. We could be obliged to *say* what the sovereign wished, where the point was to express allegiance and not to assert a matter of fact. The sovereign might require us to utter phrases expressing allegiance to God, and to worship him in sentences which were literally meaningless but expressively valuable: even if *Spirit Incorporeall* is an unintelligible epithet, it is excusable when they that so call God do so 'not *Dogmatically*, with intention to make the Divine Nature understood; but *Piously*, to honour him with attributes, of significations, as remote as they can from the grossenesse of Bodies Visible'.[9] What no sovereign can do is require us to *believe* propositions which might not in fact be true. Authority can lay

[7] John Aubrey, *Brief Lives* (Harmondsworth, 1962), 314.

[8] Edward Hyde, Earl of Clarendon, *A Brief Review of Mr Hobbes's Leviathan* (London, 1670), 'Epistle Dedicatory'.

[9] Thomas Hobbes, *Leviathan*, ed. C. B. Macpherson (Harmondsworth, 1968), 171.

down only what experience cannot decide. It is because the question whether the world has a beginning or not, to take an example from Hobbes himself, is unanswerable by human reason that authority may properly decide it.[10]

Hobbes's argument was in part political and defensive; belief is not under the control of the will, and cannot be commanded. As subjects we feel safer if we do not fear that sovereigns may command us to do what is not in our power to do. Political prudence prompts the sovereign too to self-restraint; belief can be dissimulated because the mind of man is not visible to anyone but its owner, and authority would be rash to provoke opposition by trying to discover whether people really believe what they will not avow or disbelieve what they will.

More importantly for our purposes, authority stands in the way of the growth of knowledge. Hobbes insists that each man must make up his mind for himself, and believe only what he has good reason to believe; otherwise, superstition prevails, and science is throttled. We do not *know* what we merely take on trust: 'he that takes up conclusions on the trust of Authors, and doth not fetch them from the first Items in every Reckoning (which are the significations of names settled by definitions), loses his labour; and does not know any thing; but only beleeveth it'.[11] Hobbes was not alone in taking this stand. The admired Bacon whose amanuensis he had briefly been, had said the same; the disliked Descartes did so too. Hobbes's opponents recognized the similarity. Condemning Hobbes as a monster of intellectual arrogance, they relied on Descartes's theological ill-repute to discredit Hobbes when they pointed to the similarities between his views and those of the *Discourse on Method*.[12]

The difficulty is to give a convincing account of how the various elements in Hobbes's anti-authoritarian theory of knowledge hang together. The problem is that his most salient view, and the one most loathed by his contemporary critics, is his insistence that the subject's duty is to take the sentence of the sovereign for his guide to good and evil.[13] How, in the light of that, he still insisted on the importance of judging for ourselves

[10] Ross, *Leviathan Drawn Out*, complains of this, pp. 24–5.

[11] Hobbes, *Leviathan*, p. 112.

[12] John Eachard, *Mr Hobbes's State of Nature Examined* (London, 1672), Preface.

[13] John Shafto, *The Great Law of Nature* (London, 1672), pp. A3–4.

in everything else it is not easy to see. It is quite clear that it cannot rest on an individual right to free speech or free thought. Hobbes had no time for what the Dissenters claimed as the 'right of private judgement'. The explanation must lie in his epistemology, but it is hard to find. It is not persuasive to assimilate Hobbes's philosophy of science to Baconian inductivism and empiricism; Hobbes was contemptuous of much empirical experimentation—though not of all experiment—and seems to have had no conception of inductive inference at all.[14] It looks equally implausible to suppose that Hobbes was a defender of Popper's methodology of conjecture and refutation *avant la lettre*; in Hobbes's account true science renders refutation inconceivable. Moreover one cannot suppose Hobbes a friend to Popper's programme of showing that science and liberal democracy make good bedfellows.[15] It is more persuasive to assimilate Hobbes and Galileo; Galileo thought that geometry was the key to celestial mechanics, and that experiment illuminated the operation of mechanisms whose *modus operandi*, once it was spelled out, was a matter of necessity. Hobbes's view of the relationship between the axiomatic method of geometry and our knowledge of geometry's applicability to the empirical world remains obscure; but, he may well have shared this view, even though he was prone to insist on the arbitrariness of God's decision to construct his universe at all, and on the variety of means by which he might have produced his effects. However, the analogy drawn in *Leviathan* between the art whereby God created the world, and the art whereby man creates both geometry and the state suggests a less dramatic arbitrariness behind the universe.

It is a view which surfaces again in Locke's *Essay*.[16] Geometry sets out the rules for constructing figures and therefore bodies; it is hypothetically certain in the sense that geometry shows that *if* there are cubes, spheres, or whatever, then such and such are the properties they must have. It is an applied as well as a pure science, because empirical evidence and a priori construction converge to show that we live in a Euclidean space. Locke is as emphatic as Hobbes in stressing the difference between our a

14 Watkins, *Hobbes's System of Ideas*, pp. 17 ff.

15 Karl Popper, *The Open Society and Its Enemies* (London, 1945), i. 124–7.

16 John Locke, *An Essay Concerning Human Understanding* (Oxford, 1975), 417–420.

priori grasp of geometry and our a posteriori grasp of the laws of empirical science, but they are at one in suggesting that in the eye of God at any rate, all is a priori. We see a posteriori what he constructs a priori.[17] Hobbes insisted, famously, that reason cannot tell us the nature of anything other than what we ourselves create and thus that physics could not, strictly speaking, be a science. Yet, it is not hard to see how a slightly more relaxed view would close the gap between the rational and the merely empirical while preserving the distinction between geometry and physics. Indeed, Hobbes's own discussion of the relationship between science and prudence is far from suggesting that science is wholly a priori, and far from ruling out any role for experience in science. It is not their concern for empirical evidence but their lack of concern that Hobbes complains of when he says that those who 'love to shew their reading of Politiques and History' generally 'study more the reputation of their owne wit, than the successe of anothers businesse'.[18]

The connection between this view of science and epistemological individualism is indirect, in the sense that Hobbes strongly suggests, but does not try to prove, that each of us is capable of reaching the truths both of geometry and of statecraft if we will only cleave to a good method and avoid obscure speech and obfuscating symbols.[19] Here, too, his critics objected, insisting that doctors, lawyers, philosophers, and theologians needed the specialized terminologies of their disciplines, and that Hobbes was encouraging the vulgar to set up their limited judgements as a standard to their betters, a charge anticipated and repudiated in his comments on *nosce teipsum*, 'which was not meant, as it is now used to countenance, either the barbarous state of men in power towards their inferiors; or to encourage men of low degree, to a sawcie behaviour towards their betters'.[20] The rules of good method are indeed simple enough—the avoidance of insignificant speech, the scrupulous distinguishing of words which refer to things from words which refer to words, the analytical disentangling of conceptions into their simplest elements and extreme care in their recombination. Hobbes's

[17] Roger Woolhouse, *Locke's Philosophy of Science and Knowledge* (Oxford, 1971), 10 ff.
[18] Hobbes, *Leviathan*, p. 118.
[19] Ibid. 115.
[20] Ross, *Leviathan Drawn Out*, pp. 12–13; Hobbes, *Leviathan*, p. 82.

encounter with Euclid, and with Plato's demonstration that Meno was capable of proving Pythagoras' theorem from his own internal resources would all have pressed in the same direction.[21]

Knowledge, then, is an individual possession, which each of us can secure for himself or herself. Yet Hobbes acknowledges that we need the intellectual services of others to be wholly successful in the quest for it. Each individual is to a degree at the mercy of his own idiosyncratic physiology and psychology. What we have hold of is not the world itself, but its impact on our sensory and recording apparatus; our bodies change in the same way as everything else, and with them the quality of our present grasp on the world and even on our own past thoughts and experiences. The difference between private fantasy and something we might dignify by the name of knowledge lies not only in the quality of our definitions and inferences, but also in the degree to which these are conformable to the definitions and inferences of others. Our thoughts are dictated by what we attend to and our attention is driven by our passions; out of the company of others all men are fantasists: 'the most sober men, when they walk alone without care and employment of the mind, would be unwilling the vanity and Extravagance of their thoughts at that time should be publicly seen: which is a confession, that Passions unguided, are for the most part meere Madneses'.[22] Hobbes remains an epistemological individualist, but recognizes the place of social discipline in epistemic reliability. Unless we are controlled by common standards we may fly off in all directions. Moreover, just as the passions are implicated in the unreliability of isolated individuals, so the sin of pride appears as a social and an epistemological threat, wherever men are excessively self-confident, and mistake their own reasoning for the dictates of right reason. 'And when men that think themselves wiser than all others, clamor and demand right Reason for judge; yet seek no more, but that things should be determined by no mans reason but their own, it is as intolerable in the society of men, as it is in play after trump is turned, to use for trump on every occasion, that suite whereof they have most in their hand.'[23]

This mixture of individual achievement and social control

[21] Aubrey, *Brief Lives*, p. 309.

[22] Hobbes, *Leviathan*, p. 142; cf. pp. 134–6.

[23] Ibid. 111–12.

means that the establishment of agreement can be a means to achieving a grasp of the truth, but consensus is not the test of truth. Hobbes was disinclined to trust group sentiment in this or any other area; many intellectual communities have a vested interest in teaching their members to talk various sorts of nonsense. Hobbes's view of the Roman Catholic Church's vested interest in obscurity is too well known to bear discussion. It seems that a community which can assist its members to search for the truth must have no vested interests, or an interest only in peace, security, and the advancement of humanity through the conquest of nature. Is this not in spite of everything leading us back towards an almost Popperian picture of science?

We need to belong to a community with an interest in truth; it must exercise a certain restraint on its members' fantasies, but it must not exercise a dogmatic authority over them. It is this last anti-authoritarian requirement which makes this an individualist philosophy of science whether in Hobbesian or Popperian form. Progress demands individual boldness tempered by respect for the opinions of others. What of my earlier claim that it was implausible to assimilate Hobbes's philosophy of science to Popper's? We must distinguish the tactics of scientific progress from our view of what science achieves when it is successful. We may reject Popper's description of the findings of science as no more than 'conjectures' which have thus far escaped refutation while seeing some role for his conception of the ideal scientific community in which every individual is encouraged in intellectual boldness.

If science is defined in the rationalist terms of Hobbes's account, it is still plausible to suggest that the inner resources on which the individual draws in constructing a theory are decisive, but can only adequately be exploited with the help of others. The detection of contradiction and ambiguity can be managed single-handed but is best managed by like-minded groups. A proper appreciation of the 'social' character of the creation of scientific knowledge still leaves Hobbes free to adopt the arrogant and violently anti-traditionalist approach that so distressed his contemporaries—though he is surely condemned out of his own mouth as a man who could not accurately distinguish between confidence and pride and who thus failed to live up to his own standards.

This anti-traditionalist view of knowledge is in strictly logical terms independent of the mechanical materialism to which he also subscribed. Once again, the mere mention of Popper suffices to show that epistemological individualism (in the sense of an imperative to think for ourselves) is consistent with an anti-reductive willingness to believe in minds as well as matter and even with a belief in a Hegelian Third World of Objective Mind.[24] None the less, there is an affinity between the two things in Hobbes's work. The bridge between mechanical materialism and epistemological individualism is provided by the view that men are a species of self-regulating *automata*. If the natural order contains self-maintaining bodies which preserve a complicated internal organization and which manage complex interactions with the outside world for the sake of self-preservation, we best explain knowledge of the outside world as a component of this self-maintenance. Hobbes is innocent of evolutionary speculations about just why such entities must have reliable information about the outside world, let alone of any speculations about the value of seeing such creatures as map-makers interested in continuously sophisticating their maps. Hobbes is not Karl Popper, nor even Jean-Jacques Rousseau.[25] All the same, Hobbes espoused a naturalistic and therefore an individualistic epistemology; it is individuals, in sensory interaction with the world, who are the bearers of knowledge of the world. This is the vision Hobbes shared with orthodox empiricism.[26]

Critics may by now feel that I have diluted Hobbes by first making him a precursor of Popper on the sociological front and now making him a quasi-empiricist on the epistemological, and that the bare 'affinity' suggested is too slender a basis for any very satisfying analysis. However, one can certainly say that Hobbes's vision is individualistic enough to be distinctively anti-Hegelian, and anti-Wittgensteinian; it is naturalistic enough to be decidedly anti-Kantian in spite of Kant's professedly individualist Copernican Revolution. Hobbes supposes that the interactive process between the individual and the material world provokes the conceptualizations by way of which we

[24] Karl Popper, *Objective Knowledge* (Oxford, 1972), 153–61.

[25] Popper, *Objective Knowledge*; Jean-Jacques Rousseau, 'A Discourse on the origins of Inequality', in *The Social Contract and Discourses* (London, 1973).

[26] Ernest Gellner, *The Legitimation of Belief* (Cambridge, 1974), 27 ff.

make sense of that world; but he is a naturalist in supposing that there are no privileged categories, built into the individual mind or given by 'forms of life', which we impose upon the world. The affinity with mechanism gives a distinctive content to Hobbesian epistemological individualism of a kind that sustains the earlier suggestion that Hobbes believed that membership of an intellectual community was *causally* important in keeping our thinking on the rails, but not in providing the conceptual possibility of all thinking whatever.

POLITICAL OBLIGATION REVISITED

Hobbes's account of political obligation has been so thoroughly analysed in recent years that one might reasonably despair of adding anything new to the discussion. This section sticks pretty narrowly to the 'individualist' aspect of Hobbes's theory. There are two ways in which Hobbes's account of obligation is contentious; both involve a seeming conflict between Hobbes's insistence that nobody can be under an obligation to obey another save in virtue of some previous agreement to do so, which is a piece of moral individualism *par excellence*, and his claims, on the one hand, that we are under an obligation to obey the law of nature with no suggestion of our having consented to do so, and, on the other, that 'a sure and irresistible power confers the right of Dominion, and ruling over those who cannot resist'.[27] In pursuing this issue, I take it for granted that Hobbes's understanding of obligation is that obligation is a moral, and not simply a prudential, matter.[28] That is to say, the proposition 'I am obliged to do *x*' is not reducible to 'I am forced to do *x*', and 'I ought' does not reduce to 'I had better'. The question is whether we have obligations only after imposing them upon ourselves, not whether Hobbes has a peculiar view of what obligations are. What I shall do is first show that our relations with God are so different from our relations with any earthly creature that a proper attention to that difference may

[27] Thomas Hobbes, *De Cive* (Oxford, 1983), 50.

[28] Brian Barry, 'Warrender and his Critics', in Maurice Cranston and Richard Peters (eds.), *Hobbes and Rousseau* (London, 1972); John Plamenatz, 'Mr Warrender's Hobbes', in Keith Brown (ed.), *Hobbes Studies* (Oxford, 1965), 76–8; Howard Warrender, *The Political Philosophy of Hobbes* (Oxford, 1964), 287 ff.

resolve both of the problems just stated, though I have some anxieties about the resolution. Then I revert to the question which underlies this entire section, whether Hobbes's insistence that each of us alone is responsible for his or her own allegiance and obedience represents a distinctive moral individualism.

Leviathan explains how we come to have an obligation to obey the sovereign in terms of our having promised to obey; in the unusual event of our jointly instituting a sovereign, we promise one another to obey the person or body of persons so nominated, in the more usual case of the sovereign by acquisition, we submit to the person or body of persons who could without injustice take our life, receiving our lives in return for submission. Hobbes insists that it is *submission* that creates the obligation, not merely the threat of death, nor merely defeat in battle: 'Nor is he obliged because he is Conquered; that is to say, beaten, and taken, or put to flight; but because he commeth in, and submitteth to the Victor.'[29] This is the point of his claim that nobody is obliged but by some act of his or her own. The promises involved are odd in the sense that when a sovereign is instituted, the sovereign is not a party to the covenant and therefore does not stand in any reciprocal relation of obligation to the subject; conversely, although we do covenant with the sovereign in the case of sovereignty by acquisition, the sovereign immediately performs his side of the bargain by refraining from killing us, and thereafter is under no further obligation to us. So curious is this doctrine that one can only suppose that Hobbes was drawn to it by a thought he very much did not wish to give up, namely that we really have put ourselves under an obligation which we ought to keep except where our lives would be endangered by the attempt—or more weakly, save where we fear that they would be so endangered. The polemical thrust of *Leviathan* in the Interregnum context is presumably that since the gentlemen whose minds Hobbes wishes to frame to a conscientious obedience have already as good as promised to obey the Protectorate government, they would be foolish not to make that promise articulate when asked to do so—whence Clarendon's assertion that *Leviathan* was backed by thirty legions.[30]

[29] Hobbes, *Leviathan*, p. 256.

[30] Clarendon, *Short Review*, 'Epistle Dedicatory'.

There is no analogous process in the case of our obligation to obey the law of nature. There are some interesting difficulties posed by Hobbes himself. The laws of nature are precepts or general rules 'found out by Reason, by which a man is forbidden to do, that, which is destructive of his life, or taketh away the means of preserving the same';[31] but he also describes them as being more properly theorems, an understanding of which is so to speak programmed into the self-maintaining entities that Hobbes considers us to be.[32] Under some conditions the attempt to preserve ourselves leads to the war of all against all, and reflection on the causes and miseries of that state leads to our seeing the need for some power able to overawe us all. It leads to the injunction that we should seek peace whenever possible, and to the permission to use all helps and advantages of war if we cannot safely seek peace. The obligatoriness of the law of nature has not bothered most critics of Hobbes, the one serious exception being Professor Barry.[33] Critics interested in the problem of obligation have for the past two decades worried away instead at the question of how individuals who are trying to maximize their own utilities can subscribe either to Hobbes's laws of nature or to the dictates of the sovereign. Their problem is this. Hobbes requires us to keep the laws of nature unless it is too dangerous to do so; it is this law of nature obligation which underlies our duty to obey the sovereign. But the maximizer of his or her own returns will surely obey only when it is maximally advantageous, and will disobey if it is not.[34] I do not think this was the problem that faced Hobbes. Though Hobbes indeed describes the mechanisms of desire and motivation in terms which suggest that each person is indeed bent on *maximizing* his or her own enjoyment, it emerges on closer inspection that Hobbes readily envisaged us 'satisficing'. The twentieth-century obsession with the 'prisoner's dilemma' and with the temptation to be a 'free-rider' presupposes a theory of motivation that Hobbes did not believe in. What Hobbes's individuals maximize in the state of nature is *power*. They do not do so because they like power, nor because they want to

[31] Hobbes, *Leviathan*, p. 189.
[32] Ibid. 217.
[33] Barry, 'Hobbes's Theory of Obligation', pp. 36 ff.
[34] David Gauthier, *The Logic of Leviathan* (Oxford, 1969), 76 ff.

maximize the enjoyment of anything positive. They are forced to maximize their power even though they would be content with a moderate living.[35] This is because isolated individuals have no other means of security; they are not utility-maximizing but danger-of-death minimizing creatures. Risk aversion is built in to their physical constitution, and, if they understand themselves, to their psychical constitution too. The prisoner's dilemma is thus a red herring.

Our question is not whether egoists can meet their obligations, but how 'theorems found out by reason' can impose *obligations*. Hobbes was always careful to distinguish counsel or advice which we may take or leave at our peril from law or command.[36] Hobbes's answer to the puzzle is well known; if the laws of nature are considered as the commands of God, who by right commandeth all things, they are laws and they oblige.[37] This shuffles off the problem to a different area of Hobbes's philosophy, namely the sense in which we are obliged to obey God even though we have not given our consents. Brian Barry has suggested that Hobbes ought not to have said that we have an obligation to obey the law of nature. We ought to obey, but the duty to obey the law of nature derives from its content, not from our obligation to obey its promulgator. This seems to me to be wrong, though accurate enough as an account of how we should view the duty to take notice of the law of nature considered as theorems, which are counsel not commands. Hobbes offers two possibilities; they are, I think, alternative and mutually inconsistent. Both rest on a further consideration of some interest, even if it hardly removes the inconsistency.

The first possibility Hobbes opens is one which denies the assumption we have thus far been working on, namely, that we do not consent to the government of God. In *Leviathan* Hobbes seems to say that those and those only who consent to the government of God are properly under an obligation to obey him. 'Subjects therefore in the Kingdome of God are not Bodies Inanimate, nor creatures Irrationall; because they understand no Precepts as his; Nor Atheists; nor they that believe not that God has any care for the actions of mankind; because they

[35] Hobbes, *Leviathan*, p. 161.

[36] Hobbes *De Cive*, p. 168.

[37] Hobbes, *Leviathan*, p. 217.

acknowledge no Word for his, nor have hope of his rewards, or fear of his threatenings. They, therefore, that believe there is a God that governeth the world, and hath given Praecepts, and propounded Rewards, and Punishments to mankind are God's subjects; all the rest are to be understood as Enemies.'[38] Believers alone *sin* when they violate the law of nature, though atheists are also accused of treason to the almighty because they deny his authority when they deny his existence.[39] There is another awkward question, however. In what sense do those who believe in God consent to his government? It seems that it must be, but cannot be, in the same sense as the subject consents to the government of his earthly sovereign. The motivation for submission is the same as ever, fear of death, and the believer has the added incentive that God grants and withholds eternal life, so that there is a better argument for submission to God than to any earthly sovereign. On the other hand, God does not make us an offer of life upon terms which we may accept or reject, so submission does not amount to contract.

As to the atheist who is shut out by this argument, Hobbes insists that an atheist is rightly described by the Old Testament as a 'Fool' rather than a sinner, or more exactly, as one guilty of a sin of imprudence not of injustice.[40] It is rash not to believe that there probably exists a God who brought the world into existence, and who can exercise alarming sanctions. To be on the safe side, we should believe and obey. How far we can believe in this prudential fashion is a moot point, as is its consistency with Hobbes's insistence on thinking for ourselves, and I should hesitate to go much further than suggesting that Hobbes recommended what one might call hypothetical belief—we should conform ourselves in the way belief and submission would dictate. But this account, which derives obedience from submission, is not the only one Hobbes offers. The other account derives God's legislative authority from his power, in the first place by a route which has earthly analogies, and in the background by a route which has none.

Each of us comes into the world with a right to all things. This is a useless right because we lack the power to do anything with

[38] Ibid. 396.

[39] Hobbes *De Cive*, p. 199.

[40] Ibid. 179.

it; we therefore renounce it and leave the sovereign alone in possession of this initial right, and through our submission with the power to make use of it. If any of us had sufficient power to rely on his own resources and thus to have no incentive to renounce his natural right to all things, he could become sovereign. God is uniquely in the position of requiring no earthly assistance to exercise his rights. He has no reason to renounce any of his rights, therefore he retains the right to all things, including the right to rule us as our sovereign. 'They therefore whose power cannot be resisted, and by consequence God *Almighty*, derives his Right of Soveraignty from the *power* it selfe.'[41]

But as soon as we articulate this account, we can see two alternative criteria for the existence of obligation running into head-on conflict. On the one criterion, we infer the existence of an obligation from the existence of law, and the existence of law from the existence of a lawmaker. It is God's right to rule which explains our obligation, and our submission appears not to play much role in the story. We are all born with the right to rule, that is, with authority; for human beings it is a perfectly useless right, since everyone else has the right to take no notice and we have no power to make them take notice. But God is differently situated, and can and does exercise that right. On the other criterion, the authority of any lawmaker is to be traced back to the submission of those subject to the law. What makes law law is certainly the fact that it is the word of him that by right has command, but what gives him that right is our submission; he has authority only because each of us authorizes him. The two criteria have very different implications for the concerns of this essay. When Hobbes begins with the thought that everyone has a right to all things, the notions of submission, consent, and authorization are only weakly present, and the account only weakly individualist; acts of submission do not so much transfer to another rights over our conduct he could not otherwise possess as offer him reassurance that we shall not resist the exercise of rights he already has. When Hobbes plays down this (exceedingly counter-intuitive) account of what a 'transfer' of right really means, his theory of obligation remains strikingly

[41] Ibid. 186.

individualistic. We have those obligations we impose on ourselves and no others. Sovereigns have authority because they are given it. Each man is by nature the author of his own actions only; for the sovereign to be able to be the author of the acts of all his subjects, his subjects must authorize him.

Which reading of Hobbes ought we to prefer? It is hard to tell, but a case for supposing that Hobbes is anxious to take the second route can be drawn from considering how different the earthly sovereign and God really are. Hobbes was always impressed with the story of Job. Job finally turned and reproached God, pointing out, and not before time either, that he had done all that God commanded, and what he had got out of it was bankruptcy, skin diseases, and the death of most of his household. God did not reply that Job was being sacrificed in a good cause, or that he had really behaved badly by being so proud of his own righteousness. Those utilitarian or Kantian responses are strikingly absent, especially in Hobbes's interpretation of the story. What God replied was, 'where wast thou when I laid the foundations of the earth?', which as Hobbes justly observed was not an argument drawn from his goodness or from Job's sin, but from his power.[42]

How should we understand it? What kind of argument is it? Merely to point out to Job that if God chose to behave atrociously there was little Job could do about it would have been both otiose and intellectually and morally feeble. The only answer which makes adequate sense is that God pointed out to Job that since he had created Job, *ex nihilo*, Job was wholly and entirely his to do as he chose with. Hobbes says that the right of nature whereby God reigns over men and punishes those that break his laws is not derived from the fact of his creating them. This, however, is not in conflict with my account, for what Hobbes is concerned to deny is any thought that 'he required obedience, as of Gratitude for his benefits', and my account is at one with Hobbes's in relying on God's power not his subjects' gratitude.[43] So far as earthly sovereigns go, we have to authorize them because we are by nature the authors of our own actions and responsible for them, and sovereigns can only claim authorship of our actions when we have granted them that right

[42] Hobbes, *Leviathan*, p. 398.

[43] Ibid. 397.

over us. God, on the other hand, made us; he is the author of our being and therefore without further ado the author of our actions. He cannot commit an injustice against us any more than I can commit an injustice against the clay pot which I throw on the wheel and then break up because it is ill made. As Hobbes's critics pointed out, this makes God the author of our sins and is theologically exceedingly unorthodox—but it is a point in favour of my interpretation that they should have so latched on to one of its implications.[44]

If this is right, a familiar tension in Hobbes's account of the sovereign's duties appears in a new light. When an earthly sovereign is instituted, it is entirely on the consent of his subjects that his authority depends. Each subject has a choice between staying in the state of nature and thereby risking the enmity of the sovereign and submitting to the authority of the sovereign. One might suppose that Hobbes thought that only a madman would risk staying outside the covenant and risk death by refusing to acknowledge an existing sovereign's authority or by refusing to submit on the battlefield. Hobbes did not quite say that. If someone refuses to submit because he is sincerely convinced that God will avenge the slight done to him by earthly submission to an illicit sovereign, he may be rash in drawing down death on himself—he could, after all, submit with mental reservation—but Hobbes does not suggest that the Christian martyrs were simply silly, though he does suggest that anyone so attracting death without an explicit commission from God must be more or less deranged. Again, a man might scruple to break an oath freely made in the past. So far from describing him as mad, Hobbes is quite clear that a sense of honour is an estimable character trait and useful for society. Fear may be the motive to rely on, but it is not as admirable a motive as a sense of honour or disinterested love of others.[45]

If the ordinary view of human motivation is not much damaged by Hobbes's materialism, and his insistence that each person is bound only by his own decisions is taken seriously, there remains a tension between Hobbes's insistence that subjects have no rights against their sovereigns and his insistence that subjects retain the right to decide whether the covenant is

[44] Ross, *Leviathan Drawn Out*, p. 2.

[45] Hobbes, *Leviathan*, pp. 75–6; Strauss, *Political Philosophy of Hobbes*, pp. 115 ff.

off. It is not simply that there is a tension between the utilitarian, public interest oriented prescriptions for the sovereign's conduct of government and the individualism of the story of the covenant. Certainly, recent philosophers would insist on that tension, and John Rawls's *Theory of Justice* is founded on the need to prevent individuals being sacrificed in the public interest. But just as Hobbes does not, when scrutinized, turn out to believe that individuals seek to maximize their own utilities, so, when scrutinized, he turns out not to believe that sovereigns ought to maximize the sum of the utilities of their subjects even if this entails sacrificing some of them. It is individual safety which plays the most important role, then the promotion of opportunities for individual advancement, or 'commodious living'.[46] The sovereign must above all else maintain the rule of law; what has aptly been called Hobbes's 'moral constitutionalism'[47] is a very obvious feature of the theory. However, although this means that there is no tension between a utilitarian perspective and an individualist one, there is a tension between the individualism which underpins Hobbes's prescriptions about fair trials, scrupulousness about retrospective legislation, and so on, on the one hand, and the insistence that the subject has no rights against the sovereign on the other.

It is a tension which Hobbes does his best to defuse. The sovereign has a duty to observe the laws of nature, a duty which falls on him as a private person rather than a public one; he can do more good than anyone else by so doing, because he has more power than anyone else. It may therefore be that his duty is more exacting because he has less excuse for non-observance than anyone else, being generally less at risk than anyone else. This account allows Hobbes to insist that none of his subjects can call the sovereign to account for a breach of the law of nature; the sovereign is answerable to God and his conscience alone. Conversely, this means that we have no right to have the sovereign behave in this way; it is simply that he ought to do so. If he has an obligation to do so, it is a natural law, not a positive law obligation.

None the less, what remains firmly in the hands of the individual subject is the right to decide whether obedience is

[46] Hobbes, *Leviathan*, p. 376.

[47] F. C. Hood, *The Divine Politics of Thomas Hobbes* (Oxford, 1964).

worth it. There is no right of revolution in Hobbes; but private individuals do not promise to stop thinking about their own preservation and that of their families and friends. They are obliged to obey because they have promised, but if things turn out too dangerously, they have the right to break their promises too. This has some faintly comic effects; one familiar one is the way Hobbes insists that the unusually timid should be allowed to pay for someone else to go and fight in their place and ought not to be expected to fight themselves. The non-comic effect is that creatures as forward-looking and anxious as Hobbesian men cannot be supposed to wait until the knife is at their throat until they raise the question whether obedience is too unsafe. They must surely spend much of their time watching the performance of the government in crucial respects. Certainly, '*every man is bound by Nature, as much as in him lieth, to protect in Warre, the Authority, by which he is himself protected in time of Peace*', but once they have discharged that duty, it is their right to consider their own safety.[48] To us this seems perhaps only a small concession in a generally authoritarian scheme; to some of Hobbes's contemporaries it was tantamount to denying the sovereign's authority altogether. For anyone deriving sovereignty from divine right, Hobbes's account is trebly obnoxious; the story of Job marks an absolute breach between divine power and earthly power; the sovereign is created only by the voices of the people; the sovereign's power has strict and easily recognized limits. Those who thought of the sovereign as a simulacrum of God must have thought Hobbes's 'mortall God' much too mortal and quite insufficiently God-like.[49]

'PRIVATIZATION'

This essay has been thus far engaged in arguing two cases, not exactly at odds with each other, but not usually found in company. The first is that Hobbes's view of human motivation is at an empirical level not particularly surprising, though it is novel at the analytical level because of its entrenchment in a mechanistic psychology. In the same vein, I have tried to show

[48] Hobbes, *Leviathan*, pp. 718–19.

[49] Clarendon *Short Review, passim.*

that Hobbes's 'epistemological individualism' as I have called it is not at odds with many of the commonplaces of the sociology of science, though again it has distinctive features because of the underlying mechanical psychology and Hobbes's obsession with geometry. But in the second place, I have been trying to suggest that Hobbes's contemporaries often found him alarming, not because of the authoritarianism and defence of despotism which his twentieth-century readers notice, but because of an individualism which was both like and unlike other individualisms of the time, but in being a form of individualism at all, was hostile to an emphasis on community, tradition, ecclesiastical authority, and the derivation of political authority from a Christian view of the world.

In conclusion, I should, without exaggerating the novelty of my position, distinguish if from some others which could also make these two claims. In particular, I should briefly suggest why the individualism outlined is usefully described as moral and epistemological and not as capitalist, bourgeois, or privatized. The notion that Hobbes was writing to defend or even merely to express the world-view of capitalism is implausible. The most famous argument to this effect, offered by C. B. Macpherson, is essentially circular. It starts from the assumption that Hobbes was living in a market society, either nascent or fully fledged, and from the companion assumption that political theories reflect the economic conditions associated with their production. So Hobbes's picture of human nature is not a picture of human nature, only that of market-oriented man; the undoubted contrast between Hobbes's methodology and Aristotle's has to be reinterpreted as a contrast between the outlook of market society and the outlook of a classical, non-market society. Once these assumptions are firmly in place, everything in Hobbes's theory which is friendly to capitalism becomes an argument in their favour. The circularity involved is evidently that the interpretation of Hobbes's text which supports the premisses is only reached by scrutinizing the text on the assumption that those premisses are correct.[50]

Still, there is something to be said for the interpretation. Hobbes does argue for something close to *laissez-faire* in some

[50] Hobbes, *Leviathan* 'Introduction', pp. 11 ff.

economic areas; the sovereign ought to define property rights as clearly as possible, remove uncertainty about title—for example by establishing a land register so that it was clear who owned what—refrain from unpredictable or sudden alterations in the rules, and avoid sudden and unpredictable taxes; given that, the sovereign could leave the population to get on with their economic life more or less unimpeded. Is this a positive argument for capitalism, however? There seems no reason to think that it is; Hobbes does not admire merchants, and does not admire most employers, who, he thinks, are interested in driving people to work at the lowest possible wages. Moreover, he is explicit about the need to create some sort of welfare arrangements for those who are too old or ill to work. Equally, and entirely at odds with the ethos of capitalism, he advocates sumptuary legislation to diminish class antagonisms. The belief in the virtues of unlimited accumulation that Macpherson puts at the heart of a defence of capitalism is very far from being a belief shared by Hobbes. Hobbes sees the accumulation of wealth as a threat to social harmony. People who accumulate do so to get power, to drive down wages, or to flaunt their wealth in ways which merely irritate their inferiors, an argument which Strauss struggles vainly to defuse.[51] It is this latter misuse of wealth which he particularly deplores, and which he relies on sumptuary laws to stop. Of course, a last ditch defence of an interpretation of Hobbes as an apologist for capitalism could perhaps claim that this assault on the flaunting of wealth is capitalist inasmuch as it implies that investment or some other virtuous wealth-increasing employment of funds is harmless and useful. This will not do, however, In the first place, Hobbes does not say anything of the sort. Moreover, it is essential to the picture of Hobbes as a capitalist apologist that he should assume that 'human nature' is suited to the operation of a capitalist economy. That is just what he does not seem to do; harmless, moderate persons may need no more than security and opportunity to make themselves prosperous and happy, which is an argument for a relatively *laissez-faire* policy, but they need protecting also against the arrogance, greed, and acquisitiveness of the rich.

[51] Strauss *Political Philosophy of Hobbes*, pp. 120 ff.

Now that the whole idea of a 'bourgeois revolution' in seventeenth-century England has been so thoroughly discredited, it is no argument against Hobbes-as-capitalist-apologist to show that Hobbes was both the friend and devoted employee of an aristocratic household, and that when his enemies assailed him it was for corrupting the brisk wits at Charles II's court rather than for the espousing of bourgeois and anti-aristocratic attitudes.[52] For it is equally true that the Devonshire family was an investing and improving family, as well as a landed family of great house-builders, and true, too, that those whose aristocratic pretensions amounted to pride in their descent rather than their abilities did not care for Hobbes's reminder that the sovereign was the fount of honour and that honour was a sort of price.

Still, Hobbes's defence of industry, prosperity, and science-propelled social advance was not distinctively or interestingly capitalist. It was modernizing, no doubt, and revealed a distinctively modern belief that history might be an indefinite upward path rather than a cyclical and repetitive course. It was individualistic, certainly, in its acceptance of the fact that individual intelligence and energy might take a man away from his social and geographical roots. But to have been an articulate defender of capitalism, Hobbes would have had to have had a much more calculating, accounting outlook than he actually possessed.

The same point disposes of the 'bourgeois' Hobbes, and equally of the 'privatized' Hobbes. Hobbes's bourgeois image is drawn by Leo Strauss from Hobbes's assault on pride or 'vainglory' as the great threat to civil order, and, as Strauss thinks, on the aristocratic sense of honour in consequence. Hobbes's theory of human nature gave him every reason to be insistent on this point; in terms of his account of the condition of nature, the three great causes of war are competition, diffidence, and vainglory. Now competition for the resources for survival or for a commodious living can be deflated by prosperity. If there is plenty for each of us, the only reason to struggle for a monopoly is fear that the current abundance will be cut off by physical attack. This, though, is just what the cure for diffidence also cures; once the sovereign is able to impose his will on us all, we

[52] Shafto, *The Great Law of Nature* (London, 1672), p. A2.

need neither fear immediate theft nor accumulate power in order to insure ourselves against future predations. Thus curing diffidence provides for prosperity which provides the cure for competition.

Pride is unamenable to such treatment. To be proud is to wish to emerge on top of whatever competition is at issue, to wish to have more of any good thing than anyone else; it is essentially incurable because abundance cannot choke it. There cannot be more than one summit. Hobbes's insistence on the subjective nature of value puts a distinctive extra gloss on the reasons for fearing pride; the only test of success is the envy of others. Pride demands the simultaneous abasement of others. It is therefore intrinsically antisocial and must be stamped out.

Is this a 'bourgeois' view? There seems no particular reason to think so. The truth seems rather that in Hobbes's view anyone might display pride and anyone might be decently sociable and amenable to the discipline demanded by social coexistence. The low-born fanatic insisting on the truth of his idiosyncratic illumination displayed an antisocial pride in wishing the world to bow to *his* truth and being unwilling to learn from its views. Hobbes's opponents certainly did not think of pride as a peculiarly aristocratic vice from which the bourgeois are naturally free; all rounded on Hobbes and denounced him as a monster of intellectual pride. Tenison taunted him with doing everything 'in a way peculiar to himself' and 'with such a confidence as becometh only a Prophet or Apostle'.[53] Of course, aristocrats are prone to one form of pride which nobody else is so prone to, namely pride of ancestry. The general point, however, is wholly classless; it is that we should try to purge ourselves of all those passions which are essentially antisocial, and antisocial passions are understood as those which not only set us at odds but also have a 'zero-sum' quality about them. Nor did Hobbes's opponents associate the pride he denounced with any particular social class. They thought he was absurdly hypocritical in denouncing a vice to which he was himself so prone. What they attacked was his inordinate vanity over his own originality and cleverness. As for social allegiance, they took it for granted that the people he tried to impress were 'gentlemen' and that

[53] Thomas Tenison, *The Creed of Mr Hobbs Examined* (London, 1670).

among the disagreeable sorts of pride which Hobbes himself displayed in the course of attacking that vice, boasting of his connections with the court and the aristocracy was pretty salient.

We can finally turn to 'privatization'. As will be evident, *if* Hobbes were the defender of the world-view of the capitalist bourgeoisie, he would also be a defender of a privatized world-view. That is, he would hold that our interest in government is instrumental, and that the purpose of government is to enable us to pursue private economic goals in peace; the goals would be understood in terms familiar to twentieth-century social theorists, that is, they would be inwardly directed, concerned with the welfare of the nuclear family, and it would be taken for granted that the way to achieve that welfare is by work as an employee or by profitably employing others. In Miss Arendt's essay on *The Human Condition* and Sheldon Wolin's *Politics and Vision*, Hobbes is seen as one of the founders of the liberal world-view, and the liberal world-view as essentially self-centred and apolitical. Without challenging Wolin's association of liberalism and anxiety, which cetainly seems plausible enough in Hobbes's case, I should like to enter a note of caution about the too quick move from the thought that Hobbes espoused a self-centred politics to the thought that he espoused an apolitical politics.

The caution is a double one. In the first place, Miss Arendt's vision of the politics-centred world of classical antiquity may be challenged; it is not true that Aristotle offers a particularly exuberant picture of life in the *agora*, and the undeniable zest with which Machiavelli writes of ruses, wiles, stratagems, and battles won and lost is neither based on, nor the basis of, a political theory of public man. So the contrast between a classical, publicly oriented vision of politics and a modern, privatized vision has to be treated cautiously. In the second place, Hobbes resembles Machiavelli in writing with great zest of a grim business. Hobbes's opponents never forgave him his mastery of a prose style which relied on innuendo, analogy, and metaphor to achieve what bald argument could not, but whose felicities were simply too obvious to be denied. His stylistic enthusiasms certainly encourage the 'privatized' interpretation, too. By the time Hobbes has finished suggesting that men are wolves, lions, tigers, wild cats, and whatever, we might be forgiven for thinking that Hobbes supposes we all want to become *bons petits bourgeois* and leave public life alone.

In fact, there is nothing to be said for such a view. Certainly Hobbes is hostile to 'ancient prudence' and to the view that only under democracy or some form of popular republic is there freedom; but a belief in negative liberty is no argument for or against active participation in public life. Hobbes is no liberal, but his argument is a pluralist one. Generous spirits will participate in public affairs; nobody should force the timid to join in if they do not wish to. Again, participation is subordinate to order. Sovereigns will, if they are wise, take the best advice than can get; if they do not, we have no right to insist that they should. But then again, they should recall that whatever their rights and our obligations, they cannot expect an ill-governed state to survive as long as a well-governed one. Politics in the twentieth-century sense is an optional activity in the good life, but a well-run Hobbesian state may have quite a lot of it, so long as politicians remember that they are only the sovereign's *advisers*.

Hobbes's individualism is 'private' only in the sense which Michael Oakeshott's account of the modern individual implies.[54] Mankind does not need to be told what ends to pursue, what the good life is, how private life is to be conducted; certainly, we need the company of others to get anywhere with pursuing our own intimations of the good life, but we do not need to be forced, legislated at, or to have others legislated at, in order to get on with it. Private life is not, however, 'privatized' life—it is eminently sociable, outward-looking, friendly, and spontaneously co-operative. What it demands from the *res publica*, however, is not aid or instruction in how to live it, but only a shelter within which we can pursue it. It may be that a society which understands its politics in that way will organize its economic life in a 'capitalist' fashion; it may create a social grouping properly termed 'bourgeois'; by ill luck, it may go through periods of narrowly self-centred and 'privatized' existence—but all this is contingent. What is not contingent is that distanced, self-reliant, self-conscious stance which is so distinctively Hobbesian.

[54] Oakeshott, *Hobbes on Civil Association*, *passim*.

5

Hobbes's Conception of the State of Nature from 1640 to 1651: Evolution and Ambiguities

FRANÇOIS TRICAUD

The state of nature, seen as entailing a general state of war, is probably the most widely known of Hobbes's concepts. And deservedly so, for not only is it the notion which is the main premiss of his whole ethical and political system, but it also became obligatory for later authors of the seventeenth and eighteenth centuries, when writing on similar topics, to begin their accounts from their version of the state of nature. But Hobbes's natural state is none the clearer for all that. In this paper I shall try to show the hesitations, uncertainties, and alterations it undergoes in Hobbes's different works, especially in the three political treatises: *The Elements of Law* (1640), *De Cive* (1642), and *Leviathan* (1651). That some parts of the text of *De Cive* are no older than the 1647 edition will not be ignored.[1] For the sake of brevity, chapter 14 of the first part of *The Elements*, chapter 1 of *De Cive*, and chapter 13 of *Leviathan* will occasionally be referred to as the 'Natural State Chapters'.

I shall range the problems, such as I see them, into three groups: (I) difficulties as to the exact meaning of the phrase 'state of nature'; (II) difficulties arising from two surprising explanations by Hobbes (which are often disregarded) of this

[1] It should not be forgotten that books are generally published one year or so after the author has written or revised them. For instance, as is shown by the dates of Gassendi's and Mersenne's letters inserted in the 1647 edition of *De Cive*, the text was ready to print in the first months of 1646. Another dating problem could be raised in connection with the fact that the text of *De Cive* used in this paper is the English translation published in 1651. But generally this version renders the original rather faithfully. This conformity has been checked for all the passages reproduced. In one instance only the difference was such as to require a mention (which will be found in n. 5 below).

general state of war which characterizes the state of nature; (III) difficulties linked with such causes of the state of war as are more frequently commented upon.

I

In the phrase 'state of nature', both nouns require some attention. To begin with, what does 'nature' mean in this context? Obviously, and according to a time-honoured tradition, it is contrasted with 'art' or 'artefact'. Nevertheless, no suggestion is made by Hobbes to the effect that in his state of nature men are (or were) deprived of *all* manufactured commodities, as is the case in Part 1 of Rousseau's *Discourse on the origin of inequality*. Hobbes's natural men seem to have clothes and houses, and certainly they have weapons. The artefact they are chiefly bereft of is *institution*: either the bare contract, or the social pact with its political consequences; of course, in this situation, no other technique can reach a high level of development, but this is a consequence rather than an essential part of the state of nature.

That the state of nature is inconsistent with pacts is not quite clear as early as 1640. *The Elements* Part 1, Chapter 14, describes 'men considered in mere nature' (§ 2) without explicitly stating what such a description necessarily leaves out. And, as M. M. Goldsmith has shown,[2] some passages of the book presuppose circumstances that a reader of the following treatises can find inconsistent with a state of nature. A first draft even included among the laws of nature: 'that entering into peace every man be allowed those rights which he hath acquired by the covenants of others' (*E* 1. 17. 3, editor's note, p. 89).[3] Such a law implies valid and respected covenants, antecedent to the making of

[2] 'Introduction to the second edition' of *The Elements of Law*, ed. Maurice M. Goldsmith (London, 1969), xii–xiv. I am not sure, however, that this editor must be followed when he interprets the rights mentioned in *De Cive*, 3. 14, as 'acquired private rights', meaning: acquired by contracts, prior to the making of peace. I suppose that the retained rights of § 14 are parts of the natural right to all things, and more precisely such parts as a 'moderate' man may wish to reserve for himself, because they are necessary either to life or to a tolerable life.

[3] The references are to: *The Elements of Law*, edition cited in n. 2 above (which reproduces, with a new introduction added to the first, the Tönnies edition of 1889) reference is by Part, Chapter, and Section number; *Philosophical Rudiments concerning*

[cont. on p. 109]

peace, which hardly agrees with the war of all against all. The final text has not retained this passage, but it still prescribes '*That men allow commerce and traffic indifferently to one another*' (*E* 1. 16. 12, p. 87). Now, commerce requires an acknowledged right of property, first in the seller of the goods, and after the sale in the buyer: again, such a right cannot exist, in Hobbes's system, without an organized commonwealth, and this free market clause does not reappear subsequently. More generally, the first treatise is not uniformly anxious to 'radicalize' (if I may so say) the picture of the state of nature. For instance, the law demanding '*That no man obtrude or press his advice or counsel to any man that declareth himself unwilling to hear the same*' (*E* 1. 17. 8, p. 91), as M. M. Goldsmith has pointed out, far from turning the reader's thought to some 'natural' situation, is clearly called for by Pym's and his followers' pretension to have their advice taken by the king, and by Hobbes's disapproval of such a claim.

From *De Cive* onward, the notion of a state of nature becomes clearer by an indication of what this state is *not*. The title of chapter 1 reads: 'Of the state of men without civil society'; and, as is explained in one of the 1647 footnotes, 'civil societies are not mere meetings, but bonds, to the making whereof faith and compacts are necessary' (*De Cive*, 1. 2, note, p. 110). Consequently, the absence of civil society is identified with the absence of contractual bonds: 'it was lawful for every man, in the bare state of nature, or before such time as men had engaged themselves by covenants or bonds, to do what he would' (1. 10, pp. 116–17). Here, the distinction by means of which the state of nature is defined is that which holds between a contractual relationship and a situation where the free exercise of natural right is lawful.

In 'The Author's preface to the reader' (which first appears in 1647), the dividing line is drawn in a slightly different manner: it leaves on one side the war of all against all, and, on the other, the presence of a power able to quench this war: 'the dispositions of men are naturally such, that except they be restrained

Government and Society, better known as *De Cive*, English text ed. B. Gert in *Thomas Hobbes: Man and Citizen* (Humanities Press and Harvester Press, 1978; first printings: Anchor Books, 1972); *Leviathan*, ed. C. B. Macpherson (Harmondsworth, 1968). The abbreviations used are *E* for *The Elements, De Cive* for *Philosophical Rudiments, Lev.* for *Leviathan.* The only quotation from *De Corpore* is borrowed from the Molesworth ed. (*English Works* of Th. Hobbes, London, 1839, vol. i).

through fear of some coercive power, every man will distrust and dread each other' (p. 99).

In *Leviathan*, the approach is the same: the state of nature is: 'the time men live without a common Power to keep them all in awe' (p. 185; or 'to over-awe them all', ibid., a few lines above).

I am not suggesting that on this point the doctrine has undergone a deep alteration between 1642 and 1651. In *Leviathan*, as well as in the two editions of *De Cive*, the state of nature is the situation where contracts *and* political power are lacking. But certainly a shift in the stress has occurred in 1647: before, the state of nature was defined essentially by the absence of contracts, and subsidiarily by the want of a sovereign; in 1647 and 1651, the latter point has come to the front, the former being relegated to the background.

However that may be, unquestionably the main idea conveyed by the words 'state of nature' is that of the relations between men, such as they would be *if* their behaviour were *not* controlled by a political organization based on contracts. But perhaps these curbs are not the only ones we have to eliminate mentally, in order rightly to conceive the state of mere nature. We have also to do away with every kind of affective tie or community feeling; wherever those play an important role, the typically Hobbesian reasoning is at a stop: no more war, no need of pacts, and so on. And lastly, it must be remarked that people unable to kill, either for psychological or physical reasons, cannot be let into Hobbes's state of nature. Whatever he may have said on this point, this disqualification overtakes many human beings (even though it is true that the logic of the system requires agents roughly equal as to the ability to kill).

To sum up, the state of nature is the situation that would prevail if mankind were made up of people able to slay one another, destitute of all mutual fondness, strangers to any contractual arrangements and political institutions. These suppressions necessarily result in a picture that has something unreal about it; which does not mean (this must be strongly emphasized) that it has no scientific value: it is a *model* (taking the word in such sense as physicists and economists make use of), whose function is not to *reproduce* the true condition of mankind, but to *illuminate* it. Hobbes himself was quite aware of these methodological simplifications. In *De Cive*, 8. 1, to 'return again to the state of nature' (to 'return again' meaning here to 'turn one's attention again') is equated with to: 'consider men as if but even now sprung out of the earth, and suddenly, like mushrooms, come to full maturity, without all kind of engagement to each other' (p. 205). Nothing could show more clearly that, even if 'nature' is thought of in contradistinction to 'art', the notion of a state of nature is a conceptual artefact.

This reading is particularly in agreement with *De Cive*, 1. 2, where the natural dispositions of men, or, which amounts to the same thing, the dispositions of natural men, are inferred from contemporaneous psychological observations: which strongly induces the reader to conclude that the so-called state of nature is just an artificial representation, arrived at by isolating certain fundamental and eternal features of human behaviour.

From this point of view, the word 'state' is somewhat misleading. It would have been more proper to speak of a mere risk, an abstract possibility. In later centuries, Hobbes could have offered this point of his doctrine as a 'tendential law' or a 'limiting concept'.[4] Anyway, it is easy to read the three treatises in such a way, understanding the state of nature as a representation that need not be assigned to any definite moment in historical or prehistoric times. This interpretation is supported by the (almost) constant use of an a-temporal present tense in the Natural State Chapters: 'the greatest part of men . . . do . . . provoke the rest' (*E* 1. 14. 5, p. 71); 'All men in the state of nature have a desire and will to hurt' (*De Cive*, 1. 4, p. 114); 'they are in that condition which is called *Warre*' (*Lev.*, 13, p. 185).

Nevertheless, there are in *De Cive*, chapter 1, two pages written in a different style. From § 10 to § 13 inclusive (pp. 116–18) the preterite tense predominates. The first sentence of this passage has been quoted above: 'it was lawful for every man . . .' (§ 10); the following sections afford other instances: 'But it was the least benefit for men . . .' (§ 11); 'the natural state of men, before they entered into society' (§ 12); 'that state in which all things were lawful for all men' (§ 13). Some present tenses are intermingled, but, if we except the last

[4] Paul Johnson speaks of an 'ideal limiting case' in his article 'Hobbes and the Wolf-man', in C. Walton and P. J. Johnson (eds.), *Hobbes's science of natural justice* (Dordrecht, 1987), 139–51, at p. 149.

lines of § 13, the four sections are clearly turned towards the past; or, to be more accurate, towards the state of nature conceived as a fact occurring under certain conditions, generally in a remote past, but occasionally contemporary: 'They of America are examples hereof, even in this present age: other nations have been in former ages' (§ 13, p. 118). The Red Indians reappear in *Leviathan*, 13:

the savage people in many places of *America*, except the government of small Families, the concord whereof dependeth on naturall lust, have no government at all; and live at this day in that brutish manner, as I said before (p. 187).

A comparable text occurs shortly after the beginning of chapter 17:

in all places, where men have lived by small Families, to robbe and spoyle one another, has been a Trade, and so farre from being reputed against the Law of Nature, that the greater spoyles they gained, the greater was their honour (p. 224).

In those descriptions, the state of nature ceases to be an abstract figment: it has become a descriptive sociological concept. But this conspicuous modification has required a change in the scale of the phenomenon under examination: here, the war essential to the state of nature is waged between groups, no more between individuals: besides the abstract natural state, in which man fights man, there is a concrete natural state, in which families fight one another.

However, the nature of the social link within these families deserves some inquiry. The words 'naturall lust', in chapter 13, seem to refer to sexual desire, which could more or less explain a kind of community feeling (at least temporary) between the parents. Is it possible to explain the whole family cohesion in an analogous manner? Here, one can put forward the place of chapter 17 that mentions 'the naturall inclination of Sexes, one to another, and to their children' (p. 253). But if such a sentiment can account for the parents' benevolence to the children, it is no sufficient ground for the children's obedience. This proceeds from a political bond, created by a 'supposed' promise of the child, made in return for the nurture without which he would have died: 'because preservation of life being the end, for which one man becomes subject to another, every man is supposed to promise obedience, to him, in whose power it is to save, or destroy him' (*Lev.*, 20, p. 254).

We have, then, to face the following situation: philosophy must take into account an abstract state of nature, whereas descriptive science can examine concrete ones. The concrete natural state holds between families, the cohesion of which rests on 'supposed' pacts. Of course, these pacts, which are very abstract fictions, are the supposed ending of a supposed natural war between parent and child. Thus, the analysis of the concrete state of nature brings us back to the abstract one, in its most abstract form: for a supposed Hobbesian state of nature between parent and child is much less an empirical datum than a theoretical construction, a synthetic model depicted to illustrate abstract human beings moved by one elementary passion: the fear of death. Obviously, Hobbes never meant that such a 'state' was a matter of common experience, in the relationship of fathers (or mothers) with their infant children.

II

Whatever the exact epistemological status of the state of nature may be, nobody questions its warlike character. The words 'war of all men against all men' first appear in *De Cive* (1. 12), but the idea can already be gathered from *The Elements*. More than the fact of the war, its causes are a matter of difficulty: the explanations proposed are many, but some are somewhat surprising, and the others are more fluctuating than appears at first sight.

To the first group belong the passages that ascribe the general war to a discrepancy between men's valuing judgements. Thus in *De Cive*:

> what this man commends, that is to say, calls *good*, the other undervalues, as being evil . . . Whilst thus they do, necessary it is there should be discord and strife. They are, therefore, so long in the state of war, as by reason of the diversity of the present appetites, they mete good and evil by diverse measures (3. 31, p. 150).

Literally, therefore, according to this text, men fight one another, in the state of nature, because they disagree as to good and evil. In fact, the explanation is far from satisfactory: if it means that the plunderer rejoices at a plundering that grieves the plundered, it just describes the unarbitrated conflict of desires which takes place in the state of nature. But it does not explain why the conflict arises, instead of a peaceful arrangement in which no plundering occurs. Anyhow, the corresponding passage in *Leviathan* suggests a more 'intellectual' reading:

> divers men, differ not onely in their Judgement, on the senses of what is pleasant, or unpleasant to the tast, smell, hearing, touch and sight; but also of what is conformable, or disagreeable to Reason, in the actions of common life . . . From whence arise Disputes, Controversies, and at last War (last page of ch. 15, p. 216).

I find it difficult to believe that the fundamental cause of Hobbes's primordial war is so purely doctrinal. I feel inclined to suppose that he was led astray, in such passages, by the idea (essential to his system) that 'in a civil government the reason of the supreme, that is, the civil law, is to be received by each single subject for the right' (*De Cive*, 2. 1, note, p. 123).[5] One can imagine that, starting from this conception of the sovereign's law as a 'common reason', and looking backwards to the antecedent time, he was driven to see it as the reign of conflicting individual reasons. But, considered in the general framework of the system, this conflict cannot but be interpreted as the theoretical expression of a clash of more fundamental desires, which are more clearly dealt with in the three Natural State Chapters.

The competition of appetites, however, is not represented, in any of the three political treatises, as the sole cause of the primordial war. All three also mention 'natural right' as playing a decisive part in the outbreak and persistence of violence. In *The Elements*, 1. 14, the Hobbesian notion of a natural right occupies five of the thirteen sections; in *De Cive*, chapter 1, five out of fifteen. Both books teach that every man may lawfully do whatever he deems necessary for his own defence. This point of doctrine is often shortened, not quite unambiguously, into the phrase 'right to all things'. This right is supposed to allow a man

[5] Here, 'the right' is the right reason. The Latin text explains that the 'ratio' of the city must be held 'pro recta' by the individual citizens (whereas the Latin *De Cive* speaks of 'civitas' and 'cives', the English version tends to use a more monarchical style; the passage under examination gives an instance of this difference).

to meet a pre-existing situation of strife and danger without being hindered by ill-grounded scruples. But, rather curiously, this very extensive right of self-defence is reckoned among the main causes of war:

Seeing then to the offensiveness of man's nature one to another, there is added a right of every man to every thing . . . the estate of men in this natural liberty is the estate of war (*E* 1. 14. 11, pp. 72–3).

If now to this natural proclivity of men, to hurt each other . . . you add, the right of all to all. . . . it cannot be denied but that the natural state of men, before they entered into society, was a mere war . . . (*De Cive*, 1. 12, pp. 117–18).

Thus, the right that should increase my safety is part and parcel of the circumstances that make my situation very unsafe. Perhaps this doctrine is not entirely inconsistent: the study of international relations may suggest examples in the same vein. There is, however, something circular about it, which makes it highly paradoxical. Things are not made easier if we notice that the first natural law, derived from the obligation to seek peace, demands (in both texts) that men abandon, or at least curtail, this right 'to all things' (*E* 1. 15. 2, p. 75; *De Cive*, 2. 3, p. 123). This clause presupposes that the right of nature, fully kept and exercised, is not only *a* cause of the war, but even the main one.

In *Leviathan*, chapter 13, the right of nature is not mentioned; it is just briefly alluded to in two passages in which the anticipative attacks are 'allowed' (pp. 184–5). And the war of all against all is already raging when this concept is expressly brought in, in the first page of chapter 14:

And because the condition of Man (as hath been declared in the precedent Chapter) is a condition of Warre of every one against every one; in which case every one is governed by his own Reason; and there is nothing he can make use of, that may not be a help unto him, in preserving his life against his enemyes; It followeth, that in such a condition, every man has a Right to every thing; even to one anothers body (pp. 189–90).

This text admits of no other interpretation than this: the right of nature is not a cause of war, but a philosophical conclusion concerning the actions that are made lawful by a situation of war. *Immediately* after, however, the right of nature is dealt with as a cause of war, the one that must be eradicated first in a peace-making process:

And therefore, as long as this naturall Right of every man to every thing endureth, there can be no security to any man . . . of living out the time, which Nature ordinarily alloweth men to live (p. 190).

From this point on, the reasoning is the same as in the previous treatises. Just after asserting the necessity of seeking peace, Hobbes sets forth, as a law of nature, '*That a man be willing, when others are so too, . . . to lay down this right to all things*' (p. 190).

Here, the circle is more obvious than ever: war entails right, but war is begotten by right, and the only way to stop war is to renounce right. I do not think that the charge of paralogism can here be entirely dismissed by arguing (not absurdly) that defensive steps may result in increasing the threat they are supposed to ward off. According to Hobbes's own account, men were already fighting one another, for reasons quite alien to the natural right, before there was any mention of it; and even supposing this right abandoned (wholly or partly), the first reasons for the war would still be present and active.

In fact, Hobbes seems to have mixed up two things: one of them is that all-inclusive notion of the right of self-defence which he calls 'natural right'; the other is the desire of the '*concupiscible* part' of man 'to appropriate to itself the use of those things in which all others have a joint interest' (dedicative letter of *De Cive*, p. 93). We must not be deceived by an apparently restrictive wording: in fact, 'those things' are the whole earth, which in the beginning, according to Locke's terminology, was an immense 'common'; Hobbes alludes to the same conception, when he quotes 'that common saying, *nature hath given all to all*' (*De Cive*, I. 10, p. 117). It is quite clear (1) that if a few 'commoners' claim to themselves the private and exclusive property of the 'common', war will ensue (if all are of equal strength and in the absence of an arbitrating power); (2) consequently, that peace requires the resignation of such a claim. All that has very little to do with my right of defending myself by any means, when my life is at stake. But Hobbes does not distinguish between these two problems, as can be seen, for instance, in *De Cive* I. 10–13.

It is true that both eventually merge within his political conclusions. Boundless greed begets war, then insecurity, then a desire for peace, then the mutual acceptance of limited properties, then pacts to this effect, then the setting up of a government, monopolistic holder of all coercive power, to make good the pacts. But this recourse to a protector of contractual arrangements implies the extinction of all private justice (except in cases of emergency), and consequently the transfer to the sovereign of all the 'natural rights' to self-defence. The two questions are therefore closely interwoven. But all the same, the first, dealing with the 'imperialistic' passion, concerns a possible primary cause of the war, while that of natural right deals with a consequence of it (which may act, to a certain extent, as an occasional secondary cause).

III

I shall now turn to the three Natural State Chapters, considered independently of the prominent place given to the natural right question, at least in *The Elements* and *De Cive*.

In each text, Hobbes endeavours to reduce to three the number of psychological reasons for the state of war. In *The Elements* these are 'vanity', 'comparison', 'appetite' (I. 14. 5, p. 71); in *De Cive*, chapter I: 'vain glory' (§ 4, p. 114), 'combat of wits' (§ 5, p. 114), 'appetite to the same thing' (§ 6, p. 115); in *Leviathan*: 'competition', 'diffidence', 'glory' (ch. 13, p. 185). But this ternary arrangement, as we shall see, is more apparent than real, at least in the last two treatises. And even without this complication, these three lists of three terms each call for some commentary as regards the resemblances and differences of their contents.

1. The words 'comparison' in *The Elements* and 'glory' in *Leviathan* allude to the same thing, namely, the situation where a conflict of pride results in a duel. In *De Cive*, chapter I, in spite of a pronounced parallelism with *Elements*, I. 14, this reference seems at first reading to be replaced by the 'combat of wits', which may lead to civil wars, 'where the contestation is either concerning doctrines or politic prudence' (§ 5, p. 115). But the end of the section harks back to duelling, describing the intense

'vexation of mind' and 'desire to hurt' that proceed from any sign of contempt: even though a duel is not expressly mentioned in this place (perhaps because this ill feeling may result in diverse kinds of vengeance), the idea of it is close at hand; so that the psychological causes of war, in *De Cive*, are four rather than three (in so far as a precise numbering is possible, in a domain where notions frequently overlap one another).

Almost certainly, Hobbes's attention was drawn to this murderous and/or suicidal variety of 'honourable' conduct by some characteristic features of his time. The first half of the seventeenth century may have been the heyday of duelling in Western Europe; and certainly, many moral or literary products of these years reflect what Ruth Benedict (referring to ancient Japan) has called a 'shame culture',[6] meaning a culture in which shame, and chiefly shame resulting from an imputation of cowardice, is the supreme evil, more dreaded than death. In France, Corneille's *Cid* (1636) and Descartes's *Passions of the soul* (1649) are not unrelated to this system of values. Hobbes, too, echoes it when he writes: 'most men would rather lose their lives (that I say not, their peace) than suffer slander' ('contumeliam' in the Latin) (*De Cive*, 3. 12, p. 142).

Clearly, such a feeling is, in the Hobbesian philosophy, an embarrassing object, with regard either to its origin or to its consequences. For it is not easy to understand how such a passion can arise in a psychic machine where a pleasant thing is that which helps the vital motion (*E* 1. 7. 1, p. 28; *Lev.*, 6, p. 122). Of course, it may be argued that initially men seek honour because it affords power, and therefore it is a means of increasing one's safety; subsequently the end would be forgotten, the means mistaken for an end, and the fear of being accounted a coward would prevail over any other consideration. But this interpretation is a little far-fetched, and Hobbes does not explicitly propose it. Some will find it simpler to think, as Leo Strauss did, that this anxious concern for honour is, in Hobbes's anthropology, a feature more in accordance with Descartes's *Passions* than with his materialist premisses.

Even granting that Hobbesian men can, without inconsistency, prefer death to shame, we meet with another puzzle when

[6] Ruth Benedict, *The Chrysanthemum and the Sword: Patterns of Japanese culture* (Boston, 1946). See esp. pp. 222–4.

we wonder how such men can be tamed into regarding peace as almost unconditionally good (a belief whose absence would ruin the whole system). This is no wanton cavilling: most cultures put the warrior, who has accepted the prospect of his own death, above the peaceful labourer, and 'shame cultures' tend to put war above peace. How people of such breeding can come to consider the laws of nature as a universal truth, is a question that had better be left aside.

2. The words 'vanity' (*The Elements*) or 'vain glory' (*De Cive*) refer to a passion different from that which has just been examined. Or at least, if it is the same passion, it acts under other circumstances: in a duel, the social status of the fighters is roughly equivalent; even if each of them values himself more than his adversary, he usually does not intend to rise in the social scale as a consequence of his fight. On the contrary, the vainly glorious men 'hope for precedency and superiority above their fellows' (*E* 1. 14. 3, p. 71), each of them 'challenges respect and honour, as due to him before others' (*De Cive*, 1. 4, p. 114). In *Leviathan*, chapter 13, this passion receives no name, but some men are represented as 'taking pleasure in contemplating their own power in the acts of conquest, which they pursue farther than their security requires' (pp. 184–5). It must be admitted that here we have moved from the *Ehrsucht* towards the *Herrschsucht*; but in Hobbes the frontier between the three 'cold passions' of Kant (*Ehrsucht*, *Herrschsucht*, *Habsucht*)[7] is never clear-cut. Anyhow, in *Leviathan*, the presence of these ambitious men is a fourth cause of discord, not really included in the triad competition-diffidence-glory.

Whereas the refusal to swallow affronts seems to be a nearly universal passion, the 'vanity' of *The Elements*, the 'vain glory' of *De Cive*, the nameless corresponding passion in *Leviathan*, chapter 13, only affect a limited number of men (the amount of which being nowhere precisely settled). The others, 'who are moderate' (*E*, § 3, p. 70) or 'temperate' (*De Cive*, § 4, p. 114), 'otherwise would be glad to be at ease within modest bounds' (*Lev.*, 13, p. 185). But they will be obliged, in order not to become a prey to the ambitious, to embrace a warlike way of

[7] *Habsucht, Ehrsucht, Herrschsucht*: passion for possessing, for being honoured, for dominating. See Kant, *Anthropologie in pragmatischer Hinsicht*, Pt. I, Bk. 3, §§ 80–6, 'Von den Leidenschaften', esp. §§ 84–5 (vol. vii in the Berlin edn.).

living, which includes the recourse to preventive attacks. For, as it is said in the Preface to *De Cive*,

> though the wicked were fewer than the righteous, yet because we cannot distinguish them, there is a necessity of suspecting, heeding, anticipating, subjugating, self-defending, ever incident to the most honest and fairest conditioned (p. 100).

In *The Elements*, this cause of war is the main source of men's discord, while their coexistence could otherwise have remained undisturbed. If all men were reasonable, they would live in peace, even in the state of nature, on condition that they acknowledge one another as equal (which in fact they are, at least as concerns the capacity for killing): 'men considered in mere nature, ought to admit among themselves equality' (*E* 1. 14. 2, p. 70). Granted such an acknowledgement, everyone would safely enjoy a modest property, without the help of any pact. But this will not happen, because among men 'some are vainly glorious': they will be the starting-point of a contagion of violence. In *The Elements*, in comparison with this source of war, the others seem to be additional, not fundamental, causes.

3. One of these causes (a pugnacious sense of honour) has been examined above. Another is referred to, under the names of 'appetite', as well in *The Elements* as in *De Cive*, and 'competition' in *Leviathan*. In the three books, the situation considered is the same: two men desire the same thing, which they cannot both enjoy; a strife ensues. But from 1640 to 1642 a first change has occurred. In *The Elements*, this cause of war ranks third, and seems to be mentioned chiefly for the sake of completeness; it is not insisted upon. In *De Cive*, it still occupies the third place, but now it is called 'the most frequent reason why men desire to hurt each other' (1. 6, p. 115). Nevertheless, this hint remains isolated in the book, and more numerous are the passages that emphasize the responsibility of ambitious and violent men. In *Leviathan*, 'competition' comes first; and unequivocally it is the main reason of enmity between men, bringing in either contention about a present coveted object, or anticipative aggression in order to get rid of a possible rival. This is the last stage of a reversal whose importance can only be fully realized through a comparison with *De Cive* (leaving aside the brief precursory glimpse of § 6).

In the long Section *De Cive*, 1. 2, as has been noticed in Part I of this paper, the nature of men is gathered from their contemporary behaviour. Scrutinizing the motives for their meetings, Hobbes concludes that they seek the company of one another only for 'gain' or 'glory', which will not be a proper foundation for great and lasting societies, but on the contrary explains why human encounters are naturally contentious, and pregnant with violence. This pessimistic view of man is not unlike the one that would be set forth, a little later, by French 'moralistes' such as Pascal and La Rochefoucauld, who were both, though unequally, influenced by Jansenism. In fact, the anthropology of *De Cive* has much in common with that of the Jansenists, and prompts the reader to conclude that the state of nature is bad because of a badness rooted in human hearts.

Here, precision requires two comments. First, as we have seen, the wickedness need not be universal to provoke war: some bad men can set a whole country afire. Secondly, what is really evil in the bad men is not the set of their natural impulses, but the uncontrolled vent they give to such impulses:

> For the affections of the mind, which arise only from the lower parts of the soul, are not wicked themselves; but the actions thence proceeding may be sometimes, as when they are offensive or against duty (*De Cive*, Preface, p. 100).

But, even if malice is not a general characteristic of mankind, and, when it occurs, is not 'natural' in a strict sense, it remains that man's misery proceeds from man's will, and that man's natural affections, however innocent in themselves, are the first source of these guilty volitions.

On the the contrary, in *Leviathan*, chapter 13, the problem of human wickedness has become secondary. Later in the book, the fifth law of nature will censure the 'insociable' (15, p. 210) and the tenth, the arrogant (15, p. 212), which implies that the state of nature is not a lawless place. But chapter 13, ignoring such blames, flatly contradicts, on an important point, the passage of *De Cive* that has just been quoted:

> The Desires, and other Passions of man, are in themselves no Sin. No more are the Actions, that proceed from those Passions, till they know a Law that forbids them: which till Lawes be made they cannot know: nor can any Law be made, till they have agreed upon the Person that shall make it (p. 187).

This is a very strange passage. It would be a hard task to reconcile it, not only with the doctrine of *De Cive*, but even with most statements of *Leviathan* itself, concerning the laws of nature. But in *Leviathan*, chapter 13, when he meditates on the causes of the primordial war, Hobbes is little interested in such responsibility as may rest on men for its outbreak. We have already seen that it would rage among mankind even if the race of trouble-makers did not exist. In fact, competition and diffidence (the former entailing the latter) operate like an infernal machine, without anyone's responsibility being really involved. Take two living creatures *A* and *B*, endowed with desires, destitute of all natural sympathy, able both to calculate and to kill each other; shut them up in a finite space, in which exists some scarcity of goods. Necessarily, they are rivals, and 'in the way to their End . . . endeavour to destroy, or subdue one another (p. 184). And, which makes things still worse, *A* may reckon that *B* may be reckoning that it is profitable for him (i.e. *B*) to kill *A*; and *A* will conclude that it is wiser for him (i.e. *A*) to kill *B* first. Of course, at the same moment, *B* is going through a similar reasoning: the faster reckoner will be the first striker. In other words, men are in such a situation that, the more they reason (each of them solitarily), the more they will be menaced and unhappy. This will last until they light on, and put into application, the difficult idea of reasoning *together*, entering into mutual covenants, and setting up a power able to make them good.

If such are the real data of the problem, whatever evil may ensue does not come any more from men's inner nature, but from the external (and disastrous) circumstances of their pre-contractual encounter, from 'the ill condition, which man by mere nature is actually placed in' (*Lev.* 13, p. 188). And if it is still possible to say that the primordial war proceeds from 'passions', these are passions reduced to their simplest form: appetite for such goods as are generally desired, fear of death. More than ever the concept of a state of nature appears here as a scientific diagram, in which only a few really essential forces are taken into consideration.

I do not maintain that this conception has completely superseded all other approaches, either in *Leviathan* or in the subsequent works. Let us consider, for instance, *De Corpore*, 1. 6. 7: 'the appetites of men and the passions of their minds are such, that, unless they be restrained by some power, they will always be making war upon one another.' This text is more favourable to the older, more traditionally moralistic account, than to the 'structural' one of *Leviathan* (which, however, it does not expressly contradict). Probably Hobbes did not fully realize the difference between these interpretations, and still less cared to choose between them, because on this problem, as on many other issues, his thought never came to a standstill.

Necessarily, the conclusion of this sortie into Hobbes's state of nature will be an invitation to cautiousness. My students enjoy speaking of 'la logique implacable' de Hobbes. It is a cliché they have picked up somewhere, perhaps in my teaching: for I confess I have sometimes dreamt of 'formalizing' this system, reducing it to a finite number of definitions, axioms, demonstrations, and theorems. Hobbes himself would probably have encouraged such an undertaking, agreeable to his conception of scientificity, and his pretensions to have achieved it. If one were to be successful, the only disadvantage of such a logical construction is that it would put an end to many fascinating discussions, by setting up an almost obligatory standard of interpretation. But the instance of the state of nature suggests that this prospect has very few chances of ever being carried into effect. It is beyond anybody's power to give a quasi-mathematical shape to a doctrine in which the theses are always in motion, because the author is always searching. This situation can only result in tentative expositions: which probably explains why Hobbes went to the pains of setting forth his ethical and political doctrine in three successive books. He held fast to some basic intuitions, which make him the object of a lasting and apparently increasing interest, but we have no proof that he was ever satisfied with the wording he gave them, and we even have some grounds for doubting it. That is the reason why this great philosophy lies open to such a diversity of interpretations. Hobbes conferences still have a future before them.

6

*Hobbes's Social Contract**

DAVID GAUTHIER

I

In justifying the sovereign, does Hobbes appeal to a social contract? In her new and important book, *Hobbes and the Social Contract Tradition*, Jean Hampton says 'No' ((2), cf. pp. 4, 186–8, 279). Hobbes's 'social contract' argument is unfortunately, although no doubt irretrievably, mislabelled. He appeals, not to a contract, but to a self-interested agreement or convention. And this appeal is typical of contractarian strategy; '*there is no literal contract* in any successful social contract theory' ((2), p. 4).

And in authorizing the sovereign, do the subjects alienate their rights to him? Hobbes claims that they do. But Hampton maintains that his claim is unsuccessful, and that *any* alienation theory must be unsuccessful ((2), pp. 256–66). However, beneath the surface, another, successful account of authorization may be found, according to which the subjects appoint an agent to act on their behalf. But this agent lacks many of the characteristics of the Hobbesian sovereign; he is neither absolute nor permanent. According to Hampton, the sovereign whom Hobbesian men can authorize is not Leviathan.

My concern is with the structure of Hobbes's social contract argument. Hampton's revisionist interpretation turns on two contrasts, opposing self-interested agreement to contract, and agency to alienation. Against the claim that the 'social contract' is a self-interested agreement in which the subjects appoint an agent, I shall defend the traditional account of a true contract in which the subjects alienate their rights to a ruler. This provides

* I am grateful to Daniel Farrell for comments on an earlier draft of this paper read at the University of Michigan. A shorter version has appeared in *Noûs*.

the best reading of Hobbes's argument, and the only one compatible with his political absolutism. But it offers more. For an alienation social contract theory need not be wedded to this implausible and unattractive absolutism, and Hobbes's achievement in being the first systematically to construct such a theory makes him the true parent of rational morality and politics. However, I shall not pursue this larger theme here, confining myself to analysing, not celebrating, Hobbes's argument.

My analysis will require a third contrast, also discussed by Hampton. Hobbes's social contract argument represents the sovereign as the object of a rational agreement among persons who would escape, or avoid, the state of nature—the condition of humankind in the absence of political authority. To appraise the argument, we must understand why persons would reject the state of nature. Hobbes represents the state of nature as one of conflict. How do we explain this conflict? Does it result from the *rational* interaction of persons in the absence of a sovereign, or is it an effect of their irrational *passions*? I shall begin by considering Hobbes's account of the causes of natural conflict.

II

Hobbes characterizes the natural condition of humankind as a mutually unprofitable state of war of every person against every other person. Since Hobbesian persons value self-preservation above all else, and since universal war affords each person the prospect of a life that is nasty, brutish, and short, ending in violent death, some explanation of the natural emergence of such a war is evidently needed. Hobbes's explanation has seemed plausible to some, highly implausible to others, but few commentators, until recently, have paused to consider precisely what it is. Perhaps the most straightforward way of telling Hobbes's story of the emergence of conflict is the following.

In the state of nature, the means of preservation are, or are likely to be, scarce. Hence persons find themselves from time to time in competition for these means. This sporadic conflict generates a deeper and more pervasive one. For 'there is no way for any man to secure himselfe, so reasonable, as Anticipation;

that is, by force, or wiles, to master the persons of all men he can, so long, till he see no other power great enough to endanger him: And this is no more than his own conservation requireth, and is generally allowed' ((3), p. 61). Thus, according to Hobbes, each person realizes that his best prospect of survival results from anticipating his fellows, subjecting them if he can, so that he will be assured of prevailing in the competition for the goods needful to preservation. And through anticipation, limited competition becomes universal conflict.

The state of nature thus constitutes an *n*-person Prisoner's Dilemma. Whatever others do, war is each person's best course of action. If others act peaceably, he is then master; if others are warlike, he defends himself. But the outcome, universal war, is mutually unprofitable; universal peace would offer everyone a better prospect of survival, and so would be an *ex ante* Pareto-superior state of affairs.

It would therefore seem rational for each person to agree with his fellows to end this natural condition of war. But bare agreement would merely reiterate the Dilemma. Whatever others do, violation would be each person's best course of action. If others adhere, he would take advantage of them; if others violate, he would not let them take advantage of him. As Hobbes say of such agreement, 'he which performeth first, does but betray himselfe to his enemy; contrary to the Right . . . of defending his life, and means of living' ((3), p. 68). And if neither would find it rational to perform first, or independently of the other, then agreement is of no avail. Universal war must continue until some enforceable agreement may be found; thus the need for a sovereign.

I shall call this account, representing universal conflict in the state of nature as the outcome of rational behaviour by individuals each seeking best to secure his own preservation, the *simple rationality account.* It is open to challenge at two points, whether it be considered an interpretation of Hobbes's own position, or as an independently plausible account of natural conflict given his suppositions about human motivation.

First, even if the means of preservation in the state of nature are, or may be, scarce, their scarcity need not be great enough to justify pre-emptive conflict. The costs of initiating violence on solely anticipatory grounds may outweigh the expected benefits.

If so, then the state of nature is not an *n*-person Prisoner's Dilemma. However, Hobbes recognizes a further cause of conflict in glory, the pleasure that some persons take 'in contemplating their own power in the act of conquest, which they pursue farther than their security requires' ((3), p. 61). Although those who provoke war for glory act irrationally, given their overriding concern with their own preservation and well-being, yet they provoke retaliatory, and anticipatory, responses from others who 'otherwise would be glad to be at ease within modest bounds' (ibid.), and these responses are themselves rational. And so universal war develops, not as the outcome of each person's rational endeavour to preserve himself, but as the outcome of the rational endeavours of some to preserve themselves against the irrational pursuit of glory and domination by others.

There is no doubt that Hobbes considers glory a contributory cause of universal conflict in the state of nature. But, at least in *Leviathan*, he does not rely on it as primary; instead, he places the rationality of anticipating one's fellows at the core of his argument. Thus those who claim that, according to Hobbes, universal conflict arises because of the irrational desire of some for glory, rather than because of the concern of each to maximize rationally his prospect of preservation, are mistaken. But there is a second and more substantial challenge to the simple rationality account of the origin of conflict.

Grant that in the state of nature war is a more rational strategy for each person than is merely peaceable behaviour. It does not follow that war is the most advantageous or most rational strategy, or that the state of nature actually constitutes an *n*-person Prisoner's Dilemma. Hobbes describes the laws of nature as 'convenient Articles of Peace', suggested by *reason*, 'upon which men may be drawn to agreement' ((3), p. 63). But if it is rational for everyone to agree on articles of peace, then why is the state of nature one of universal war? On the simple rationality account of conflict, the answer is that agreement would be rational were compliance also rational, but in the absence of effective enforcement, compliance is not rational and so agreement would be pointless. The second challenge rejects this explanation, maintaining that compliance is in principle rational. Hobbes claims that in an agreement 'where one of the parties has performed already', it is not 'against reason, that is, against the benefit of the other to performe' ((3), p. 73). But if second performance is rational, then so is first performance, since by performing first one elicits the performance of the other and so obtains the benefit for which one entered into agreement. Agreement does not give rise to a Prisoner's Dilemma; compliance is each person's best response to the compliance of others.

But does Hobbes not insist that 'he which performeth first, does but betray himselfe to his enemy'? We have already noted that he does. But why does he say this? His reason is that 'he that performeth first, has no assurance the other will performe after; because the bonds of words are too weak to bridle mens ambition, avarice, anger, and other Passions, without the feare of some coercive Power' ((3), p. 68). It is rational for persons to comply with their agreements provided that their fellows have already done so, yet Hobbes argues that in the absence of coercion such compliance cannot be expected, since it is contrary to the natural, but irrational, 'Passions, that carry us to Partiality, Pride, Revenge, and the like' ((3), p. 85).

Mutually agreed peace would be the outcome of rational interaction in the natural condition of humankind. But persons are not sufficiently rational to adhere voluntarily to their agreements; hence mutually agreed peace, without enforcement, is unattainable. Faced with the choice between anticipatory violence and passive acquiescence in or mere retaliation against whatever one's fellows do, anticipatory violence is rational. The state of nature is not a true Prisoner's Dilemma, but it presents itself as such a Dilemma, because of the subversion by the passions of what would otherwise be rational agreement on peace. This second challenge to the simple rationality account of conflict in the state of nature yields what I shall call the *subversive passions account*.

An explanation of universal conflict in the state of nature must answer two questions. First, it must show why persons are violent rather than naturally peaceable. Second, it must show why persons remain violent rather than becoming peaceable by agreement. On the simple rationality account, both of these questions are answered by an appeal to individual rationality. The first challenge addresses the first question, claiming that persons are naturally violent because of their irrational passions. The second challenge addresses the second question, claiming that persons remain violent because agreement would be subverted by their irrational passions. Unlike the first challenge, the second seems to succeed; it provides a more plausible interpretation of Hobbes's overall position, by reconciling his insistence, in replying to the Foole, that it is rational to adhere to an agreement in which the other party has already performed, with his equal insistence, in showing the inadequacy of agreement alone to being about peace, that it is not rational to adhere to an agreement in which the other party has yet to perform.

But why does Hobbes hold that it is rational to adhere to one's agreement provided the other party has already done so? On the face of it such compliance is irrational. For the benefit of agreeing is to obtain the performance of the other party; one's own performance is the cost one pays. If the other party has already performed, then one has gained the benefit without paying any cost; why then should one gratuitously pay it? Surely the original claim that adherence to agreement poses a Prisoner's Dilemma-type problem is correct, even if Hobbes rejects it in replying to the Foole.

Hobbes has an answer to the charge that second performance is irrational. 'He therefore that breaketh his Covenant, and consequently declareth that he thinks he may with reason do so, cannot be received into any Society, that unite themselves for Peace and Defence, but by the errour of them that receive him' ((3), p. 73). Hobbes does not deny the short-term cost-avoidance in violation, but claims that it is outweighed by the expectation of the long-term cost of being considered an enemy of those who unite to bring about peace. As several recent commentators have noted, we may think of Hobbes as here appealing to the idea of an iterated Prisoner's Dilemma. If we consider each particular agreement in isolation, then we have a simple Dilemma in which the net benefit of violation is greater than that of compliance. But if we consider the effect of any particular agreement on the later agreements that one will wish and need to make, then the expected benefit of compliance outweighs the immediate advantage of violation.

But is this so? And even if this is so within society, would it hold in a state of nature? Whether it is rational to keep an agreement despite the immediate gain from violation must depend on the magnitude of the reputation effect on one's subsequent interactions. And in a state of nature this effect may be quite small. If there is little communication among persons, and if interactions involving any particular pair or group of persons are relatively infrequent, then reputation effects will be of only minor importance.

Hence we may suppose that Hobbes should have taken a more complex view of the rationality of adhering to agreements. Against the Foole, he could rightly insist that if agreements are generally kept, so that a state of peaceful co-operation exists, then a unilateral violator may reasonably expect to lose more through punishment or ostracism by her fellows, than to gain through her violation. And he could add that if there is a real possibility of joining a group that can provide peace and security to its members, then someone who violates her agreements may reasonably expect to lose through being excluded. But otherwise, Hobbes should have admitted that a person who fails to take advantage of compliance by another, when she can benefit from that compliance without carrying out her part of the agreement, must expect to incur unnecessary costs. To that extent the Foole is right; second performance, and so first performance, would then be irrational.

On this *modified rationality account*, interaction in the state of nature has two possible outcomes such that both are rational in constituting equilibria in which each person's behaviour maximizes her prospects of preservation and well-being given the behaviour of her fellows. One of these equilibria is universal war resulting from anticipatory violence; the other is universal peace resulting from mutual adherence to agreements ensuring peace and co-operation. The latter is Pareto-superior to the former. But without enforcement universal peace is unstable, for we may suppose that the defection of only a few persons would make it disadvantageous for others to continue their peaceable, agreement-keeping behaviour, so that degeneration to universal war would rapidly ensue. Granted, a lone defector, or a very small number of defectors, must expect to lose. But if compliance, although the individually rational response to compliance by most others, is individually rational *only* as a response to compliance by most others, then we may suppose both that persons in a state of nature will not initially find themselves in a peaceable state of affairs, and that they will not be able rationally to attain it without some coercive device to ensure that their agreements are kept.

The modified rationality account thus requires the supposition that in a situation in which there are two equilibrium outcomes one of which is Pareto-superior to the other, the superior outcome may be rationally inaccessible. Persons, even if fully rational, may be unable to co-ordinate their actions to bring it about. In an ideal world with no costs for communication and decision-making, this supposition may not hold. But in the real world it does. There may be no direct route from the natural condition of humankind to a state of affairs that would be in equilibrium and that would be better for each person than the state of nature.

Were Hobbes to accept this modification of his argument, then he could say both that the laws of nature are rational prescriptions, and that individuals behave rationally in a state of nature even though they act without reference to these laws. For although a rational individual must be willing to seek peace and to adhere to the conditions of peace provided almost all of his fellows may reasonably be expected to do likewise, yet such an expectation is not reasonable in the state of nature. Hobbes would then have the distinction he wants between the *in foro interno* validity of the laws of nature in all circumstances, and their *in foro externo* inapplicability in the state of nature. And he would not need to appeal to the irrationality of some persons at any point in his account. Universal conflict in the state of nature can be explained on the suppositions that persons are fully rational but must make decisions and communicate with their fellows in real space and time, and that universally peaceable behaviour is fully rational and Pareto-superior to universal conflict. The state of nature does not constitute a true Prisoner's Dilemma, but the co-ordination problem faced by real persons who seek the superior, peaceable state of affairs, has no rational, non-coercive solution.

Attractive as this modified rationality account of conflict may be, it has embarrassing consequences for Hobbes's account of sovereignty. For if universal conflict results from the inability of rational persons to solve a co-ordination problem in the state of nature, then, although a coercive force—and so, we may say, a sovereign—will be needed to solve that problem and bring about peace, yet, once peace is attained, further coercion, or at least the extensive coercion practised by an absolute and permanent sovereign, should not be necessary to maintain it. For if compliance with agreement is rational in a context of general compliance, then *rational* persons should remain in such a context once they find themselves there. And this will defeat Hobbes's defence of *permanent* absolute sovereignty.

Such a defence, if it is possible at all, seems to require an appeal to irrational passions. For if some persons are unable to curb the natural passions that carry them to pride and partiality in order to keep their agreements with their fellows, then coercive force will continue to be needed to maintain a context of general compliance, and perhaps a permanent and absolute sovereign will be the best coercive device. (We may doubt this, but we may nevertheless grant that Hobbes's case is at least arguable.) So perhaps we should conclude our discussion of the causes of natural conflict in the following way. Hobbes has available to him an explanation of the emergence of the war of every person against every other person that is consistent with the assumptions that persons are fully rational and that the laws of nature are rational prescriptions. We have called this the modified rationality account. It establishes the need for a coercive power to bring about peace, but not for a permanent and absolute sovereign to maintain peace. To defend Hobbes's view of sovereignty in a manner consistent with his premisses, we must supplement the modified rationality account with the claim, central to the subversive passions account of conflict, that without coercive force some persons are unable to control their passions in order to comply with the agreements that establish and maintain peaceful co-operation, despite the advantageousness, and so rationality, of their compliance.

III

The state of nature lacks any institutional structure. To introduce such a structure is to convert it into society. In our account of conflict in the state of nature, we have abstracted from the possibility of this conversion. Thus the modified rationality account states that, if fully rational persons were in, *and could not exit from*, a state of nature, then they could not effectively agree on peace, and universal conflict would emerge. But of course Hobbes supposes that persons can exit from the state of nature, and his account of conflict is intended to establish, not that rational persons would face universal conflict, but that they would accept an institutional structure that provides the coercive force needed to motivate compliance with the laws of nature, and so to establish and maintain peaceable co-operation.

How do persons exit from the state of nature, converting it into society? What institutional structure must they adopt, to resolve their problem of compliance? According to Hobbes, what is needed 'to make their Agreement constant and lasting . . . is a Common Power, to keep them in awe, and to direct their actions to the Common Benefit' ((3), p. 87). The second task—the direction of actions to the common benefit—is essentially one of co-ordination. But to ensure that persons follow the directions given, 'to secure them in such sort, as that by their own industrie, and by the fruites of the Earth, they may nourish themselves and live contentedly' (ibid.), the first task—to keep them in awe—is necessary. And it is this task that requires a sovereign—someone who rules.

Hobbes's procedure for instituting a sovereign has two parts. The first is a covenant of every person with every other person. The second is the authorization, by every person, of some one person (or group). The authorization provides the content of the covenant; each person covenants, with every other person, to authorize some one person or group, which is to say, to treat the acts of that person or group as her own.

For Hobbes a covenant is a type of contract. And so the institution of a sovereign is effected by a social contract. But Hampton finds this terminology misleading. She claims that the institution of the sovereign requires only a self-interested agreement. What is the point here at issue? And is Hampton correct? She claims that 'SI [self-interested] agreements differ from contracts in being coordinations of intentions to act that are kept by both parties *solely for self-interested reasons*, whereas contracts are trades of *promises* that introduce moral incentives that either *supplement* or *replace* each party's self-interested motivations' ((2), pp. 145, 147). A social contract provides a moral basis for sovereignty; a self-interested agreement provides a purely prudential basis.

But Hampton's distinction needs modification. Consider an agreement made within a framework providing for legal enforcement. And suppose that without the prospect of such enforcement, compliance with the agreement would not be adequately motivated. This is surely a paradigmatic contract. But the incentive provided by legal enforceability need not be thought of, by the parties to the agreement, as moral. Rather, their agreement simply calls into play a supplementary but necessary incentive, and in so doing reveals its contractual character.

Or consider this situation. Your crops will be ready to harvest next week, and mine the following week. Each of us will benefit if we harvest together, rather than each working alone. It is then in the interest of each of us to agree to assist the other in return for obtaining the other's assistance. But suppose that, after the crops are in, you will move from this area and our paths are unlikely to cross again. Straightforward agreement may then seem insufficient, since if I help you next week, you will gain the benefit you seek, and have no reason to accept the cost of assisting me the following week. Hence we must expand the agreement to introduce a further incentive, itself quite irrelevant to the primary objective of mutual assistance. I may propose that you deposit some article with me as surety, in the belief that you will prefer to assist me rather than to forfeit the article. The resulting agreement is one that each of us keeps for purely self-interested reasons; it introduces no moral incentives. But the point of the agreement is to bring about mutual assistance in harvesting, and this is not in itself directly and sufficiently supported by self-interest. And what must be added to the agreement, so that the primary objective may be achieved, is itself unwelcome; each of us would prefer an agreement without surety, were that feasible. Such an agreement, some part of which exists only to afford incentives for compliance not sufficiently motivated by straightforward coordination on the primary objective, is a contract.

I propose to distinguish contracts from other agreements by characterizing the former as exchanges of intentions to act that introduce incentives, whether internal or external, moral or other, to supplement or replace each party's motivation to attain the true objective of the agreement. In particular, I distinguish contracts from purely co-ordinative agreements. Both require that each person prefers the outcome of agreement to that of no agreement. In purely co-ordinative agreements, each also prefers compliance with the agreement to non-compliance, given compliance by her fellows, and this preference for compliance is not induced by sanctions, external or internal. Furthermore, each expects the others to comply, and intends to comply herself. No part of the agreement exists solely to ensure compliance with the remainder, so that, leaving compliance aside, omitting any of the terms of the agreement would be regarded as undesirable by at least one of the parties.

A contract is only partially co-ordinative. Again, each prefers the outcome of agreement to that of no agreement. (If this preference is induced by threats, then the contract is coercive.) But either someone does not expect compliance by the other or others, or would be unwilling to comply herself, in the absence of sanctions or terms introduced solely for the purpose of ensuring compliance with the remainder. Rather, someone expects compliance by the other or others, or intends to comply herself, only because of the additional incentives that the agreement calls into play.

Note that in so characterizing contract I say nothing about a preference for non-compliance over compliance, given that others comply. If each person chooses on the basis of her preferences, and if no problem is created by decision-making or communication costs, then a contract is required only in those cases in which some would prefer non-compliance, given compliance by the others, in the absence of sanctions or specially created incentives. But my characterization of contract allows for cases in which, even if each person would prefer, in some not strictly behavioural sense, to comply given compliance by the others, yet sufficient compliance would nevertheless not be expected in the absence of additional terms or incentives, whether because of the costs of making a purely co-ordinative agreement, or because of the irrational refusal of some to comply with such an agreement. For in these cases co-ordination must be induced by supplementary incentives, and this is what distinguishes contract.

Given Hobbes's insistence, whatever his reason for it, that agreement alone does not suffice to achieve peace in the absence of a common power, we should interpret the covenant of every person with every other person as a contract, and not as a purely co-ordinative agreement. For even if we suppose that everyone keeps this covenant for purely self-interested reasons, yet these reasons stem, not simply from the concern to achieve the primary objective of agreement, peace and security, but rather from the power of the sovereign, an incentive called into play, and indeed created, by the agreement itself.

We may draw a parallel with our example of the agreement for mutual assistance in harvesting. There, reasons stemming from the primary objective of agreement were recognized by the parties as insufficient to ensure compliance. Hence a further incentive was created by expanding the agreement to embrace surety. In the same way, among persons who seek peace, reasons stemming from their primary objective of agreement are recognized as insufficient to ensure compliance, and so a further incentive is created by enlarging the agreement to include the institution of a sovereign, who has the power to enforce adherence to the conditions of peace. The institution of a sovereign is not the primary objective of agreement, or part of this objective. Were mere agreement on conditions of peace sufficient—were the covenant a purely co-ordinative agreement—then the sovereign would be not merely unnecessary, but positively undesirable. Hobbes himself admits that the institution of the sovereign is not without costs, noting 'that the Condition of Subjects is very miserable; as being obnoxious to the lusts, and other irregular passions of him, or them that have so unlimited a Power in their hands' ((3), p. 94).

Hampton claims that the agreement to institute a sovereign, considered in itself, is kept for purely self-interested reasons. If she is right, then the institution of a sovereign, *as such*, is purely co-ordinative and fits her model of self-interested agreement. But to suppose that Hobbes does not appeal to a social contract is to overlook the context of the institution of the sovereign, and to fail to recognize that it is part of a larger agreement, whose primary objective is peace and security, and that in relation to this larger agreement, it is accepted, despite its cost, to ensure compliance. Everyone agrees to the conditions of peace, which are the laws of nature. But this agreement is not in itself effective. Everyone agrees that her actions should be directed to the common benefit, in so far as she shares in it. But this agreement, to create a co-ordinator, is not in itself effective. To provide sufficient incentives for adhering to the laws of nature and accepting the directives of a co-ordinator, everyone must also agree to authorize one person or group, who is then sovereign, with sufficient power to enforce both adherence to the laws of nature and obedience to his commands. Sovereignty is created only to provide sufficient incentives so that persons will act to attain their primary objective, peace. And so the overall agreement, of which institution of a sovereign is only part, is contractual.

IV

Is sovereignty successful? Does it create the incentives needed for peace? Will each person be sufficiently motivated by considerations of her own interest to obey the sovereign's directives and adhere to the laws of nature? If this is what is required for success, then sovereignty fails. The sovereign's attempt to make his subjects secure gives rise to a free-rider problem which cannot be solved by a direct appeal to self-interest.

If the sovereign is to provide security, what must his subjects do? Hampton argues, plausibly, that a subject must (1) 'not interfere with the sovereign's punishment of anyone other than himself', (2) 'actively assist the sovereign when ordered to do so in punishment and enforcement activities involving others', and (3) 'be disposed to obey the punishment orders of only the sovereign' ((2), pp. 174–5). We may agree with her that the first and third of these raise no problems in plausible circumstances; no one would have an interest in opposing an effective sovereign or in supporting a rival. But to give the sovereign active assistance is to risk one's own safety and security. Will not each subject prefer to free-ride, letting others (should they so choose) actively assist the sovereign? Will not each subject reason that the incremental effect of adding her assistance in support of the sovereign would yield her so little expected benefit, in comparison with the expected cost to herself of providing the assistance, that it is not in her interest, and so not rational, to assist?

This reasoning seems sound. Each subject's active assistance yields a slight increase in the overall level of security, while decreasing her own security level. Assume that the total gross increase in the overall level of security—the sum of the increases provided if each assists the sovereign—exceeds the total gross decrease—the sum of the risks each runs in giving assistance. And assume that this holds on every occasion in which the sovereign demands assistance. Thus on every such occasion, if everyone assists the sovereign there is a net increase in security. Assume also that the gross total increase in each person's security level—the sum of the increases provided to her if everyone assists the sovereign whenever he demands assistance—exceeds the gross total decrease in her own level resulting from the assistance she gives whenever the sovereign demands her assistance. Thus if everyone always assists the sovereign there is a net increase in security to each subject. Not only society as a whole, but every member of it, may expect to gain on balance. Nevertheless, it is surely likely that each person loses from her own active assistance; the slight increase in her level of security resulting from her own actions is less, and quite possibly much less, than the risks she runs in performing those actions.

In attempting to obtain the active assistance of his subjects, the sovereign thus seems to face the usual problem involved in supplying an incremental public good—a good that is non-excludable, so that if it is supplied to one person, it is supplied to all. But Hampton denies that the sovereign need face this problem, because security is not an incremental good, but a step good. The security level is not increased incrementally by each individual act of assistance to the sovereign, but in discrete steps each of which requires the acts of several individuals. And the sovereign can exploit the step character of security to arrange it so that each subject will find it rational to obey his orders, and provide the active assistance he needs.

Consider her example ((2), pp. 176 ff.). The sovereign wants a law-breaker apprehended, and selects a group of persons to carry out the task. If the group is too small it will fail, and no increase in security will result. If the group is too large, no greater increase in security will result than if it were just large enough to carry out the apprehension successfully. Hence if the sovereign commands a minimally sufficient number of persons to constitute the apprehending group, each person selected will reason as follows: 'It is very likely that the others selected, and no one else, will participate in trying to apprehend the lawbreaker. Hence if I participate, very likely the group will succeed and security will increase. If I do not participate, very likely the group will fail and security will not increase. So the expected value, to me, of my participation is almost equal to my expected gain in security from apprehending the lawbreaker, and this exceeds my cost of participation. Therefore it is rational for me, because in my interest, to obey the sovereign's command and give him my active assistance.'

But is Hampton's argument plausible? Suppose that the society contains n persons. Let the increase in security that would be afforded to the i-th person by the cost-free apprehension of the law-breaker be b_i. Thus the total gross benefit $B = \sum_{i=1}^{n} b_i$. Let the minimal group appointed by the sovereign to apprehend the law-breaker contain m persons; without loss of generality assume that these are persons $1, \ldots m$. Let the loss in security to the i-th person from the risks involved in seeking to apprehend the law-breaker be c_i; for persons $m+1, \ldots, n$ not in the appointed group $c_i = 0$. Thus the total cost $C = \sum_{i=1}^{m} c_i$. As before, we assume B is greater than C. But given that the task of apprehending the law-breaker is assigned to a small group of persons, is it plausible to suppose that for each person i, b_i is greater than c_i? To be sure, the average gain B/n must be greater than the average loss C/n. And since the increase in security is a non-excludable good, so that for each person i, b_i is positive, for any person not in the selected group, b_i is greater than c_i. But what about those persons commanded by the sovereign to undertake the task of apprehension? If it is to be rational for each of them to obey his command, then it is necessary (but not sufficient) that each expect that the group's activity if she participates will increase her security to an extent that more than offsets the risk she runs in participating. But we may easily show that in general, the prospective members of the group will not expect to gain this much.

Suppose otherwise. Then for each person i in the group, b_i is greater than c_i, and so the sum of the gains in security to those in the group, $\sum_{i=1}^{m} b_i$ must exceed the total cost C of providing those gains. If we assume that each person in the society may expect roughly the same gain in security as her fellows from the apprehension of the law-breaker, then the total benefit B must be roughly equal to $(n/m) \sum_{i=1}^{m} b_i$ and so must be greater than $(n/m)C$. But since n is much greater than m, the total benefit B must be much greater than the total cost C. Indeed, suppose that the sovereign appoints one person out of every hundred members of society to the apprehending group. Then the benefit from apprehending the law-breaker must be at least one hundred times the cost, for it to be plausible to suppose that each person named to the apprehending group will find it in her interest to offer her assistance.

Can the sovereign provide his subjects with peace and security, if he may expect their active assistance only when the good to be provided is so much greater than the cost of providing it? The answer is surely that he cannot. The sovereign cannot motivate the members of a small group voluntarily to provide a non-excludable public good, albeit a step good, unless that step good offers a net benefit to the small group alone. And such goods will not suffice for peace and security. Hobbes has no general solution to the free-rider problem that confronts a sovereign in need of the active assistance of his subjects, if we assume, as Hampton does and as we have done implicitly in our discussion, that each subject will decide whether to assist the sovereign by a direct appeal to her overall self-interest.

V

Our discussion of the failure of sovereignty would not surprise Hobbes. Indeed, he might agree that he has no solution to the free-rider problem as we have posed it. For he never claims that the sovereign must gain the assistance of each subject by making a direct appeal to his self-interest. Such an appeal treats each individual's 'private Appetite' as 'the measure of Good', and Hobbes insists that so long as this is done 'a man is in the condition of meer Nature' ((3), p. 80). Authorizing the sovereign commits the subject to more than self-interestedly assisting him in his punishment and enforcement activities. It commits the subject to accept the sovereign's *judgement* in place of his own, so that when the sovereign requires his active assistance, he obeys directly and not only if a self-interested calculation shows obedience to be advantageous. We must explain the role of authorization in Hobbes's argument.

Although Hobbes insists that 'all men equally, are by Nature Free', yet he treats authorization as limiting that freedom ((3), p. 111). He distinguishes two ways in which such a limitation might arise, either 'from the expresse words *I Authorise all his Actions*' by which the subject places himself under the sovereign, or 'from the Intention of him [the subject] that submitteth himself to his [the sovereign's] Power (which Intention is to be understood by the End for which he so submitteth . . .)' (ibid.). And this end, Hobbes goes on to say, is 'the Peace of the Subjects within themselves, and their Defence against a common Enemy'. But the first way, the words themselves, do not limit freedom, or put the subject under any obligation, for in these words 'there is no restriction at all, of his own former naturall Liberty' ((3), p. 112). And so Hobbes concludes 'that the Obligation a man may sometimes have, upon the Command of the Soveraign to execute any dangerous, or dishonourable Office, dependent not on the Words of our Submission; but on the Intention; which is to be understood by the End thereof. When therefore our refusall to obey, frustrates the End for which the Soveraignty was ordained; then there is no Liberty to refuse: otherwise there is' (ibid.).

In deciding whether actively to assist the sovereign, the subject is to consider whether refusal to assist frustrates the end that sovereignty exists to realize. How are we to interpret Hobbes's position here? There are at least three possibilities. If, first, we focus on Hobbes's previous statement of the end, then we might read the last sentence quoted as saying: 'When an individual's refusal to obey frustrates the maintenance of peace among the subjects, and their defence against an enemy, then the individual must obey (i.e. has an obligation to obey, or has no liberty not to obey); otherwise he may refuse.' This treats the end as collective. And it would, seemingly, require a particular individual to sacrifice himself for that end, if we suppose, as surely we must, that peace and defence may require some persons to perform dangerous and even fatal tasks. Thus Hobbes says, 'when the Defence of the Common-wealth, requireth at once the help of all that are able to bear Arms, every one is obliged; because otherwise the Institution of the Common-wealth, which they have not the purpose, or courage to preserve, was in vain' ((3), p. 112).

But second, we may recall that Hobbes maintains that each individual is concerned to preserve himself, and has no natural care for the preservation of well-being of his fellows. And so we may suppose that the end is to be undestood not collectively but individually; each seeks to be maintained in peace among the other subjects, and to be defended against their common enemy. We might then read the sentence as saying: 'When an individual's refusal to obey frustrates his prospect of living in peace among his fellow subjects, or being defended against their common enemy, then he must obey; otherwise he may refuse.' On this reading no individual would be obliged to sacrifice himself, since even if his sacrifice would help to preserve the general peace, it would frustrate his own prospect of living in peace. Thus Hobbes says that those, even criminals, who resist the sovereign's sentence of death, 'but defend their lives, which the Guilty man may as well do, as the Innocent' ((3), p. 114).

There is a third interpretation, which may be motivated by reflecting on the significance of commitment in our interactions. Showing this requires a brief detour in our interpretation of Hobbes's text. Suppose that at time t I may choose between two actions, X and Y, and if I choose X, then at a later time t' you may choose between two actions, A and B. Thus there are three resulting prospects, XA, XB, and Y. Suppose that I prefer XA to Y to XB, and you prefer XB to XA to Y. So if you were to have a choice at t' you would prefer the outcome of choosing B. But if I were to expect you to choose B should you have a choice between A and B, then I should deny it to you by choosing Y at t, since I prefer *Y* to *XB*, and so you would get your least preferred prospect. However, If I were to expect you to choose *A* at *t′* despite your preference for *XB* to *XA*, then I would choose *X* at *t*, since I prefer *XA* to *Y*, and you would get your second-best prospect. Clearly then you want to commit yourself in advance to choosing *A* at *t′*. Note that this corresponds to my previous example of harvesting, if we let *X* be that I help you next week, *Y* be that I don't, *A* be that you help me a fortnight hence, and *B* be that you don't.

Again, suppose the same abstract choices as before, with my preferences unchanged, but you now prefer *Y* to *XA* to *XB*. So if you were to have a choice at *t′*, you would prefer the outcome of choosing *A*. And if I were to expect you to choose *A* should you have a choice between *A* and *B*, then I should give it to you by choosing *X* at *t*, since *XA* is my most preferred prospect, and you would get your second preference. However, if I were to expect you to choose *B* at *t′* despite your preference for *A*, then I should choose *Y* at *t*, which I prefer to *XB*, and you would get your most preferred prospect. Clearly then in this case you want to commit yourself in advance to choosing *B* at *t′* should you have a choice.

Let us now put flesh on these skeletal choices, and in so doing exhibit the relevance of commitment to Hobbes's concerns. Suppose I am a potential law-breaker, who prefers law-breaking with impunity to law-abiding, but law-abiding to law-breaking and being caught. You prefer that I be law-abiding, but if I break the law, you then prefer that I do so with impunity, to spare you the danger in having to apprehend me. You prefer not to be part of the group that the sovereign selects to assist him in maintaining law and order. If I expect you to react to my law-breaking in accordance with your preferences, I shall blithely go ahead. This is disadvantageous for you. But if you are committed to apprehending me, then I shall remain law-abiding. Your commitment to act against your preferences yields your best prospect.

More generally, to maximize his expectation of living in peace among his fellows, and being defended against their common enemy, a subject may do best to commit himself to perform certain actions in conditions in which, should he actually then perform them, would not best ensure his living in peace and security. The best deterrent, against the potential hostility both of one's fellows and of external enemies, may be a readiness to retaliate which in itself would be disadvantageous. This suggests that we read Hobbes's sentence as saying: 'When an individual's refusal to obey would violate the commitments that maximize his prospect of living in peace among his fellow subjects, or being defended against their common enemy, then he must obey; otherwise he may refuse.' This requires each subject to run real risks, but only those to which he would rationally have committed himself as maximizing his expectation of peace and security. It does not require anyone to sacrifice himself for the general peace and security of his fellows. But it does afford the sovereign the assistance that he needs, to punish offenders and maintain peace and security for his subjects.

This third interpretation enables us to make best sense of Hobbes's argument, although he does not introduce the vocabulary of commitment needed to formulate it. For there is no ground for supposing that he would have accepted the collective concern necessary to the first interpretation; his account of individual motivation is directly incompatible with it. And the second interpretation leaves the obligation to obey the sovereign too weak, in making it depend directly on one's present interest. If each subject decides whether or not to obey by considering whether or not, in each particular situation, obedience is to his own interest or advantage, then private appetite remains the measure of good and evil, and the sovereign will be unable to elicit the degree of obedience requisite for him to bring about and maintain peace. Each subject must realize that his prospect of living securely and at peace with his fellows is maximized if he is commited to offering active support to the sovereign, even when giving that support is not itself maximally conducive to his peace and security.

We may apply this interpretation of Hobbes's position on our obligation to assist the sovereign to his discussion of law and right reason. Obedience to the sovereign is obedience to the law, which is the expression of his will. Hobbes says that 'It is the law from whence proceeds the difference between the moral and the natural goodness: so that it is well enough said . . . that "moral goodness is the conformity of an action with right reason"; . . . for this *right reason*, which is the law, is no otherwise certainly right than by our making it so by our approbation of it and voluntary subjection to it' ((4), p. 193). Each person voluntarily subordinates his own natural reason, by which he distinguishes good and evil, to the law, thus making it a common reason that distinguishes moral good and evil.

And why does each person so subject himself? 'The reason . . . is this, that because neither mine nor the Bishop's [Bramhall, with whom Hobbes is disputing] reason is right reason fit to be a rule of our moral actions, we have therefore set up over ourselves a sovereign governor, and agreed that his laws shall be unto us, whatsoever they be, in the place of right reason, to dictate to us what is really good' ((4), p. 194). Each person's own natural reason would direct him on each occasion to what appears to him as his greatest benefit. But since, as we have seen, it is not always to each person's greatest benefit to be so guided, an alternative guide must be found. And this guide is the will of the sovereign. His laws provide a basis, not only for co-ordinating the actions of the members of society for their common benefit, but for overruling the judgements of each member when his own expectation of greatest benefit so requires.

But no person would have an interest in subordinating his own reason to that of the sovereign were not his fellows to do likewise. This is not to say that each would then lack reason to restrain any self-interested behaviour. But the particular form of restraint—the acceptance of the will of a single person or group as authoritative—demands mutuality; otherwise it would constitute a mere one-sided subservience of one individual to another.

Nor would any person have an interest in totally subordinating his reason to that of the sovereign. Hobbes does not disagree, allowing that one may rightly disobey or ignore the sovereign's commands in some circumstances. In our interpretation, these will be situations in which obedience would be contrary to one's present interest in peace and security, *and* would not be required by any prior commitment based on one's expectation of peace and security. There is then a line between those contexts in which a person has resigned his private judgement as his guide to action and those in which he has retained it.

In authorizing the sovereign, each subject intends to commit himself to accepting the sovereign's judgement and will, as expressed in his laws, in those respects in which such acceptance affords the subject the greatest expectation, *ex ante*, of living in peace and security with his fellow subjects and with the members of other societies. It is this intention which puts him under obligation to obey the sovereign even when free-riding would be in his direct interest. No weaker obligation would suffice for Hobbes's purposes, since no weaker obligation would enable the sovereign to gain sufficient active support for him to achieve and maintain peace and security among his subjects.

Against this interpretation of Hobbes's account of authorization and obligation, it may be objected that Hobbesian persons are psychologically incapable of the degree of commitment required to override self-interested free-riding. A Hobbesian person, it may be urged, cannot commit himself, even in his own interest, to perform actions that would not be in his interest at the time of performance. Although Hobbes does not discuss this matter explicitly, he does insist that 'of the voluntary acts of every man, the object is some *Good to himselfe*' ((3), p. 66). However, we may suppose that the problem of commitment was not fully clear to Hobbes (and indeed, that it has become clear to us only in the light shed by the Prisoner's Dilemma). In *The Logic of Leviathan* I endorsed the view that Hobbesian individuals are so conceived that they would be psychologically incapable of a commitment to actions not in their interest at the time of performance ((1), pp. 93–9). But I now believe that the Hobbesian text gives no real guidance on this matter. It is clear that for Hobbes a person's interest must enter at some point into an explanation of each of his voluntary actions; a commitment against interest, to perform an action against interest, would be incompatible with his psychology. But this leaves room for a commitment based on interest. Whether Hobbes would have accepted it we cannot say.

Furthermore, we should note that commitment poses a problem for Hobbes, however he views human psychology. If persons are incapable of commitment to actions not directly in their interest, and so of undertaking interest-overriding obligations, then, as I have argued, sovereignty must prove ineffectual. But if persons are capable of commitment, then absolute sovereignty, which Hobbes defends, is unnecessary and indeed indefensible. The sovereign's role will be limited to co-ordinating the actions of his subjects for their mutual benefit, and providing the residual enforcement needed to assure each that his obedience to the sovereign's laws will not be exploited to his disadvantage by less obedient fellows.

But the defence of absolute sovereignty is an acknowledged weakness in Hobbes's argument. And so if we find that in assuming that persons are capable of commitment, we undermine that defence, we also open the door to a much more interesting and defensible interpretation of much of Hobbes's moral and political theory. Supposing persons to be capable of commitment has the evident advantage of reflecting what seems true of human psychology. We may then be able to construct an adequate moral and political view by employing commitment, but not by dismissing it.

In section III I argued that the covenant should be considered a contract rather than a purely co-ordinative agreement because the primary aim of the parties cannot be realized without providing for enforcement. And in sections IV and V I have argued that the authorization of the enforcer, to be effective, requires a commitment to obedience that overrides self-interest. But such a commitment cannot be part of a purely co-ordinative agreement. Thus both parts of the procedure for instituting a sovereign fit the model of a social contract rather than that of a mere convention, adhered to because each party considers it in her interest given her expectation of adherence by her fellows.

VI

I turn to the contrast between an alienation social contract theory and an agency theory. The distinction, as formulated by Hampton, is between 'the position that the ruler is instituted when the people surrender their power to him' and 'the position that the ruler's power is only loaned to him' ((2), p. 3). To authorize someone to act in one's name is to appoint her as one's agent. The subjects authorize the sovereign to act in their name. But this does not suffice to make Hobbes's account an agency theory. The issue is not whether the sovereign is the agent of his subjects, but whether he is *only* their agent. But surely there is no doubt about this; he is more than his subjects' agent and they do surrender their power to him. Hobbes formulates the covenant by which the sovereign is instituted in these words: '*I Authorise and give up my Right of Governing my selfe, to this Man, or to this Assembly of men, on this condition, that thou give up thy Right to him, and Authorise all his Actions in like manner*' ((3), p. 87). To authorize the sovereign is to give *up* one's right to him, and this is surrender, not loan.

Hampton does not deny that Hobbes formally espouses an alienation contract, but she denies that he needs it, since she supposes that the sovereign can gain the support he needs by a direct appeal to the self-interest of his subjects, and she denies that an alienation contract is possible, because 'the cost [of alienation] would always be greater than the increment of benefit attained' ((2), p. 257). We have seen that she is mistaken on both counts. The sovereign would be ineffective, were the subjects not to commit themselves to an obligation, overriding considerations of self-interest, to obey him, and the prospective subjects may expect to benefit by making such a commitment. And if the subjects commit themselves to an overriding obligation to obey the sovereign, then they give up to him some portion of their right to govern themselves, and accept his judgement as determining good and evil.

However, although Hobbes uses the *words* of alienation in his account of the authorization of the sovereign, yet two quite different objections may be brought against understanding Hobbes's account as an alienation theory. The first is that Hobbesian persons are incapable of surrendering or alienating their rights to the sovereign. This is simply the objection that commitment is incompatible with Hobbesian psychology, and I have already responded to it. If Hobbes rejects the possibility of commitment, then his account of sovereignty fails. The second objection is that, whether or not the subjects must give up their right to govern themselves for the sovereign to be effective, authorization cannot be correctly understood as the giving up or surrendering of right. To authorize someone is to appoint her as one's agent, but this is only to loan her one's right. As Hobbes says, an act '*done by Authority*' is 'done by Commission, or Licence from him whose right it is' ((3), p. 81), There is no suggestion or implication that the person 'whose right it is' has given *up* that right to the agent. If I authorize you to act on my behalf, then I must acknowledge, or as Hobbes would say, own what you do, as my action. But this does not preclude me from acting on my own behalf, unless I have specifically committed myself, by covenant, not so to act, or from withdrawing my authorization, and subsequently acting on my own behalf, although I may not retroactively *disown* your action if performed with my authorization, any more than I may disown my own action. As Hobbes insists, from the words of an act of authorization 'there is no restriction at all, of his own former naturall Liberty', and so no giving up of right ((3), p. 112).

But an act of authorization may involve the giving up of right.[1] Whether any right is given up must be determined, as Hobbes says in the particular case of authorizing the sovereign, by the intention of the act. If the end for which I authorize someone to act on my behalf requires me not to act on my own behalf, then I do indeed give up the right so to act. The subject authorizes all of the sovereign's actions. To determine whether she thereby gives up any of her natural right, we must consider her intention. For she retains the right to do whatever is compatible with her end, which is her own peace and security. And she retains the right to withdraw her authorization from the sovereign, not simply if it pleases her to do so, but rather if neither being committed to maintain her authorization nor actually maintaining it is required by her end. But since her peace and security require that she commit herself to assist the sovereign in his efforts to maintain internal order and defend the society against external enemies, in authorizing the sovereign she does give up some portion of her natural liberty, or her right to do whatever seems best to her for her own preservation and well-being.

In so interpreting Hobbes, I am departing from the position I took in *The Logic of Leviathan*. There I claimed that an act of authorization in itself never involves giving *up* one's right, and that Hobbes could speak as if it did in the case of authorizing the sovereign, only because each person is obligated, by covenant with her fellows, to maintain that authorization ((1), p. 155). Not being free to withdraw, she in effect gives up her right to govern herself. But although Hobbes does indeed speak of the obligation assumed by each subject to all of her fellow subjects,

[1] The following argument was suggested by a seminar presentation on the relationship of sovereign and subject by Terry Moore.

and does insist that 'every Subject has Liberty in all those things, the right whereof cannot by Covenant be transferred', yet he claims that 'in the act of our *Submission*, consisteth both our *Obligation* and our *Liberty*' and appeals to our end in submitting to determine the actual extent of the right given up ((3), p. 111). Thus although each person obligates herself by covenant with her fellows, yet the obligation she thereby assumes is in effect simply to undertake a further obligation, to be governed by the sovereign, which is itself based not on her covenant but on the intention in her act of authorization.

Hobbes must espouse an alienation social contract theory in order to defend absolute, permanent sovereignty. If the subjects merely loan their rights to the sovereign, then he is assured neither absolute nor permanent power. But an alienation social contract theory is not therefore incompatible with limited sovereignty. Indeed, if persons have the capacity to alienate certain of their rights in order better to further their interests by undertaking overriding commitments, then internal, moral constraints, holding them to their commitments, will do much of the work that Hobbes assigns to external, political constraints, and, as we should intuitively suppose, *only* limited sovereignty is defensible. An absolute sovereign is neither needed nor wanted among persons who have some capacity to commit themselves to what their peace and security demand.

Hobbes represents himself as timorous, the twin of fear. He is frightened by the potentially destructive effects on peace and order of the individualism which he saw unleashed in his time. He recognizes, clearly, that each person has reason, based in her own interest, to acknowledge constraints on the pursuit of that interest. He underestimates (or denies) the potential efficaciousness of internal or moral constraints, and so overstates the necessary extent of external or political constraints. Thus he is led to create Leviathan. But he asks the right questions, and begins to understand the form that the answers must take. The idea of an alienation contract—a device by which persons mutually agree to give up certain of their natural liberties, and in particular their self-oriented judgement of good and evil as their sole guide to action—is his enduring contribution to our thought. No secular and rational morality and politics can be built without it.

REFERENCES

(1) David Gauthier, *The Logic of Leviathan* (Oxford, 1969).
(2) Jean Hampton, *Hobbes and the Social Contract Tradition* (Cambridge, 1986).
(3) Thomas Hobbes, *Leviathan* (London, 1651).
(4) Sir William Molesworth (ed.), *The English Works of Thomas Hobbes of Malmesbury*, vol. v (London, 1841).

7
Hobbes on Justice

D. D. RAPHAEL

Hobbes has a distinctive view of justice. His most explicit statement of it comes at the beginning of chapter 15 of *Leviathan*, where justice is identified with the third law of nature, '*That men performe their Covenants made*'. In making the identification Hobbes does not immediately speak of definition: he says, in the English version, that 'the Fountain and Originall' of justice consists in this third law of nature, while the Latin version abbreviates 'Fountain and Originall' to 'natura'. A couple of sentences later, however, it is plain that for Hobbes these terms are tantamount to, or include, the notion of definition; he says that 'the definition of INJUSTICE, is no other than *the not Performance of Covenant*. And whatsoever is not Unjust, is *Just*'.[1]

If we were to follow everyday usage of the word 'definition' and suppose that the definition of a common word gives its normal meaning, we should find Hobbes's statement puzzling. To say that 'justice' means the performance of covenants (or promises and contracts) seems not only excessively narrow but positively untrue. The categories of action to which we apply the terms 'just' and 'unjust' do not even include the keeping or breaking of promises and contracts. We would say that the breaking of a promise or contract is 'wrong' but we would not naturally use the word 'unjust'. We would say that there is an 'obligation' to keep a promise but we would not naturally say that it is a requirement of 'justice'.

J. S. Mill evidently thought otherwise. In chapter 5 of *Utilitarianism* he analyses six classes of action to which the term 'justice' is commonly applied, and one of these six is the keeping of promises (or of faith). I do not think that Mill reached this

[1] *Leviathan*, ed. C. B. Macpherson (Harmondsworth, 1968) (hereafter cited as *L*), p. 202.

view from attention to actual usage; it is not borne out by the classifications of the *Oxford English Dictionary*, which are genuinely based on a survey of usage. Mill probably reached his view because he was arguing towards the conclusion that the idea of the just always connotes the idea of a right, and it is easy to suppose (I have done it myself in the past) that the two ideas are coextensive in their application. It is indeed the connection between justice and rights that led Hobbes to his distinctive view of justice, and it is possible that Hobbes's account, which certainly influenced Hume, may have had some influence in leading Mill to assume that the concept of justice includes the keeping of faith within its ambit even though the two cannot simply be identified, as Hobbes had argued.

Hume is more circumspect. His complex analysis of justice in the *Treatise of Human Nature* does not treat the keeping of promises as a species of just action but it does, more reasonably, regard the two as being closely allied so that the analysis of promises can shed light on the nature of justice. There is, I think, no doubt that, consciously or unconciously, Hume was stimulated to this line of enquiry, and to his characterization of both justice and promise-keeping as 'artificial virtues', by Hobbes's argument that 'Humane Justice'[2] is not 'natural justice' but depends upon convention in the form of covenant.[3]

After giving his definition of justice in chapter 15 of *Leviathan*, Hobbes goes on to argue that, although covenants can be made in the condition of nature, they are invalid until and unless backed up by the coercive power of a commonwealth; consequently there cannot 'actually' be injustice or justice in the absence of a State. He then adds that this conclusion can be drawn also from 'the ordinary definition of Justice in the

[2] The term is used, to distinguish human from natural justice, in *A Dialogue between a Philosopher and a Student of the Common Laws of England*, ed. Joseph Cropsey (Chicago, 1971) (hereafter cited as *D*), p. 73.

[3] John Laird, *Hobbes* (London, 1934), 286–7, noted that Hume's theory of artificial virtue, and especially of justice, was 'intentionally Hobbian'. In an article, 'Obligations and Rights in Hobbes', published in *Philosophy*, 37 (1962), I suggested (p. 351) that the distinction which I found in Hobbes between natural and artificial obligation was 'the source from which there arose, consciously or unconsciously, in Hume's mind the idea of a distinction between natural and artificial virtue. Both philosophers treat the obligations of justice, and especially of promise-keeping, as artificial, and artificial in the special sense of depending upon a *verbal formula*.' I repeated this briefly in my book *Hobbes: Morals and Politics* (London, 1977), p. 100.

Schooles', namely that '*Justice is the constant Will of giving to every man his own*'.[4] Hobbes takes the term 'own' to mean property and recalls that in the condition of nature every man has a right to all things, so that there is no property, no exclusive right which assigns a thing to one man and excludes other men from it. Hobbes accordingly regards it as immaterial for practical purposes whether justice be defined in terms of covenant, as he defines it, or in terms of property, as he understands the traditional formula to define it.

Hobbes's explicit definition of justice as the performance of covenants appears only in *Leviathan*. The corresponding passages in *The Elements of Law* (1. 16. 2) and *De Cive* (3. 3) touch lightly upon one half of it, the identification of unjust action with the breach of covenant or contract. Even then the mention of injustice is secondary to the definition of 'injury', which Hobbes regards as synonymous with unjust action. The point that Hobbes chiefly wants to make is that injury is action *sine jure*, without right, and can therefore be connected with a previous renouncement of natural right, leaving the renouncer 'without right'. As for an explicit definition of the positive term 'justice', *De Cive* simply accepts, in the Epistle Dedicatory, the traditional view that '*Justice* . . . signifies a steady Will of giving every one his *Owne*'.[5] So does the later *Dialogue between a Philosopher and a Student of the Common Laws of England*.[6]

The point of Hobbes's definition of justice in terms of covenant is twofold. In the first place, it brings out Hobbes's view that 'Humane Justice'[7] exists by convention and not by nature. The new definition, however, is not essential for this purpose. The point is made quite clearly without it in the Epistle Dedicatory to *De Cive*, where Hobbes conducts his argument from the traditional definition. He says that when he thought about natural justice, he was led by the 'very word *Justice* (wich signifies a steady Will of giving every one his *Owne*)' to consider the idea of 'one's own' (property) and 'found that this proceeded not from Nature, but Consent'.[8]

[4] *L*, p. 202.

[5] *De Cive EV*, p. 27; cf. Latin version, p. 75, where, however, 'his own' is rendered 'Ius suum', and not 'suum' simply, as in the usual formulation.

[6] *D*, p. 58.

[7] See n. 2 above.

[8] *De Cive EV*, p. 27.

The second purpose of Hobbes's definition is to support the absolute authority of the sovereign. Hobbes wishes to argue that the sovereign has a right to do whatever he thinks fit, so that his commands are never a breach of justice. Since justice depends on covenant and since the obligation of subjects to sovereign arises from the social contract or, in the case of an acquired commonwealth, from an implicit covenant, the subjects can be guilty of injury or injustice, but the sovereign cannot, because he has not made any promise under the social contract or in response to an implicit covenant undertaken by his subjects.

The scope of Hobbes's conception of justice is therefore much wider than it looks at first sight. John Laird[9] wrote that Hobbes had both a narrower and a wider sense of justice and that he confused the two. The narrower sense was that given in *Leviathan*, chapter 15, the performance of covenant; the wider sense, according to Laird, was 'whatever was done "with right" ', and this Laird professed to find in the corresponding passage of *De Cive*, 3. 5, where Hobbes distinguishes two uses of 'just' and 'unjust', one applied to persons, the other to actions. Of the latter Hobbes writes: 'When they are attributed to Actions, *Just* signifies as much as what's done with Right, and *unjust*, as what's done with injury.'[10] This is not in fact a wider definition or meaning than the one given in *Leviathan*, chapter 15. Hobbes explains in all three statements of his political theory that action 'with right' and action 'without right' (injury) involve covenant or contract, so that for him a definition of justice in terms of covenant and a definition in terms of a right come to the same thing. Laird might have done better to refer to a slightly later passage in the *Leviathan* chapter itself (para. 9), where Hobbes repeats the distinction between the justice of persons and the justice of actions which he drew in *The Elements of Law* and in *De Cive*. In the *Leviathan* formulation of this distinction, the terms 'just' and 'unjust' are said to mean 'Conformity, or Inconformity to Reason',[11] which might well be called a wider meaning than a definition either in terms of covenant or in terms of a right. It is probable, however, that

[9] *Hobbes*, p. 183.

[10] *De Cive EV*, p. 64. The Latin version, p. 110, defines just action as 'quod iure factum' and unjust action as 'quod *Iniuriâ*'.

[11] *L*, p. 206.

Hobbes did not intend a wider scope; he says here that the justice (or righteousness) of a man is the conformity to reason of his 'Manners, or manner of life', while the justice of an action is the conformity to reason of that particular action. What he wants to stress is the distinction between a tendency and a particular instance; the use of the word 'reason' is of no special consequence in this passage.[12]

There is, then, no confusion of a wider and a narrower meaning, but rather a deliberate extension by Hobbes of what in other hands would be a narrow meaning. Hobbes links *effective* justice with the social contract or with the implicit covenant that takes the place of the social contract in a commonwealth by acquisition. In consequence, effective justice covers the whole field of positive law. This does indeed give justice a wide sense, though still tied to the idea of covenant. Although Hobbes's actual discussion of justice is brief, the concept itself has a vital role in his ethical and political doctrine, and it is an advantage for his theory to show that an apparently narrow definition turns out to give justice a wide range. The resulting wide scope of the term has the added advantage of conforming to common usage; we often apply the term 'justice' to the system of law as a whole, as when we speak of the courts of justice.[13]

Hobbes's definition of justice in terms of covenant has a further consequence of capital importance for his theory of obligation. He points out an interesting logical feature of promise-breaking and then uses it to portray the obligation of promises, and of justice, as having a different character from the obligation of natural law. A. E. Taylor was led by some of Hobbes's remarks about obligation into suggesting that Hobbes's 'ethical doctrine proper . . . is a very strict deontology, curiously suggestive . . . of some of the characteristic theses of

[12] As F. C. Hood, *The Divine Politics of Thomas Hobbes* (Oxford, 1964), 113, has observed, Hobbes writes loosely here but his meaning is clear enough. He is thinking of the third law of nature and so speaks of the performance of covenant as conforming to reason, but does not imply that this is the only kind of action which conforms to reason (i.e. to a law of nature). My comments on Laird can be applied also to the more guarded criticism of Hobbes's usage made by Howard Warrender, *The Political Philosophy of Hobbes* (Oxford, 1957), 132.

[13] The lawyer in *A Dialogue* defines a just action as 'that which is not against the Law' (*D*, p. 72). The philosopher does not himself adopt this definition but uses it to argue that law must be logically prior to (human) justice.

Kant'[14] That judgement, in my opinion, mistakes a part for the whole, but it is true that Hobbes indicates a radical distinction between prudential obligation and a form of non-prudential obligation which shares something of the logical features of Kant's conception of moral obligation. Hobbes's notion, however, does not apply to the whole of moral duty but to that large part of it which can be assigned to justice. Nor does it have the kind of absolute metaphysical status that Kant gave to the claims of morality. On the contrary, non-prudential obligation for Hobbes is to be contrasted with the more fundamental obligation of natural law. It is the result of convention and so can be classed with the notions of the ancient Sophists. But it has a distinctly original feature in fastening upon logic and language as being responsible for the formation of this peculiar kind of obligation. I believe we are justified in calling it artificial obligation.[15] It foreshadows Hume's notion of artificial virtue.

Hobbes makes the initial logical point about promises by comparing injury or injustice to 'absurdity', that is to say, self-contradiction.[16] In *The Elements of Law* he says flatly that 'there is in every breach of covenant a contradiction properly so called',[17] and in *De Cive* that it is 'no lesse contradiction' than denying what has previously been affirmed.[18] In both places Hobbes's ground for the assertion is that the making of a promise is willing an action in the future, while breaking the promise is willing the omission of that action in the present. The result, says Hobbes, is that the promise-breaker has willed the doing and the not doing of the same action at the same time. In *Leviathan* Hobbes is more cautious and restricts himself to saying that injury is 'somewhat like' absurdity; 'to contradict what one maintained in the Beginning' is compared but not fully equated with 'voluntarily to undo that, which from the beginning he had

[14] A. E. Taylor, 'The Ethical Doctrine of Hobbes', *Philosophy*, 13 (1938), 408 ff.; reprinted in Keith C. Brown (ed.), *Hobbes Studies* (Oxford, 1965), 37 ff.

[15] I used the term 'artificial obligation' in my article, 'Obligations and Rights in Hobbes' (published in *Philosophy*, 1962) in order to describe covenantal obligation, which Hobbes distinguished from '*naturall obligation*' in *De Cive*, 15. 7. In ch. 10 of *The Divine Politics of Thomas Hobbes* (published in 1964), F. C. Hood, quite independently (for he knew nothing of my article at that time), and more elaborately, described a distinction in Hobbes between natural and artificial obligation, associated with a distinction between natural and artificial rights and justice.

[16] *The Elements of Law*, 1. 16. 2; *De Cive*, 3. 3; *Leviathan*, 14, para. 7.

[17] *Elements*, p. 82.

[18] *De Cive EV*, p. 63.

voluntarily done'.[19] Even if the facts were as Hobbes represents them, a willing or a doing of mutually exclusive actions is not the same as self-contradiction, the utterance of mutually exclusive statements. Perhaps Hobbes realized this when he came to write *Leviathan* and therefore confined himself to a comparison with contradiction. However, the facts are not as Hobbes represents them. While the precise characterization of promising is notoriously difficult, promising is certainly not the doing or the willing of the action promised; if it were, promise-breaking would be impossible, for an action that has been done cannot be literally undone.

Nevertheless there is a logical peculiarity about promises and it seems likely that this is what caught Hobbes's attention. The making of a promise is the voluntary creation of an obligation by the use of words. To promise is to undertake an obligation. Consequently the statement that a person is obliged to do what he has promised is an analytic statement and the denial of that statement would be a self-contradiction. Since incurring the obligation is voluntary, breaching the obligation is a voluntary act that opposes or cancels (one might say metaphorically that it 'belies') the earlier voluntary act of promising.

The *Leviathan* (ch. 14) version of this logical feature of promise-breaking is followed by a characterization of the bond or obligation which is produced by promises or similar acts.

> And the same are the BONDS, by which men are bound, and obliged: Bonds, that have their strength, not from their own Nature, (for nothing is more easily broken then a mans word) but from Feare of some evill consequence upon the rupture.[20]

A similar remark is made in chapter 18 (para. 4): 'Covenants being but words, and breath, have no force to oblige, contain, constrain, or protect any man, but what it has from the publique Sword.'[21] In *The Elements of Law* (2. 3. 3) Hobbes had drawn a distinction between the 'natural bonds' of chains or imprisonment and the 'verbal bonds of covenant'.[22]

The verbal act of promising produces a verbal bond or obligation, one that does not have the force to 'oblige' in the

[19] *L*, p. 191.
[20] *L*, p. 192.
[21] *L*, p. 231.
[22] *Elements*, p. 128.

sense of 'constrain' a man. It is not a real bond or chain in the actual world of things and actions. When Hobbes says in chapter 18 of *Leviathan* that covenants 'have no force to oblige', he is using the word 'oblige' as synonymous with 'contain' and 'constrain', while when he says in chapter 14 that 'men are bound, and obliged' by the bonds of covenant, he is using the term 'obliged' in a different sense to mean a verbal or metaphorical bond that is 'easily broken'. He tries to bring out the difference between the two kinds of obligation in a note to *De Cive*, 14. 2, where, having distinguished between contracts, which 'oblige', and laws, which '*tie* us fast, being obliged', he proceeds to this explanation:

> *To be obliged*, and *to be tyed being obliged*, seems to some men to be one, and the same thing, and that therefore here seems to be some distinction in words, but none indeed. More cleerly therefore, I say thus, That a man is obliged by his contracts, that is, that be ought to performe for his promise sake; but that the Law tyes him being obliged, that is to say, it compells him to make good his promise, for fear of the punishment appointed by the Law.[23]

Hobbes's comparison of the verbal bond or obligation of a promise with the verbal bond or necessity of logic is apt. Logical necessity, too, can be contrasted with the effectively forceful necessity of the real world. If a person contradicts himself, one might object: 'You cannot say that.' Logically or rationally he cannot (or, in 'more correct' speech, he *may* not). Physically, however, he *can* say it; he has just done so. Anyone *can* use language arbitrarily, but in the interests of communication, the main point of having a language, there are rules which we are told we 'cannot' violate. 'Cannot' means 'should not'; the rules lay obligations upon us. These obligations, however, do not have the power to constrain us physically; they do not remove our ability to break the rules.

The full implications of the comparison between promise-breaking and self-contradiction are not brought out, and were probably not realized, by Hobbes himself. But there are certain straws in the wind which are worthy of notice. In chapter 17 of *Leviathan* (para. 12) Hobbes calls covenant an 'Artificiall' agreement in contrast to the 'Naturall' agreement or sociability

[23] *De Cive EV*, pp. 169–70.

of bees and ants.[24] Then, in chapter 21, he writes of liberty, and in the course of doing so he discusses the relation between liberty and necessity. This involves an understanding of different kinds of necessity. There is natural or physical necessity and there is the different necessity or bond of laws. Hobbes describes civil (i.e. positive) law as 'Artificiall Chains' which men have made by mutual covenants (para. 5). He then repeats what he has said earlier about the intrinsic weakness of such covenantal bonds: 'These Bonds in their own nature but weak, may neverthelesse be made to hold, by the danger, though not by the difficulty of breaking them.'[25] The marginal heading to the paragraph summarizes its content as 'Artificiall bonds, or Covenants'. The artificial bonds or chains of covenant and civil law are plainly to be contrasted with the natural bonds of real chains or imprisonment. They are also to be contrasted with the constraining or persuasive power of natural laws.

In the first sentence of the Introduction to *Leviathan*, Hobbes contrasts Nature with Art. Nature is the art of God. Human art or artifice is an imitation of nature. The State is an artificial man. The natural man is made by God; the artificial man is made by human beings in imitation of the natural man. So, too, the laws of the State are artificial chains or bonds, made by men, in imitation of the natural chains of the laws of nature. Although Hobbes does not say so explicitly, I think that the verbal or logical bond or obligation which he attributes to covenant is a form of artificial bond or obligation, to be contrasted with the natural obligation of natural law.

The obligations of natural law have a genuine force. If we go against the precepts of natural law, we find ourselves in trouble; we get into the competitive condition of war, in which we are liable to lose our lives. Laws of nature are for Hobbes rules of a prudential morality. The artificial laws of the State acquire their constraining power from the sanctions of 'the publique Sword', that is, from enforcement by a system of authorized officers and punishments. Without the sanctions, either of natural consequences or of civil penalties, the obligations of law and covenant would be ineffective. Yet, from a *logical* point of view, there are (verbal) bonds or obligations created by covenants. They are

[24] *L*, p. 226.
[25] *L*, pp. 263–4.

not effective on their own but need to be backed up by the force of the penal system. They make up a logical system of duties and so they constitute a system of morality, the code of justice. They differ from the system of morality made up by the laws of nature. The obligation of the laws of nature is fundamentally an obligation of prudential morality: this is what you ought to do in order to preserve your life. The covenantal obligation of the system of justice is an obligation of logic, comparable with logical necessity, depending on rules about the use of words. If you say that *S* is *P*, you may not combine this with the statement that *S* is not *P*; if you express a will to do *X*, you may not combine this with a will to refrain from doing *X*.

Although the artificial system of morality, built on covenant, is intended to be an imitation of the natural system, there is a significant difference which Hobbes appears to have overlooked. The obligations of natural law, as Hobbes understands them, are not obligations towards other men, with correspondent claim-rights held by those other men. They are obligations to act for the sake of one's own interests. Even if they are treated as commands of God, the fundamental reason for obedience is still self-interested, an acknowledgement of the power of God to preserve our lives or to end them. Natural right for Hobbes is divorced from natural obligation, being a liberty-right, a freedom from obligation to do or to forbear. The artificial obligation created by covenant, however, is not merely an obligation to do a specified action, and so a curtailment of the natural right to do whatever one thinks fit. It is an obligation *to* the person with whom one has covenanted, and in consequence that person has a claim-right against the covenantor that the action be done. Hobbes tries to confine his use of the noun 'a right' to liberty-rights and to describe the possession of claim-rights by the different expression 'has it as due'. He does not altogether succeed in this endeavour, but that is by the way. However, a necessary feature of his conception of justice as depending on covenant is that the artificial obligations and rights which are created by covenant are obligations to other persons and claim-rights possessed by those other persons. Hobbes's failure to perceive this is responsible for his error in saying that injury is acting 'sine jure', without a liberty-right to act thus. The original meaning of the Latin word *injuria* seems to have been acting contrary to what *is* right or just; but if we think of the developed conception of injury in relation to the concept of 'right' used as a noun, we must say that injury is acting so as to invade or breach another person's claim-right.

Despite this lack of congruence between artefact and the natural system which it is supposed to imitate, Hobbes's account of justice and covenant is clearly of much theoretical interest. His own concern, however, in entering upon civil philosophy is not simply theoretical but practical. If the logical obligation of covenant or justice has no force to make people act, what is the point of it? The answer to that question is to be found in understanding the point of Hobbes's social contract. It used commonly to be said that Hobbes's political theory expressed the doctrine that might is right, putting all the emphasis on the role of force. In particular it was said that the social contract was superfluous in his theory. He describes two ways in which a State can come into existence, by 'institution' (agreement and contract) and by 'acquisition' (conquest). Since, being a realist, he acknowledges that States usually arise by the latter method, there is no point (it was said) in his hypothesis of a social contract, which has no real application. In a State which comes into existence by conquest, force is all that matters.

This is a serious misunderstanding of Hobbes's position. Hobbes certainly does stress the necessity and the importance of force and of the fear of force in politics. His grim picture of the condition of nature concentrates on the fearful prospect that we face in the absence of a settled organized State. Again, he emphasizes more than once, as I have noted earlier, the fact that law and contract are ineffective unless they are backed by the power of a strong political authority. Nevertheless this is not the core of Hobbes's doctrine. Hobbes's greatness as a political philosopher lies in his perception that although physical power is necessary, it is not enough.

When Hobbes describes the setting up of a State by conquest, he asks us to imagine the victor standing over one of the vanquished wth a drawn sword, in a position to take away his life. If the victor spares the life of the vanquished, we must suppose, Hobbes says, that the vanquished has implicitly promised obedience in return for having his life spared; and having made this promise, the vanquished individual becomes a subject, bound by the same obligations of covenant as apply to the citizens of an instituted commonwealth, who covenant together by a social contract to vest authority in a sovereign and to obey him. The purpose of the unreal hypothesis of a social contract is to bring out clearly the nature of the moral obligation of covenant which the subjects of a State have incurred. Without the supposition of an implicit covenant made by the vanquished to the victor, Hobbes maintains, the members of a vanquished group would not be subjects but captives. They could be held in fear by chains and weapons but they would not be under any moral obligation to obey.

You may ask, what does it matter? Since Hobbes agrees that force is essential and that the subjects of a State must be faced with the prudential obligation of being moved by fear of force, why should he set so much store by an additional obligation of non-prudential morality depending on a promise? The reason is that the sovereign cannot be exerting his physical power on all his subjects all the time. Hobbes compares a captive to a slave and a subject to a servant. Captives or slaves will take the opportunity to escape if the immediate threat of swords or guns is removed or if they are not kept in chains or prisons. Subjects or servants, on the other hand, can generally be trusted to obey the rules, though there had better be sanctions in the background to remind everyone that there will be trouble for any person who breaks the rules. A sovereign must have the willing obedience of at least a good many of his subjects if his exercise of power is to be effective. It is not possible, even in a totalitarian State, to rely simply on force and fear.

This is why Hobbes stresses the importance of covenant and of the morality of justice, depending on covenant, as a necessary addition to the exercise of force and the threat of force. The purely moral obligation of a covenant, a verbal bond of logical consistency, will not be effective unless the force of the State is there to back up the requirements of the law when the law is broken. But the whole system depends on the fact that for most people, most of the time, the exercise of force is not necessary. It depends on their willing obedience. According to Hobbes, it depends on their acceptance of the moral obligation of an implicit promise to obey the law.

The weakness of Hobbes's theory is that his moral, non-prudential obligation is made to depend on a mythical promise. Some citizens—naturalized immigrants, volunteer members of the armed forces—do promise obedience to the law and loyalty to the State. But most people do not undertake voluntarily the obligations of a citizen. They are born in a particular jurisdiction and automatically acquire both the obligations and the benefits of citizenship. Hobbes would have done better to think of a different basis for a moral obligation to obey the law. The most obvious candidate is the notion of general utility. It is obvious when we think of Hobbes's picture of the condition of nature. Hobbes did not take that line because he started off with an egoistic psychology. (He does not retain a completely egoistic psychology in *Leviathan*, but enough of his original view remains to make it virtually impossible for him to think of people being motivated by regard to the general interest rather than their own interest alone.) There is also the fact that Hobbes did perceive a peculiarity in the logic of promises, and so he thought that the idea of covenant and contract could serve his purpose. One can see from *The Elements of Law*, 2. 3. 3, that this purpose was in Hobbes's mind right from the start when his attention was drawn to the logical character of covenantal obligation. In that passage he describes covenantal obligation as a 'verbal bond', to be contrasted with the 'natural bonds' of chains and imprisonment.[26] He uses the distinction to explain the difference between a servant, who is trusted, and a slave, who is not. All this is intended to illustrate the main subject of the chapter, 'dominion, or a body politic by acquisition' (2. 3. 1).[27]

So much for Hobbes's distinctive definition of justice. It is worth noting, by way of supplement, what Hobbes has to say about traditional notions of justice. I have already discussed the relation of Hobbes's definition in *Leviathan* to the traditional definition which he accepts in *De Cive* and in *A Dialogue*. (The *Dialogue*,[28] incidentally, says that the traditional definition, 'giving to every Man his own', is Aristotle's, although it is in fact from Ulpian's *Digest*.) Hobbes does have something to say about other traditional doctrines concerning justice.

[26] *Elements*, p. 128.
[27] *Elements*, p. 127.
[28] *D*, p. 58.

In the first place he criticizes the traditional classification, derived from Aristotle, of commutative and distributive justice. Commutative justice is said to require equality of value in the exchange involved in a contract. Distributive justice is said to be the award of benefit in accordance with merit.

Hobbes rejects the stock idea of commutative justice, pointing out that it is not unjust to sell at a higher price than one buys. Value depends on the desire of those who agree to a contract, so that any kind of agreement can be just or fair so long as it is made voluntarily. Hobbes obviously has a point here. The merit of Aristotle's discussion of 'commutative' justice lies in his giving an *explanation* of what constitutes economic value, and not, as Aristotle himself originally intended, in giving a *justification* of one kind of exchange rather than another. The fairness of a contract does indeed depend on the wishes of the parties, provided that they each have a reasonable knowledge of what is involved and provided that they really are free agents. In the *Leviathan* statement of his position (ch. 15, para. 14), Hobbes goes on to say that commutative justice, properly speaking, is simply the justice of a contractor, that is, the keeping of covenants made in a contract for the exchange of goods. This assimilates commutative justice to Hobbes's own definition of justice as the performance of covenant. But he did say, earlier in this paragraph, that the 'just value' in a contract is what the parties 'be contented to give';[29] so he has there implicitly admitted an idea of 'the just' as meaning 'the fair' and not simply the performance of covenant.

He criticizes the stock concept of distributive justice, again in the *Leviathan* statement, on the ground that to give people benefits because of their merit is not justice at all but 'grace'; it is a matter of free gift and not of obligation. Distributive justice, in Hobbes's view (para. 15), is to distribute to every man 'his own', as the traditional definition of justice requires. More properly, he adds, this is to be called equity.[30]

Hobbes draws a firm distinction between justice and equity. Justice, the performance of covenant, is assigned to the third law of nature in *Leviathan*, corresponding to the second law in *De Cive*. Equity, equal or impartial treatment by a judge, is assigned

[29] *L*, p. 208.
[30] *L*, p. 208.

to a separate law of nature, the eleventh in *Leviathan* and the tenth in *De Cive*. In *Leviathan*, chapter 15 (para. 15), Hobbes says that distributive justice is 'the Justice of an Arbitrator', whose function is 'to distribute to every man his own: and this is indeed Just Distribution, and may be called (though improperly) Distributive Justice; but more properly Equity',[31] a separate law of nature. There is in fact a difference between this formulation of distributive justice or equity and the later formulation of equity as the eleventh law of nature in paragraphs 23–4.[32] The earlier formulation is not confined to equal distribution; it follows the traditional definition of justice as the distribution or rendering to each man of what is 'his own', which might be an equal or an unequal distribution, according to circumstances. The later formulation fixes upon equality; it says that a judge or arbitrator must '*deale Equally*', must not be 'partiall in judgment', must produce 'equall distribution to each man, of that which in reason belongeth to him'. This is partly because Hobbes thinks of *aequitas* as meaning equality, and partly because he disagrees with Aristotle's meritarian (and so inegalitarian) account of distributive justice. As a mater of fact Aristotle does not use the term 'distributive justice' to refer to the just (impartial) treatment of litigants by a judge. For Aristotle, equal or impartial treatment by a judge is an element of 'corrective' or 'rectifying' justice.

Having distinguished between justice and equity, Hobbes is able to say, in *Leviathan*, chapter 18 (para. 6), that a sovereign 'may commit Iniquity; but not Injustice, or Injury in the proper signification'.[33] This is because the sovereign has, like any man, a natural obligation to obey the laws of nature, including the law that prescribes equity, but he has no covenantal or artificial obligation towards his subjects as the result of their social contract or implicit covenant of obedience. To be sure, the sovereign has a natural obligation to obey the third law of nature that prescribes the performance of covenant; but the covenants made in the course of instituting or acquiring a commonwealth are all covenants undertaken by the subjects; the sovereign has not bound himself by any promises to them.

[31] *L*, p. 208.
[32] *L*, p. 212.
[33] *L*, p. 232.

Consequently the sovereign has absolute authority, retaining the original natural right to do whatever he thinks fit. So if the sovereign orders a citizen to be arrested and executed, he does no injustice or injury since he has the full right to do it. But he may be acting inequitably. If the citizen has not broken any law or, in breaking a law, has not done anything that merits so severe a penalty as death, then the sovereign, in his capacity as supreme judge of the State, is not dealing equitably with that citizen as compared with others. The sovereign is bound by the laws of nature, which prescribe measures to avoid slipping back into the condition of war. He therefore has a natural duty of equity, but no obligation of justice, to refrain from treating a citizen in this way.

Hobbes does not explain how the earlier remarks on distributive justice, which he thinks should be called equity, fit in with his later account of equity. In the later passage (*Leviathan*, ch. 15, paras. 23–4), we are told that a judge or arbitrator should deal with people equally or impartially; that is equity. But Hobbes goes on to say that equity is also 'the equall distribution to each man, of that which in reason belongeth to him'.[34] This is plainly related to the traditional definition of justice which Hobbes interpreted as being concerned with property. But it is not at all clear why the distribution of 'that which in reason belongeth' to a man should be an equal distribution. Hobbes has told us in chapter 13 that all men are roughly equal in natural powers, and here in chapter 15 he says that the ninth law of nature requires men to acknowledge their natural equality. But he cannot think that the possession of property should always 'in reason' be equal. He simply does not explain what he thinks.

Before leaving the eleventh law of nature, prescribing equity or distributive justice, we should note two corollaries of it, which Hobbes gives as the twelfth and thirteenth laws (eleventh and twelfth in *De Cive*). The twelfth says that if goods cannot be divided, they should be enjoyed in common because equity requires it. And the thirteenth says that if goods can neither be divided nor enjoyed in common, then they should be allocated by lot. Both of these provisions are egalitarian, but Hobbes

[34] *L*, p. 212.

interprets the idea of lot as allowing for a right of primogeniture and a right by first possession.

One other feature of Hobbes's political theory that is relevant to justice is his view of punishment. He does not call this an aspect of justice, which he wants to confine to the performance of covenant. He deals with the matter first in enunciating the seventh law of nature (sixth in *De Cive*), which requires '*That in Revenges* (that is, retribution of Evil for Evil) *Men look not at the greatnesse of the evill past, but the greatnesse of the good to follow*' (*Leviathan*, ch. 15, para. 19).[35] In consequence, Hobbes says, punishment must have for its purpose the 'correction of the offender, or direction of others'. He is putting forward a reform plus deterrence theory of punishment, and this is elaborated in *Leviathan*, chapter 28, a valuable discussion of the nature and justification of punishment. Although Hobbes does not consider this to be a part of his account of justice, the chapter does in fact make a significant contribution to the subject of criminal justice.

Hobbes there (para. 1) defines punishment as '*an Evill inflicted by publique Authority, on him that hath done, or omitted that which is Judged by the same Authority to be a Transgression of the Law; to the end that the will of men may thereby the better be disposed to obedience*'.[36] This is a deterrence theory but not a straightforward consequentialist theory; for the definition of punishment requires that it can be inflicted only for a breach of the law, so that the infliction of such an evil on the innocent would be contrary to the definition. When Hobbes comes to explain this part of his definition (para. 22),[37] his grounds for it are partly consequentialist, partly not. He gives three reasons: (1) harming the innocent cannot be useful to society; (2) harming the innocent goes against the natural law of gratitude, which requires a requital of good for good and of evil solely for evil; (3) it goes against the natural law of equity, which requires 'an equall distribution of Justice', i.e. impartiality. The second and third reasons are non-consequentialist. They are also reasons which we should normally assign to the concept of justice, and indeed Hobbes himself here refers to equity as 'an equall distribution of Justice'.

Western political thought about justice has always, from

35 *L*, p. 210.
36 *L*, p. 353.
37 *L*, pp. 359–60.

Plato onwards, included two opposed conceptions of distributive justice, one egalitarian, the other meritarian. The egalitarian conception made its way into natural law doctrine as the normative principle that all men 'are by nature' (meaning that they are entitled to be) free and equal. When Hobbes gives his version of the natural law doctrine of human equality, he changes it from a normative idea to a positive one: all men are roughly equal in power, so that no one man is strong enough to dominate all the rest. Yet he derives from this a normative rule, a law of nature, that the equality of all men should be acknowledged; and he pokes fun at Aristotle for saying that men are unequal by nature, some being fit to rule and others unfit, the fit ones being philosophers like Aristotle himself. From this and from Hobbes's account of equity and its corollaries, it is clear that he follows the egalitarian conception of human entitlement and rejects the meritarian. But he does not assign these ideas to the notion of justice, because he wants to use that notion to support his chief aim in political theory, namely to show that power in politics is essential but not enough.

8

Hobbes and the Problem of God

ARRIGO PACCHI

This paper deals with the question of the relation between Hobbes's philosophy and theology. There are some scholars who have tried to answer this question denying any link between Hobbesian thought and Christian, or even natural, religion, emphasizing the significance of the openly declared materialism and of the supposed atheism of Hobbes, and considering his theological statements as merely opportunistic ones; others sift and peruse each Hobbesian writing, in search of every hint made by Hobbes at the existence of God, or at the coincidence of natural and divine law, in order to show that he was in all respects a Christian thinker. The first group is very large, and is supported by a tradition beginning with Hobbes's contemporaries. It includes the most representative scholars of Hobbesian thought, from Strauss to Polin, which last, for instance, recently published a book largely concerned with this problem and this kind of interpretation.[1] The second group is comparatively small, and lately formed: its leader, so to speak, is F. C. Hood, who in his book *The Divine Politics of Thomas Hobbes*, pursuing the tracks of a more famous—and more moderate—book by Howard Warrender,[2] tried to show that in Hobbes's political philosophy the laws of nature oblige *only* because they are the commands of God revealed with certainty in Scripture. The 'Hood thesis' gave rise to serious disagreement, not only in England (Skinner's review being a notable example of this

[1] R. Polin, *Hobbes, Dieu et les hommes* (Paris, 1981) (see esp. the first part, 'Hobbes et Dieu', pp. 5–72). Polin had expressed in shorter form the same ideas in *Politique et philosophie chez Thomas Hobbes* (Paris, 1953), esp. pp. xv and xx.

[2] F. C. Hood, *The Divine Politics of Thomas Hobbes* (Oxford, 1957). H. Warrender, *The Political Philosophy of Hobbes* (Oxford, 1964).

dissent),[3] but also in France and in Italy, where what I called 'the first group' is very powerfully represented indeed.

A number of critics[4]—among whom I myself stand—are becoming more and more convinced that neither of these critical alternatives really does Hobbes's thought complete justice: the one, because it ignores its theological implications; the other, because it forces Hobbes to say what he doesn't say. In my opinion, a better understanding of the question must necessarily involve a careful analysis of what Hobbes writes about the relation between philosophy, its objects, and the objects of theology, keeping Hobbesian thought, generally considered, and Hobbesian philosophy accurately separated; for Hobbesian thought may comprehend philosophy *and* theology, though philosophy excludes theology from itself. I will therefore in the first place analyse what Hobbes states about the aforesaid relation between philosophy and theology, in a discussion implying strong connections with Hobbes's conception of natural science; then, I will briefly consider the strictly theological expression of his thought, in order to verify its significance and extent; eventually, I will try to show that there is no real contradiction in Hobbes applying himself very seriously to theological studies, though he resolutely excludes theology from philosophy.

Everybody knows the reasons offered by Hobbes in his *De Corpore* for arguing the absolute divorce between philosophy and theology: in the eighth paragraph of the first chapter of the book, he emphasizes that philosophy cannot study the nature and attributes of God, because this everlasting, ingenerable, and incomprehensible being is not knowable by means of the usual

[3] Q. Skinner, 'Hobbes's *Leviathan*', *The Historical Journal*, 7 (1964), 321–33.

[4] To show the growing balanced and undoctrinaire interest in Hobbes's thought on religion the following examples can be cited: S. I. Mintz, *The Hunting of Leviathan* (Cambridge, 1962), esp. 41–5; W. Förster, *Thomas Hobbes und Puritanismus* (Berlin, 1969); K. M. Kodalle, *Thomas Hobbes: Logik der Herrschaft und Vernunft des Friedens* (Munich, 1972), esp. chs. II and III; J. G. A. Pocock, 'Time, History and Eschatology in the Thought of Thomas Hobbes', in *Politics, Language and Time: Essays on Political Thought* (London, 1972), 148–201; H. W. Schneider, 'The Piety of Hobbes', in *Thomas Hobbes in his Time*, ed. R. Ross, H. W. Schneider, and T. Waldman (Minneapolis, 1974), 84–101; P. J. Johnson, 'Hobbes's Anglican Doctrine of Salvation', ibid. 102–25; H. G. Reventlow, *Bibelautorität und Geist der Moderne* (Göttingen–Zürich, 1980), 328–70 (now also in Engl. trans. (London, 1984), pp. 194–222); M. Bertozzi, *Thomas Hobbes: L'enigma del Leviatano*, Pugillaria 3 (Bologna, 1983), 3–34; M. Malherbe, *Thomas Hobbes* (Paris, 1984), 217–49.

scientific methods of resolution and composition, and cannot be investigated with respect to his possible generation.[5]

What is somehow striking in this passage, is the fact that Hobbes settles the question in a few lines, as if such an opinion were widely shared, and therefore did not require detailed explanation; or as if he had explained it more exhaustively elsewhere. In point of fact, if one carefully peruses Hobbesian works published before *De Corpore*, one will find very few statements—mostly indirect ones—which relate to this question. On the other hand, a clear distinction between philosophy and theology was not universally shared, in spite of being one of the chief principles of modern lay thought: and even the most remarkable thinkers of the time had made use of it with some flexibility: Francis Bacon did not consider a marriage of philosophy and theology to be quite proper,[6] he did not, nevertheless, exclude natural theology from philosophy; Descartes described it as 'entièrement contre mon sens' to mingle 'la religion avec la philosophie',[7] but this did not hinder him from working out his arguments for God's existence with very great care. The truth is that Hobbes *had* actually exhausted such a theory, but in a never published work, intended to demolish Thomas White's *De mundo dialogi tres*, a manuscript that saw the light only in 1973, thanks to the care of Jacquot and Jones.[8] Therefore the assertive conciseness of *De Corpore* finds its background in the detailed discussion of *AntiWhite*. For this reason, I think it not superfluous to recall some features of this very important Hobbesian work.

AntiWhite is now fairly well known and therefore there is no need to describe it in detail.[9] It is enough to be reminded that it was probably written about 1643, and that Hobbes dealt with White's *Dialogi* as with a kind of target, to test the strength of his

[5] *De Corpore*, I. 8 (*LW* i. 9–10).

[6] F. Bacon, *Cogitata et visa*, in *The Works of F.B.*, ed. J. Spedding and others (London, 1857–59), iii. 596.

[7] Letter to Mersenne (27 Aug. 1639), in R. Descartes, *Œuvres*, ed. C. Adam and P. Tannery, new edn. by B. Rochot and others (Paris, 1964–74), ii. 570.

[8] From now on, referred to in the text as *AntiWhite*.

[9] Besides the long introduction by the editors (*AntiWhite*, 9–97), see also: J. Bernhardt, 'L'Anti-White de Hobbes', *Archives Internationales d'Histoire des Sciences*, 25 (1975), 104–15; M. Brini Savorelli, 'Hobbes e White', *Rivista di Filosofia*, 5 (67) (1976), 335–48; E. G. Jacoby, 'Der "Anti-White" des Thomas Hobbes', *Archiv für Geschichte der Philosophie*, 59 (1977), 156–66.

own theories, and to train himself in the art of confuting. Perhaps this training feature of the manuscript—and some not very orthodox statements contained in it—led Hobbes to leave it unpublished. So the work, though it was very carefully read and very well appreciated by Mersenne, fell into oblivion.

In fact, it has been a quite undeserved oblivion, because *AntiWhite* is a very interesting book, supplying precious indications about Hobbes's thought, with special regard to his gnoseology and epistemology, at that stage of their development.[10] Moreover, on the question of the relation between theology and philosophy, White's work was a perfect target for Hobbes's polemics, for the third dialogue of White's *De mundo* is entirely devoted to demonstrating God's existence, in terms that may be summarized as follows: the world is not boundless, nor eternal; its motion comes from an external principle: we must therefore postulate of necessity the existence of an everlasting single being, having in itself its own cause and principle and being the cause of all the rest; and this being is God.

White develops his a posteriori arguments through a certain number of *quaestiones*, referring to a conceptual background and to a language which is mainly Aristotelian, and which does not forget the medieval speculative heritage; for he was as interested in that as he was in the discoveries and assumptions of Galilean science, and endeavoured to make them agree. Within this framework, Hobbes organizes his confutations, intended to show the incoherence of White's statements, in a cogent succession of analyses and new definitions of terms, invalidations of inferences, refutations of arguments, and so on. Beyond these technicalities, however, this dispute reveals a substantial disagreement on the specific subject of the demonstrability of God's existence in a philosophical context. In Hobbes's opinion, if one does undertake such an endeavour—as White did—one will offend, not only philosophy, but theology too, and religion, and providence; for the logical necessity of demonstrations is in opposition to God's omnipotence and indeterminableness. On the other side, the demonstrative pretence changes faith into

[10] Cf. above all *AntiWhite*, 1. pp. 105–7, and 14. 1, pp. 201–2, where the very important definition of philosophy as 'nomenclatura' is set forth.

something like natural science, removing all merit from the believer.[11]

These are, so to speak, parade arguments; but Hobbes also carefully explores the question in a specific philosophical sense, referring to the main principles of his conception of science and reason. Scientific discourse is, as he will exemplify later in *Leviathan*, only conditional: 'if This be, That is; if This has been, That has been, if This shall be, That shall be'.[12] Its truth being merely propositional, it never is about existence, which can be certified only by sense experience. But God, a not-extended being (here, in *AntiWhite*), is not subject to sense-experience, not imaginable or conceivable, and therefore it is ἀφιλόσοφον to try to demonstrate his existence;[13] all the more so since such an endeavour implies our engaging in a lot of insoluble problems: for instance, whether the world be finite or infinite, whether corporeal beings—and incorporeal too, of which no adequate definition can be given—are eternal or not.[14] At this time, Hobbes does not dare to say that the expression 'incorporeal substance' is a logical nonsense, as he will do in *Leviathan*,[15] and prefers referring to revelation.[16] He is likewise inclined to believe, by faith, that God is the world's primary mover,[17] but resolutely denies that the relation between God and the world may be philosophically elucidated: that would be an anthropocentric point of view, involving the question of God's design with reference to a solely human conception of the usefulness of creation, and so mortifying the divine incommensurability and incomprehensibleness.[18]

Essentially, Hobbes aims at demonstrating that all endeavours to apply philosophical ways of thinking to the problem of God's existence, or of God's relation to the world, are destined to arouse inextricable contradictions and paralogisms, mainly where there is an undue conflation between physics and

[11] *AntiWhite*, 26. 3–5, pp. 309–10.

[12] *Leviathan*, 7, ed. C. B. Macpherson (Harmondsworth, 1968), 131. All further references are to this edition.

[13] *AntiWhite*, 26. 2, pp. 308–9; 27. 1, p. 312.

[14] *AntiWhite*, 2. 3, p. 111; 26. 2, p. 309.

[15] *Leviathan*, 34, pp. 428–9.

[16] *AntiWhite*, 4. 3, p. 127.

[17] *AntiWhite*, 27. 14, p. 323.

[18] *AntiWhite*, 13. 6, p. 198.

metaphysics, with the worst consequences for metaphysics itself, and even for Christian faith.[19] One may give a very typical example of Hobbesian procedure of confutation: analysing White's arguments for demonstrating that the universe derives from an external principle, Hobbes works as follows: first of all, he subjects some thirty *voces*—that is, words he judges White introduced in an improper or confused sense—to very precise new definitions. This series of words begins with *ens, corpus, materia*, ending with all possible specifications of cause and power. On this ground, after a pressing sequence of arguments, Hobbes will conclude that, if the thesis of a self-created world is logically inconsistent, there remain only two possible consequences: the world had not a beginning; or it had its beginning from something, that cannot be a body, all bodies being parts of the same universe; otherwise, we would fall again into the first thesis.[20]

Here, Hobbes's reasoning follows Aristotelian ways of thinking: nothing can produce itself, and everything that moves is moved by an external mover. But in this assumption of the speculative proceedings adopted by his adversary, in this somehow peculiar *argumentum ad hominem* consists the force of Hobbes's case: for he is in a very good position to raise a number of contradictions concerning the notion of God: for example, he demonstrates that this not-corporeal, world-originating principle is, because of its very immateriality, inconceivable; nor can it be defined as 'external' to the universe, this definition being invalidated by its spatial connotation. Moreover, if this principle cannot be a body—otherwise, as it has already been said, it would be numbered among the objects compounding the universe itself—it will be nothing at all, White himself having already demonstrated that nothing exists beyond the universe.[21] In his conclusions, Hobbes emphasizes, then, the inconceivableness, not only of the supposed world-originating principle, but also of all possible relations between such a principle and the world, invalidating every endeavour to conceive the subordi-

[19] *AntiWhite*, 2. 8, p. 115; but the whole of part 3 of the work is devoted to arguing this background idea. In particular, see 27. 14, p. 323; 28. 3, p. 333; 29. 2, p. 340; 32. 2, p. 373.

[20] *AntiWhite*, 27. 1–5; see in particular the conclusions to para. 5, p. 317.

[21] Ibid. For a development of the argument, see para. 6, pp. 317–18.

nation of the universe to God, in a cognitive and rational manner, and stressing the danger that such a demonstrative ambition may even question God's existence itself.

As it has been rightly noted,[22] a rather similar statement about the same questions can be found—many years later—in *De Corpore*.[23] But it may appear even odder that, in those same years when he denied White all possibility of rationally proving God's existence, elsewhere Hobbes expressed an opinion which is not fully in agreement with that which he expounded in *AntiWhite*. In *Elements of Law*, for instance, written about 1640, Hobbes clearly distinguishes between the knowledge of God's attributes, and that of God's existence. On the first, he is as drastic as he will be little later in *AntiWhite*, pointing out that God is incomprehensible, and that 'all his attributes signify our inability and defect of power to conceive any thing concerning his nature';[24] here he is following the pattern of that negative theology he will afterwards express, not only in *AntiWhite*, but also in *De Cive* and in *Leviathan*.[25] But on God's existence Hobbes's opinion is very different: in *Elements*, he writes that the statement 'there is a God' may be demonstrated, by a posteriori reasoning, easily reducible to the classic causal argument:

> the effects we acknowledge naturally, do necessarily include a power of their producing, before they were produced; and that power presupposeth something existent that hath such power; and the thing so existing with power to produce, if it were not eternal, must needs have been produced by somewhat before it; and that again by something else before that: till we come to an eternal, that is to say, to the first power of all powers, and the first cause of all causes. And this is it which all men call by the name of GOD.[26]

This is not an isolated thought: in the first edition of *De Cive* (1642), we can find an allusion, perhaps only a pleonastic one, to God as 'first mover of all things', producing all natural effects by secondary causes;[27] but in the same book, Hobbes very openly states that 'by the light of nature it may be known that there is a

[22] By Jacquot and Jones, *AntiWhite*, p. 111 n. 21.

[23] *De Corpore*, 26. 1 (*LW* i. 334–6).

[24] T. Hobbes, *The Elements*, 1. 11. 1, p. 53.

[25] *AntiWhite*, 35. 16, pp. 395–6; *De Cive*, 15. 14 (*LW* ii. 340–2); *Leviathan*, 31, pp. 402–3.

[26] *Elements*, 1. 11. 2, pp. 53–4.

[27] *De Cive*, 13. 1 (*LW*, ii. 298).

God'.[28] And if we have any doubts about the weight of this remark, we may refer to a footnote in the 1647 edition, where he pointedly confirms his statement, in spite of limiting its pertinence to men not too busy at pursuing pleasures, riches, and careers.[29] To sum up, in *Elements* and *De Cive* Hobbes opines that natural reason, though it is not able to define divine attributes, may at least lead men to the persuasion of God's existence: and that, in evident opposition to the thesis so polemically expressed in *AntiWhite*.

In Hobbe's subsequent writings, this way of thinking will be confirmed many times: we have only the embarrassment of choosing, among a very large number of possible citations, almost entirely already utilized by Brown, and Hepburn[30] in their analytical essays on the question. In the Hobbesian writings on the free-will dispute, in *Leviathan*, in *De Homine*,[31] these scholars have identified occasional references to the problem, and also more substantially supported statements, and they have treated all this material as being at the same documentary level. Although they do not entirely agree in their conclusions,[32] they may nevertheless be associated together because of their critical method, which consists in thoroughly examining several passages to point out their demonstrative implications, with no regard for their context, even though their opposition to Hobbes's scepticism and fideism is clearly stated elsewhere, sometimes in the same works.

Before going on, it is therefore useful to reject the supposed contrast between Hobbes's enunciation of arguments for God's existence, and the fideistic scepticism somehow underlying his philosophical thinking. In fact, the theory expounded in *AntiWhite* on the conditional nature of scientific reasoning is

[28] Ibid. 2. 21 (*LW* ii. 179).

[29] Ibid., note to 14. 19 (*LW* ii. 326).

[30] K. C. Brown, 'Hobbes's Grounds for Belief in a Deity', *Philosophy*, 37 (1962), 336–44; R. W. Hepburn, 'Hobbes on the Knowledge of God', in *Hobbes and Rousseau: A Collection of Critical Essays*, ed. M. Cranston and R. S. Peters (Garden City, NY, 1972), 85–108.

[31] Brown rightly calls attention to Hobbes's use of the teleological argument in *De Homine* (*LW* ii. 6 and 106–7) and in *Decameron Physiologicum* (*EW* iii. 380–1).

[32] Brown appears to oppose Polin's thesis about Hobbes's assumption of God's foreignness to philosophy with great strength. Less lively, but better argued, is Hepburn's essay which, whilst amply taking into account Brown's suggestions, simply weighs the pros and cons of the matter.

never denied by Hobbes; on the contrary, it is confirmed in *Leviathan*[33] as one of the most important supports of the epistemology outlined in it; moreover, in the whole of Hobbes's writings the existence of God is never qualified, although there are many references to his inconceivableness and his incomprehensibleness; and yet Hobbes was quite aware that there might be a contradiction between stating God's inconceivableness and trying to demonstrate *ratione naturali* his existence; so much aware of it was he, that he specified very clearly his thought on the question. We must state in advance that Hobbes constantly keeps his distinction between demonstrating God's existence and knowing his attributes, except in *AntiWhite*, where, as it has been remarked, he excludes them both from a philosophical consideration, perhaps for incidental polemic reasons.[34] The supposed contradiction will then be only on the asserted demonstrability of God's existence, that may appear in opposition to the equally asserted claim of God's absolute inconceivableness. Now, there is a passage (in the *Objectiones* to the Cartesian *Meditationes*), often neglected by critics, that seems to provide a highly significant explanation of Hobbes's way of conceiving of that demonstrability, distinguishing, so to speak, between *knowing* God and *thinking* of him:

It is the same way with the most holy name of God; we have no image, no idea corresponding to it. Hence we are forbidden to worship God in the form of an image, lest we should think we could conceive Him who is inconceivable.

Hence it appears that we have no idea of God. But just as one born blind who has frequently been brought close to a fire and has felt himself growing warm, recognizes that there is something which made him warm, and, if he hears it called fire, concludes that fire exists, though he has no acquaintance with its shape or colour, and has no idea of fire nor image that he can discover in his mind; so a man, recognizing that there must be some cause of his images and ideas, and another previous cause of this cause and so on continuously, is finally

33 *Leviathan*, 7, p. 131, where a distinction is made between *absolute* (or factual) and *conditional* (or scientific) knowledge.

34 It should nevertheless be noted that in *AntiWhite* Hobbes also maintains that of God at least one can say on a rational level of consideration, that he exists: '. . . in eam opinionem propendeo, nullam propositionem veram esse posse circa naturam Dei, praeter hanc unam: Deus est; neque ullam appellationem naturae Dei convenire praeter unicum nomen, *ens*.' (*AntiWhite*, 25. 14, pp. 395–6.)

carried on to a conclusion, or to the supposition of some eternal cause, which, never having begun to be, can have no cause prior to it; and hence he necessarily concludes that something necessarily exists. But nevertheless he has no idea that he can assert to be that of this eternal being, and he merely gives a name to the object of his faith or reasoning and calls it God.[35]

This passage clarifies, I think openly enough, that in Hobbes's opinion rational discourse may start from the existence, certified by sense-experience, of certain facts, or events, to attain the *hypothetical*, only supposed, existence of a being connected to them by a causal relation, without requiring direct experience of the being itself. Referring to a concept of hypothesis very near to that repeatedly referred to in his *philosophia prima*,[36] Hobbes avoids contradicting the principle, stated by himself, of the pure conditional nature of scientific reasoning, for in this case sense experience provides the start, the existing fact: *if* this fact exists, *then* a primary cause for it exists. But it must be remarked that Hobbes attains this primary cause in a merely hypothetical way, resolutely denying any possibility of referring to such a cause by way of a full knowledge and, thus, of any possibility of knowing God's attributes. In fact, Hobbes was very fond of this explanatory theory; for, after having expounded some rudiments of it in *Elements of Law*,[37] he also confirmed it in *Leviathan*, adding a somewhat pre-deistic hint about the 'admirable order' of Nature, and emphasizing that 'it is impossible to make any profound enquiry into naturall causes, without being inclined thereby to believe there is one God Eternall; though they cannot have any idea of him in their mind, answerable to his nature'.[38]

In my opinion, this last observation offers a considerable insight into the understanding of the real meaning of Hobbes's statement about achieving a rational persuasion of God's existence: they are not 'arguments' in a theological sense, but only remarks about the feelings to which a student of natural causes of phenomena necessarily inclines. A mechanistic

[35] *Objectiones ad Cartesii meditationes*, ob. V (*LW* v. 260). English trans. ('Objection V of the Objections III') in *The Philosophical Works of Descartes*, rendered into English by E. Haldane and G. R. T. Ross (Cambridge, 1934), ii. 67.

[36] For Hobbes's notion of 'supposition' see chs. 2 and 3 of my *Convenzione e ipotesi nella formazione della filosofia naturale di Thomas Hobbes* (Florence, 1965).

[37] *Elements*, I. 11. 2, p. 54.

[38] *Leviathan*, 11, pp. 167–8.

philosopher is led, so to speak, to seek a general warrant and frame for the system of natural causes, since it is, in its necessary chain, the proper object of science. So, if we turn the apparent purpose of Hobbes's discourse upside down, we may assume that his arguments are not aimed at the existence of God in a theological or traditionally religious sense, but at some kind of reassurance that a conception of Nature and of man—as part of mechanically regarded Nature—grounded on a deterministic principle of causal necessity, is really well grounded. Furthermore, this reassuring reasoning will also strengthen the arguments denying human free will.

One of the most significant passages in this sense may be found in *Of Liberty and Necessity*, published in 1654, but written about eight years earlier. As is well known, in this concise but very clear pamphlet, Hobbes polemizes against Bishop Bramhall, aiming to demonstrate that human will cannot be free because of the necessity of causal chains in the material world, a world including man as an equally material component. Now, one of the main points of Hobbes's argument is the passage at issue, clarifying that the necessary sequence of causes, embracing every human action, must be referred to a primary and eternal cause, that 'set and ordered' this determined causal system:

> That which I say necessitateth and determinateth every action, that his Lordship may no longer doubt of my meaning, is the sum of all things, which being now existent, conduce and concur to the production of that action hereafter, whereof if any one thing now were wanting, the effect could not be produced. This concourse of causes, whereof every one is determined to be such as it is by a like concourse of former causes, may well be called (in respect they were all set and ordered by the eternal cause of all things, God Almighty) the decree of God.[39]

The same opinion is expressed by Hobbes in his later book on *Questions Concerning Liberty, Necessity, and Chance*,[40] where he confirms, against Bramhall's renewed objections, that God is

[39] *Of Liberty and Necessity* (*EW* iv. 246).

[40] *The Questions Concerning Liberty, Necessity, and Chance* (they take up the whole of vol. v in the *EW*). A discussion on the issue of free will in the same terms can also be found in *AntiWhite*, 37. 3 ff.; particularly interesting conclusions in para. 14 (the last one) of the same chapter (p. 411). On the matter of free will in Hobbes, penetrating pages are to be found in S. Landucci's book, *La teodicea nell'età cartesiana* (Naples, 1986), 99–126.

'the cause of all motions and of all actions', so that even sin 'must derive a necessity from the first mover';[41] for, human election

> is always from the memory of good and evil sequels; memory is always from the sense; and sense always from the action of external bodies; and all action from God; therefore all actions, even of free and voluntary agents are from God, and consequently necessary.[42]

One may notice this recurrent reference to God in Hobbes's observations on the necessary causal context underlying the course of facts in the natural and human world: 'if liberty cannot stand with necessity, it cannot stand with the decrees of God',[43] assuming we ascribe 'all necessity to the universal series or order of causes, depending on the first cause eternal'.[44] These are the principal references to the question, accompanied, as usual, by repeated statements about the inconceivableness and ineffableness of divine attributes. 'We ought not to dispute of God's nature', Hobbes concludes polemically in the final pages of *Questions*: 'He is not fit subject of our philosophy.'[45]

In these passages, the properly ascending structure of the a posteriori argument vanishes, to emphasize, on the contrary, the descending movement of this unavoidable causal sequence, from God, warranting it, to all natural and human events. More explicitly than elsewhere, God is then conceived as the highest sanction of the validity and coherence of the mechanical order of the material universe. After having dismantled the Aristotelian and scholastic theory maintaining the identification of knowing and known, Hobbes was called upon to answer for the grounds and objective significance of his own epistemology, and then to legitimate the unconditioned validity of the causality principle, the causal relation being the only plausible link between a subject and the world sending to it its messages.

It may be observed that this divine warrant—so important in Descartes's conception of Nature—has in Hobbes's work a

41 *Questions*, XII (*EW* v. 138–9).

42 *Questions*, XXXIV (*EW* v. 338).

43 Ibid. 340. Spinoza too employs the phrase 'decree of God' to mean the very strong determination that governs Nature's events in their necessary chain: cf. *Tractatus theologico-politicus*, iii (in *Opera* im Auftrag der Heidelberger Akademie der Wissenschaften, ed. C. Gebhardt (Heidelberg, 1925) iii. 46).

44 *Questions*, XXXVIII (*EW* v. 366).

45 Ibid. 436 and 442–3.

wider role, giving both a general and a generic reliability to the subject–object relation, that Hobbes seems to think is already granted by his definition of *causa integra*. But we must also note, that from Locke to Berkeley British empiricism will afterwards stress more and more the significance of an appeal to God, to argue—as in Locke's case—the asserted conformity between ideas and things, that is that the connection between primary and secondary qualities is 'regular and natural'. And if God is a veritable pillar of Locke's realism, he is even more significant for supporting the physical coherence of the world dematerialized by Berkeley's radically subjectivist reduction.

I think it not entirely groundless to regard Hobbes as the first term in a course of thought which progressively becomes aware of the difficulties arising when realism attempts to rest upon merely subjective empirical foundations. Hobbes's God is the hypothetical last term of human reasoning, a supposition never verifiable, the unified expression of the rationality pervading the external world and of the intelligibleness of it to the human mind. Though he cannot be considered—technically speaking—in a philosophical perspective, God is a kind of transcendent warrant of Hobbes's conception of reality as a material world of moving bodies, causally connected in a necessary determined sequence of events. So, paradoxically, Hobbes's God appears lastly to be the highest warrant of two of the main principles of *Hobbism*, so execrated by theologians of every time and faith: the materialistic view of reality and the denial of human free will.

In other words, having recourse to the well-received frame of the traditional argument for God's existence, Hobbes is here expressing an intellectual inclination which is not in opposition to his statements as declared in *AntiWhite*: appealing to a general reassurance about the rationality of reality does not contrast with denying technical validity to a specific demonstrative procedure, aiming at God's existence in a properly theological sense. Moreover, it must be noted that Hobbes denies White the possibility of demonstrating the existence of a God that *created* the world, while he constantly refers to a *mover* God. Similarly, it is of interest, on the one hand, to relate Hobbes's 'proof' to Ockham's proof of God as world-conserving cause, and on the other hand, to analyse how far the reduction of the whole of reality to movement, which can be found in a famous page of *De Corpore*, can appear as further support to Hobbes's notion of God.[46] It may anyway be observed that the double movement of Hobbes's 'proof', an ascending one as an argument and a descending one as a warrant, produces a kind of circle: for God should warrant the necessity of that causal connection by which he himself is warranted. But I think we must speak of an identification, rather than of circularity, Hobbes's philosophical God being the same as the necessity itself of a causal process; it is for this reason that he looks so little like the personal God of the Hebraic–Christian tradition.

This perspective is seen to change if we turn our attention away from the field of natural philosophy, and therefore of natural theology, to that of the political system, to consider the historically given religion and the historically given God of the Old and New Testaments, as they appear in the third part of *Leviathan*. If one looks with an unbiased eye at those pages in *Leviathan* that consider religion both as a psychological attitude and as a historical fact, one can come away convinced that Hobbes did consider man's religious attitude and motivations with the utmost seriousness. In maintaining that man's religiousness rises on the one side from an inborn striving to know 'the causes of the events', and on the other from an anxiety over his future, Hobbes reveals that he can acutely observe religiousness whilst avoiding any devaluation of it.[47]

Of course, as the range of scientific explanation of events broadened, Hobbes believed, the margins of the supernatural are inexorably narrowed down, thus doing away with any explanation in the area of superstition, magic, or miracles.[48] It nevertheless does not corrode the very essence of the naturalness of a religious attitude as such, albeit allowing a distinction between an as it were correctly addressed religiousness and one which can be just as legitimate in its psychological motivation, but which evaporates, because it addresses itself to the wrong objects. The latter mainly refers to the inventions of pagan

[46] Cf. *De Corpore*, 6. 5 (*LW* i. 62). For Ockham's argument see, for example, *Scriptum in librum primum Sententiarum: Ordinatio*, lib. I, dist. ii, q. X (in the crit. edn. by S. Brown and G. Gàl (St. Bonaventure, NY, 1970), 355–6.

[47] *Leviathan*, 12, pp. 168–73.

[48] Suffice it to consider chs. 36 ('Of the Word of God, and of Prophets') and 37 ('Of Miracles, and their use') of *Leviathan*.

priests,[49] although the falsehood of many Christian priests may be as misleading.[50] The former expresses itself in revealed religion, in which by means of the word of God a sort of material and political bond is established between God and Abraham and Moses, indeed between God and men at large.[51] I used the term 'material' intentionally, because the entire interpretation of the Bible as suggested by Hobbes consists of a systematic bringing of the supernatural, the rationally inexplicable, down to the natural, to what is earthly material, explicable in rational terms. What Hobbes is after is the bringing of Christianity down to earth, by means of a naturalistic and materialistic interpretation of biblical terminology, in constant opposition to Greek philosophy, held responsible for having unduly spiritualized that Christianity which had on the contrary risen out of the fundamentally non-spiritualistic attitude of Hebrew culture.[52]

It is of course impossible to proceed here to a detailed analysis of how Hobbes read the Bible and of the result of his peculiar and aimed interpretation; it is enough to point out in passing that Hobbes's criticism also yields remarkable philological

[49] 'For these seeds have received culture from two sorts of men. One sort have been they, that have nourished, and ordered them, according to their own invention. The other have done it, by Gods commandement and direction . . .', *Leviathan*, 12, p. 173. Hobbes then goes on to illustrate the 'absurdities' of pagan religion.

[50] Cf. again *Leviathan*, 12, pp. 181–3, and more generally the fourth part of the work, devoted to 'The Kingdom of Darknesse', that is to say, to an ideological-based analysis of the catholic religion, its rites and its symbols. Here, in particular, see *Leviathan*, 44, pp. 628–9.

[51] 'But where God himselfe, by supernaturall Revelation, planted Religion; there he also made to himselfe a peculiar Kingdome; and gave Lawes, not only of behaviour towards himselfe; but also towards one another . . .', *Leviathan*, 12, p. 178. Cf. also ch. 40, 'Of the Rights of the Kingdome of God, in Abraham, Moses, the High Priests, and the Kings of Judah' (*Leviathan*, pp. 499–512).

[52] Cf. chiefly ch. 34 ('Of the signification of Spirit, Angell, and Inspiration in the Books of Holy Scripture') and 44 ('Of Spirituall Darknesse from Misinterpretation of Scripture') of *Leviathan*, where this thesis comes out more clearly: but Hobbes's dislike for classical learning is a recurring theme in all his political works. See remarks on this point in *Elements* and *De Cive*. Not as well known (and often much more meaningful) are the remarks that can be found in the *Historia ecclesiastica*, in the short treatise *Concerning Heresy*, and in the *Answer* to *The Catching of Leviathan* by Bishop Bramhall; in all these works, Hobbes develops a proper doctrine of the incompatibility—on a theoretical and historical level—between Greek philosophy and Hebrew–Christian religion, whose disastrous yoking generated theology. In the two latter writings, Hobbes also develops an outspoken materialistic notion of God. But to all these most important topics I shall devote further specific work.

results.[53] In any case, this process seems to me to bear witness to an interest in the subject on Hobbes's part, although the outcome of these efforts of his could not but appear unwelcome to contemporary theologians. It is not my intention here of course to deny the great novelty of the rationalistic criticism operated by Hobbes on the Bible, on the churches, and even on religion itself as a psychological, social, and political phenomenon, neither do I intend to turn Hobbes into a champion of Christianity or into a sort of *defensor fidei*: I nevertheless feel one can admit that Hobbes's attitude to religion and theology appears at present to be much more multifarious that it might have been accepted as being in the past.

As we have seen, Hobbes's philosophy and Hobbes's theology give us two different images of God: the philosophical God is the final, purely supposed term of a chain of material causes, the merely hypothetical conclusion at which natural reason arrives in its conditional proceeding from experience of facts; on the other hand, the God of *Leviathan* is the biblical God, a physically personal and theologically identified being which stimulates and warrants any orderly human society and is the unavoidable reference for any political theory. However, if Hobbes's two gods do not exactly overlap, neither do they contradict each other, sharing as they do a subordination to a universal rationalistic ideal. Moreover, what Hobbes says of the faulty possibility of knowing God in a philosophical way does not clash with a larger possibility of being known, by God himself conceded in a theological way, i.e. when we are discussing by means of a critical rational approach a revealed text, one in which God accounts for himself. If philosophy refers man to faith, theology picks up the hint. If natural reason, to quote Bacon's *Advancement of Learning*, 'sufficieth to refute and convince atheism', but not 'to establish religion',[54] biblical criticism,

[53] Hobbes, for instance, was one of the first (preceded only, among non-Jewish scholars, by Andreas Bodenstein or Carlostadius, Andreas Masius, and Jacques Bonfrère) to argue against Moses' authorship of the Pentateuch.

[54] In *Works* ed. cit. iv. 341. See a similar passage in the *Confession of Faith* of the Parliament's Assembly, where it is stressed that: 'Although the Light of Nature, and the works of Creation and Providence do so far manifest the Goodness, Wisdom, and Power of God, as to leave men inexcusable; yet are they not sufficient to give that knowledge of God and of his Will, which is necessary unto salvation.' In *The Humble Advice of the Assembly of Divines, Now by the authority of Parliament sitting at Westminster* (London and Edinburgh, 1648), A2.

moving as it does within the bounds of faith, can, on the contrary, verify the whole range of relations established in time between God and the world, between God and man.

Was Hobbes sincere in this reference to faith, to the biblical God, albeit reconsidered in a materialistic way, in the light of an already advanced philological criticism? A comparison with the way in which a few years later Spinoza will deal with the same issues might show that Hobbes stops quite short of the Dutch thinker in the way of a complete devaluation and desecration of the Hebrew–Christian tradition.[55] In fact, we can never know what really was in Hobbes's mind, but we *do* have his writings, which are what he wanted us to believe was on his mind. What is certain is that he was not only a philosopher, in the sense in which we now academically term this branch of learning: he was a philosopher, a mathematician, an optician, and a little bit of a theologian too, because theology exists in his thought next to philosophy, albeit fundamentally distinct from it. That his theology was strongly conditioned by the rationalistic bent of his thinking is something that, obvious as it may sound, would require much further arguing.

[55] On some aspects of this subject see Richard H. Popkin, 'Hobbes and Skepticism', in *History of Philosophy in the Making*, ed. J. Linus and S. J. Thro (Washington, 1982), esp. 138–40.

9
Hobbes's Hidden Influence

G. A. J. ROGERS

INTRODUCTION

Hobbes's *Leviathan* is recognized as one of the glories of the seventeenth century and Hobbes's place as one of the giants in an age of giants is for us assured. Yet it was not always so, as we all well know. To be identified as a follower of Hobbes was to be identified as an atheist and a lecher, at least for some period of time in the second half of the seventeenth century, and unless one were seeking notoriety, as some undoubtedly were, then it was as well to distance oneself from his name.

We shall come to examples of these responses shortly. However, before we do I wish to identify a likely consequence of this reputation for the reception of Hobbes in later seventeenth-century England. With such a reputation it seems reasonable to suppose that even when people read Hobbes they were unlikely to admit that they had been influenced by him, except in the sense that they might denounce him or at least one of his accursed doctrines. Few, we might suppose, who had regard for their reputation, would admit either openly, or even to themselves, that Hobbes might have exercised any positive influence on them. Few, that is, would have been prepared to acknowledge that they might be in any way indebted to him. But the question which arises, and to which this paper is addressed, is whether Hobbes was nevertheless influential, albeit unacknowledged and unacknowledgeable. May we detect the fingerprint of Hobbes in the writings of those who would have wanted no such thing?

Clearly there is a problem about any such detection. In the very nature of the case there is likely to be little or no direct evidence. For those so influenced will not have gone out of their way to declare it. It will be found, if anywhere, either in the secret notebooks and diaries of the age, or, less securely, in the style of presentation or the method of argumentation of those who openly rejected him. We can be sure that it will not be found in the titles and dedications of the writers seeking to obtain or retain respectability. There was no *Festschrift* for Hobbes on his seventieth, eightieth, or even his ninetieth, birthday. The evidence for this kind of Hobbist impact will in large measure be circumstantial, and therefore to that extent will not be conclusive. But if the probabilities rise sufficiently, even if we allow that we have something less than knowledge, we may well agree a reasonable certainty.

THE REPUTATION OF HOBBES

Let us begin, then, with Hobbes's reputation. The first point to notice is the apparently obvious one that Hobbes took some time to become notorious. Notoriety is rarely an innate property of human beings: it usually has to be worked for! The relevance of this is that long before the name of Hobbes was notorious he had established a name with some which remained unshaken and probably unshakeable for the duration. It would be easy to make quite a long list of the famous for whom this remained true, but at least these three examples are sufficient to give the claim a good base: the Cavendish family, John Aubrey, and, perhaps most important of all, Marin Mersenne. The Cavendishes remained loyal to Hobbes throughout. Their intellectual regard for him is well illustrated by the words of Sir Charles Cavendish, who in August 1644, soon after the publication of Descartes's *Principia Philosophiae*, could write in terms which implied that he regarded Hobbes as intellectually comparable with Descartes. He hoped that Hobbes and Descartes would soon be acquainted, 'and by that meanes highlie esteeme one of another'.[1] Aubrey's regard for Hobbes is

[1] *A Collection of Letters Illustrative of the Progress of Science in England From the Reign of Queen Elizabeth to that of Charles the Second*, ed. James Orchard Halliwell (London, 1841), 83. According to John Aubrey, Lord Cavendish bought books for the library at Chatsworth on Hobbes's advice. (Cf. *Aubrey's Brief Lives*, ed. Oliver Lawson Dick (Harmondsworth, 1962), 231.)

too well known to need much comment, stretching as it obviously did from Aubrey's first meeting with him in 1634, when Aubrey was a schoolboy in Wiltshire and Hobbes, then already forty-six, came to visit Malmesbury for a week. Hobbes, Aubrey tells us, was 'pleased to take notice of me'.[2] and his friendship for the older man was to last to the end. And Mersenne not only presided over the convent in which Hobbes lived in Paris from 1640, but invited him to write the set of objections to the *Meditations* and also, in 1644, published Hobbes's *Tractatus Opticus*. To Mersenne he was 'that incomparable man Mr. Hobbes', the author of 'that outstanding work the *De Cive*'.[3]

These friends of Hobbes were therefore well acquainted with him before he acquired any widespread notoriety. But a notoriety was to grow rapidly from the publication in 1642 of *De Cive*, and even before this Hobbes had allowed manuscripts of his writings to circulate which brought opposition in their wake. Early hostility showed itself at his appointment as mathematics tutor to the Prince of Wales, which Robert Baillie in Scotland reported as being ill-taken because of Hobbes's supposed atheism.[4] By 1652 Hobbes had been banned from Charles's Paris court, probably under pressure especially from French Jesuits and English Catholics around the Queen.

Another early manifestation of the opposition yet to come was nothing directly to do with Hobbes at all. It was the unauthorized publication in 1654 of *Of Liberty and Necessity* and the response this evoked from Bishop Bramhall, with whom Hobbes had debated free will; there had been a mutual agreement not to publish their written exchanges. Incensed by what he believed to be a breach of trust on the part of Hobbes, Bramhall responded with his own views on free will and also an attack on Hobbes's religious views as he detected them in the now published *Leviathan*. Hobbes's shift from comparative obscurity to notoriety was by now well under way.

The attacks mounted against him were, of course, to continue

[2] *Brief Lives*, p. 229.

[3] Mersenne to Samuel Sorbière, 25 Apr. 1646. The English translation of this letter is published in Thomas Hobbes, *De Cive. The Latin Version*, A Critical Edition by Howard Warrender (Oxford, 1983), Appendix A, pp. 297–8.

[4] Cf. Samuel I. Mintz, *The Hunting of Leviathan* (Cambridge, 1962), 12.

throughout his life and beyond. He was continually denounced as an atheist, but he was also protected by his intimacy with the Cavendish family and the warmth of feeling for him of his former pupil the King. His public reputation, was, however, clear. For many in the clergy and in the court he was the atheist and immoralist, the paradigm of everything which should be pronounced anathema.

And so it was that those who wished to shock their elders or their colleagues declared themselves Hobbists, and were as surely in their turn subject to attack. There are, perhaps, not a large number of examples of such poses being struck. But one famous incident well illustrates the way in which the name of Hobbes had become linked with immorality and atheism (the two were scarcely separated) in the public mind. In 1669 a Fellow of Corpus Christi College, Cambridge, one Daniel Scargill, who had offered to defend positions taken from *Leviathan*, was removed from the university, in part for his Hobbist beliefs.[5] Scargill was clearly a reprobate, and his own behaviour, linked by himself to what he claimed were Hobbist principles, is a measure of what many by then regarded as the moral and theological implications of Hobbes's philosophy. As others have shown, by the 1660s and 1670s there was in any case evidence of a rising tide of such generally unacceptable beliefs and a corresponding reaction to them.[6] The result was, of course, even more determination on the part of most aspirants to intellectual pretension to distance themselves from any sort of identification with the 'Monster of Malmesbury'.

We may observe such behaviour at close hand in an exchange between two of the century's greatest intellectual figures. It is, I believe, a telling illustration of the reputation of Hobbes into the 1690s. On 16 September 1693 Isaac Newton, by now the author of the *Principia*, and rapidly becoming the most famous natural philosopher in the world, wrote to the almost equally illustrious author of *An Essay Concerning Human Understanding*, his intimate

[5] On this event see James L. Axtell, 'The Mechanics of Opposition: Restoration Cambridge v. Daniel Scargill', *Bulletin of the Institute of Historical Research*, 38 (1965), 102–11.

[6] Cf. Quentin Skinner, 'The Context of Hobbes's Theory of Politial Obligation', in *Hobbes and Rousseau: A Collection of Critical Essays*, ed. Maurice Cranston and Richard S. Peters (New York, 1972), 109–42.

friend John Locke. The letter is extraordinary on several counts, written as it was whilst Newton was undergoing a mental crisis, which some have seen as approaching a mental breakdown. In it Newton apologizes for some bad behaviour towards Locke, engendered by false suspicions of Locke's intentions towards him. He continues:

I beg your pardon for my having hard thoughts of you . . . and for representing that you struck at the root of morality in a principle you laid down in your book of Ideas and designed to pursue in another book and that I took you for a Hobbist.[7]

I have elsewhere attempted to identify the parts of Locke's *Essay* which offended Newton from a study of Newton's own copy of Locke's book.[8] It does, I believe, relate particularly to Locke's hedonism. But for our purposes Newton's reasons for using the word 'Hobbist' are less important than the reaction they engendered in Locke. Clearly Locke is concerned at Newton's criticism, for after a placatory paragraph assuring Newton of his continued friendship he turns to the matter of the *Essay Concerning Human Understanding*, which is going to the press for a second edition. If Newton 'would point out . . . the places that gave occasion to that censure' Locke will 'by explaining my self better . . . avoid being mistaken by others . . .'.[9] We should notice that Locke himself avoids the word 'Hobbist' in his reply. One detects here, perhaps, a dislike of even using the term. For certainly it is remarkable that in Locke's published writings the name of Hobbes scarcely features at all. As Peter Laslett pointed out many years ago, Hobbes's name does not appear in either of the two *Treatises of Government*. In the *Essay Concerning Human Understanding* the name of Hobbes is mentioned but once, and then only in the context of repudiation.[10] Yet, as all students of political theory know, there seem to be many passages in the *Treatises* which sound as though they are a dialogue with Hobbist theories of government. As Laslett neatly expressed it,

[7] *The Correspondence of John Locke*, ed. E. S. de Beer, 9 vols. (Oxford, 1976–), iv. 727, Letter No. 1659.

[8] Cf. G. A. J. Rogers, 'Locke's *Essay* and Newton's *Principia*', *Journal of the History of Ideas*, 39 (1978), 217–32.

[9] Locke, *Correspondence*, iv. 729.

[10] Cf. *An Essay Concerning Human Understanding*, 1. 3. 5, ed. Peter H. Nidditch (Oxford, 1975), p. 68.

'Locke never escaped the shadow of *Leviathan*'.[11] And yet he scarcely mentions his name. And why not? Can it be that the explanation lies in the very Hobbist emotion of fear? Or perhaps it is the Lockian virtue of prudence. Certainly both would have been justified. For without any overt references, Locke was to be accused by others besides Newton of showing Hobbist tendencies, especially in his theological writings.[12]

We may begin to wonder if the reason Locke himself was almost unable to bring himself to mention Hobbes by name was because he was well enough aware that there were sufficient similarities between some of his own views and those of his predecessor to make life uncomfortable for him with any overt show of association. It has been suggested by Noel Malcolm, in his paper in this volume, that the reason why Fellows of the Royal Society maintained an exclusion on Hobbes was not because they were so opposed to all his views, but rather, that because they shared some of them, they feared too close an identification.[13] The suggestion is plausible. And when we remember that Locke was one of the Fellows, and sometime a member of its Council, we may perhaps suspect a similarity of explanation.

We shall return to the relationship between Hobbes and Locke below. Let us for the moment just agree that from the mid-century on—i.e. from about the date of the publication of *Leviathan*—there was strong reluctance on the part of almost anybody to be publicly identified with its author.

THE METHOD OF HOBBES

I begin with a quotation. '[C]ertain it is that words, as a Tarter's bow, do shoot back upon the understanding of the wisest, and

[11] John Locke *Two Treatises of Government*, A Critical Edition with an Introduction and Apparatus Criticus by Peter Laslett (Cambridge, 1964), 72.

[12] Ibid. 72–3. Dr M. A. Stewart has also drawn my attention to Locke's response to Stillingfleet's attempts to read him as having Hobbist tendencies on the issue of immortality. Locke replies that 'I am not so well read in *Hobbes* or *Spinoza*, to be able to say what were their Opinions in this matter.' *The Works of John Locke Esq. in Three Volumes*, 2nd edn. (London, 1722), i. 566.

[13] Noel Malcolm, 'Hobbes and the Royal Society', above, esp. pp. 60–61.

mightily entangle and pervert the judgement; so as it is almost necessary in all controversies and disputations to imitate the wisdom of the Mathematicians, in setting down in the very beginning the definitions of our words and terms. . . .'[14] The writer, you may be surprised to learn, is not Hobbes, but his one-time master Francis Bacon. We may be sure, though, that Hobbes had read these words of Bacon before he so famously set eyes on Euclid in the gentleman's library, though that event not only confirmed the Baconian remark but opened Hobbes's mind to the full potential of its application. In *Leviathan* we may perhaps detect the echo of Bacon's remarks: 'The first cause of Absurd conclusions I ascribe to the want of Method; in that they begin not their Ratiocination from Definitions; that is, from settled significations of their words: as if they could cast account, without knowing the value of the numerall words, *one*, *two*, and *three*.'[15]

The remarks of both Bacon and Hobbes might be dismissed as a commonplace. But to do so would, I believe, be to misread the force of the mathematical, and particularly the geometrical, model as it entered from the mathematicians and astronomers into the wider intellectual consciousness. In short, I wish to suggest that it was only in the seventeenth century that the possibility of applying the geometrical model outside of geometry and its close relative astronomy, became widely recognized. Before that could happen geometry's full potential had itself to be more widely acknowledged.

The full story of that awakening is clearly a major event in early modern intellectual history. Surprisingly it remains still somewhat obscure. The printing of the text of Euclid in Venice in 1482 is obviously in some sense the beginning. The revival of Plato in Florence was no doubt an aid. And then there was the new astronomy of Copernicus and all that followed from that. In England a beautiful piece of propaganda in favour of geometry appeared in 1570 in the form of a preface to the first English edition of Euclid. It was written by Queen Elizabeth's court astrologer (hinting at another important source for the rising

[14] *Of the Advancement of Learning, The Philosophical Works of Francis Bacon*, ed. J. M. Robertson (London, 1905), 120.

[15] *Leviathan*, I. 5. Reference is to the Penguin Books edn., ed. C. B. Macpherson (London, 1968), p. 114.

influence of geometry), the fabulous John Dee. Dee's Preface depicts geometry, not theology, as the queen of the sciences. For it is through its mastery that we may climb to the highest intellectual heights and even reach heaven itself. Echoing the platonic ideals Dee describes the way in which a knowledge of geometry will enable us to rise above the transient earth to the eternal form of forms.[16] Not only is geometry seen as a key to unlocking the secrets of nature for man's benefit—the Baconian message which predates Bacon—but it is also seen as revealing the eternal forms lying beyond and behind transient experience.

When, or even whether, Hobbes read Dee's Preface we do not know. However, we do know that similar views about the place of geometry were held by thinkers for whom Hobbes showed the greatest respect. As leader of that school we should place Galileo. His famous words about the place of geometry in relation to our understanding of the physical world are engraved on the mind of every student of the scientific revolution:

> Philosophy is written in this grand book, the universe, which stands continually open to our gaze. But the book cannot be understood unless one first learns to comprehend the language and read the letters in which it is composed. It is written in the language of mathematics, and its characters are triangles, circles, and other geometric figures without which it is humanly impossible to understand a single word of it: without these, one wanders about in a dark labyrinth.[17]

The nature and depth of Hobbes's debts to Galileo is a subject on its own. But we all know that Hobbes himself acknowledged Galileo's achievement and saw his own work in political philosophy as exemplifying similar virtues as a science.[18] But his originality lay in applying this method not to the natural world but to the world of men, or rather, to put it in terms which Hobbes would surely have preferred, he argued that men too were capable of being comprehended according to the geometri-

[16] *The Elements-of Geometrie of the most ancient Philosopher Euclide of Megara, Faithfully (now first) translated into the English toung, by H. Billingsley . . . With a very fruitfull Praeface made by M. I. Dee . . .* (London, 1570). The pages of Dee's preface are not numbered, but the relevant passages are on what would be pp. 2–4.

[17] *The Assayer*, as in *Discoveries and Opinions of Galileo*, trans. with an Introduction and Notes by Stillman Drake (New York, 1957), 237–8.

[18] The famous reference is in the Epistle Dedicatory to the *Elements of Philosophy. The First Section Concerning Body, EW* i. ix.

cal method. There is a story that Galileo was the original source of this idea, the suggestion that it would be possible to have a deductive system of ethics based on the model of geometry. Hobbes visited Galileo at Arcetri in 1635 or 1636. It is said that Galileo put the idea to Hobbes as they walked in the grounds of the grand-ducal summer residence of Poggio Imperiale.[19] The oral tradition on which this story is founded, for that reason, if no other, is not conclusive evidence. But it has a ring of plausibility. True or not, we know full well that from about this time the idea of an axiomatized system of ethics was firmly in his mind.

SYSTEMS OF ETHICS

The paradigm of moral philosophy for the seventeenth century was of course set by the ethical works of Aristotle. Departure from that paradigm was no easy matter. Bacon, for example, could not do it, and the little he wrote that may be considered moral philosophy presents nothing of the serious challenge to Aristotle that compares with his radical proposals for the reform of the investigation of nature. Rather similar remarks might be made about Descartes. But no one can doubt that a new prospect is opened with the publication of *De Cive* and *Leviathan*. That Hobbes himself saw his work as one of ethics should be in no doubt. He could write in the Epistle Dedicatory to *De Cive* that philosophy consisted of three branches, that treating of figures, called geometry, that of motion, called 'Physick', and finally that of natural right, called 'Moralls'. He goes on to praise the geometers in ways which might remind us of Dee:

> And truly the Geometricians have very admirably perform'd their part. For whatsoever assistance doth accrew to the life of man, whether from the observation of the Heavens, or from the description of the

[19] The source for this is A. G. Kastner's *Geschichte der Mathematik* (Göttingen, 1800), iv. 186. The remark is quoted in Frithiof Brandt, *Thomas Hobbes' Mechanical Conception of Nature* (Copenhagen and London, 1928), 393. It runs, in English translation: 'John Albert de Soria, a former teacher at the University of Pisa, affirms that it is known through oral tradition that Galileo first gave Hobbes the idea of bringing moral philosophy to a mathematical certainty by working according to geometrical principles, when they were taking a walk at the grand-ducal summer residence of Poggio Imperiale.' (I am grateful to Mrs Wendy Cox for the translation of this passage.)

Earth, from the notation of Times, or from the remost experiments of Navigation: Finally, whatsoever things they are in which this present Age doth differ from the rude simplenesse of Antiquity, we must acknowledge to be a debt which we owe meerly to Geometry.[20]

Hobbes then goes on to explain what he understands by moral philosophy and its tasks: if the moral philosophers had been nearly as successful (as the geometers), he says, he knows not what might have been the benefits for human happiness: 'For were the nature of humane Actions as distinctly known, as the nature of *Quantity* in Geometrical Figures, the strength of *Avarice* and *Ambition*, which is sustained by the erroneous opinions of the Vulgar, as touching the nature of *Right* and *Wrong*, would presently faint and languish; And Mankinde should enjoy such an Immortall Peace that . . . there would hardly be any pretence for war.'[21]

It was just this distinct knowledge of the nature of human actions which Hobbes attempted to achieve in his works, and from that deduce the consequences for how we ought to behave. And it was from clear and settled definitions of terms, just as in Euclidean geometry, or Copernican astronomy (or, later, we might add, Newtonian mechanics) that the whole system was to be inferred.

Here was quite an original conception of ethics. But Hobbes was able to show that the deductions made often coincided with well-established tenets of Christian doctrine and were encapsulated in the general principle: '*Do not that to others, you would not have done to your self.*'[22] It was a principle, he held, which followed logically from the nature of man and the primary injunction, the fundamental law of nature, to seek peace.

Another important feature of Hobbes's account of ethics is that it is that branch of philosophy, moral philosophy, which admits of two quite different forms of demonstration. For, as he explains, 'the causes of the motion of the mind are known not only by ratiocination [as in natural philosophy] but also by the experience of every man that takes the pains to observe those motions within himself'.[23] It was to that extent more certain

[20] *De Cive EV* 25.
[21] Ibid. 25–6.
[22] Ibid. 72.
[23] *De Corpore, EW* i. 73.

than natural philosophy. The same point is made somewhat differently in other works. Thus he writes:

> Geometry is . . . demonstrable, for the lines and figures from which we reason are drawn and described by ourselves; and civil philosophy is demonstrable because we make the commonwealth ourselves. But because of natural bodies we know not the construction, but seek it from effects, there lies no demonstration of what the causes be we seek for, but only of what they may be.[24]

Precisely what Hobbes means by 'because we make the commonwealth ourselves' is difficult to say. He may mean, on the one hand, that because we have constructed it we know its causes, in the way that the watchmaker knows the causes of the motions of the watch which he has made with his own hands. Or he may mean something rather different, namely that the commonwealth is in some strong sense a product of the mind, or if you like, a social fact, rather than a natural fact, with a reality determined by us rather than by the way the world is independently of all human wishes. If the latter is indeed his position, then Hobbes may be seen as to some degree anticipating Locke's account of the distinction between nominal and real essences.

THE RECEPTION OF HOBBES'S SYSTEM AGAIN

There can be no doubting the originality of Hobbes's ethical system. The application of the geometric method, the axiomatization of moral principles, was a powerful new weapon in the armoury of the philosopher. The only problem was that as it had been produced by a man widely considered to be the arch atheist-materialist of the age it would hardly do to give him due acknowledgement. What then happened, I believe, is what one would in these circumstances expect. People borrowed Hobbes's good ideas without acknowledgement, and even used them to attack him.

Central to the Hobbesian analysis was the concept of reason. it was reason which enabled man to comprehend the right course of action, to follow the argument and recognize the truth

[24] Epistle Dedicatory to *Six Lessons to the Professors of Mathematics*, *EW* vii. 184.

of the laws of nature. In the early decades of the later seventeenth century the group most closely identified with reason were the loosely associated group of thinkers known as the Cambridge Platonists. Their founder, Benjamin Whichcote, had in his sermons and teachings made reason the central human faculty: 'To go against *Reason* is to go against God,' he said. 'There is nothing proper and *peculiar* to Man but the Use of Reason and the Exercise of Virtue.'[25] The other leading figures of this school also gave high priority to reason. And amongst them were some of Hobbes's strongest opponents.

The depth and extent of their hostility to Hobbes has been charted elsewhere.[26] My interest in them lies, not with that, but with whether they adopted any of Hobbes's central ideas. And my contention is that at least one of them did. The man I have in mind is Henry More.

More was by far the most prolific of the Cambridge school. Like his fellow philosopher at Christ's College, Ralph Cudworth, much of his writing was directed against the threat of atheism as he saw it especially in Hobbes, but also in Descartes, and the Epicurean revival. It was the materialist ontology of these philosophers, actual or potential, that particularly concerned him. But he was also uncomfortably aware, or at least made aware by others, of their implications for moral theory. He was, in this connection, as we shall see, especially aware of Hobbes.

Hobbes, the non-Platonist, was profoundly impressed by geometry. The Cambridge Platonists give it no special place, and none of them had pretensions to great mathematical skill. Such are the vagaries of intellectual history. Yet in 1668 we find Henry More at long last publishing his moral philosophy, and the form in which he chose to exhibit it is that of the geometrical method. We may agree immediately that the content of the work is far from the ethics of Hobbes. But the form of its presentation is similar, and I believe significantly so.

It is said that More refrained from writing a work on ethics because his friend Ralph Cudworth (who had published almost nothing) was intending to do so. However, frustrated by the

[25] *Moral and Religious Aphorisms*, collected by Dr Jeffery, republished with large editions by Samuel Salter (London, 1753), Aphorisms 76 and 71.

[26] See esp. Mintz, op. cit., ch. V.

delays in Cudworth's work, and encouraged by others, he at length published his own views. The opening words of his Epistle to the Reader immediately raise the issue of the influence of Hobbes. He writes that he was with difficulty persuaded by his friends to a work 'of this Nature'. And by this he means a work set out *more geometrico*, for he goes on: 'as having first a very mean Opinion of those Systems for Moral Philosophy, which pretend to overthrow Iniquity by *Definitions* and *Divisions*'.[27]

We may immediately ask: of which systems did More have such a low opinion? The answer appears to be that, when he wrote these words in 1667, there was only one that he could have known, that of Thomas Hobbes. The Epistle Dedicatory goes on to tell us that More believed that, for the Godly, knowledge of good and evil was not difficult, but that his friends persuaded him that there was a great need for a work set out in the new style 'as might not bear down Opposition by some new Advantage in the Method, but in carrying Proofs for every Precept, and Conviction for every Rule'. It is not unreasonable to suppose that the 'great need' for such a work arose in those who sought a suitable intellectual response to what they took to be the ethics of Hobbes.

More's work makes no attempt to confront Hobbes's moral theory directly. And it is worth remembering that it was Epicureanism in general for which he had the lowest regard.[28] In fact, in the book Hobbes is mentioned by name only in connection with the issue of free will, More claiming that he had already refuted him on this issue in his treatise *Of the Immortality of the Soul*. But the geometrical style is unmistakably, if reluctantly, present. It makes itself apparent from the first definition of Ethics as 'the art of living well and happily' through the twenty-three 'Noemata' or axioms, offered as clear and self-evident truths, no sooner understood than agreed. After that we may be forgiven if we find the presentation *more geometrico* less overt. Certainly the work does not attempt the highly deductive form of Spinoza's *Ethics*, and we may well be tempted to believe

[27] Quotations are taken from the English translation of More's *Enchiridion Ethicum* published as *An Account of Virtue: or Dr. Henry More's Abridgement of Morals,—put into English* (London, 1690), cited as *Virtue*. The pages of the Epistle Dedicatory are not numbered.

[28] He thought that atheism was 'first norished up in the stie of Epicurus'. Cf. C. A. Patrides in the Introduction to *The Cambridge Platonists* (London, 1969), 27.

that More's heart was not wholly in his stated task. If we set aside the form, then the most overt influences on the content are those of Aristotle, particularly the Eudemian Ethics, other classical authors, especially Cicero, and Descartes's account of the passions. But even in the content we might detect something of Hobbes in the style of presentation and even in the choice of words. Thus, as an example, we may take More's account of cupidity:

The kinds and Species of *Cupidity* are, in the First Rank, *Hope*, *Fear*, *Jealousie*, Security, and *Despair*: In the next are *Irresolution*, *Animosity*, *Courage*, *Emulation*, *Cowardise*, and *Consternation*.

Hope, he goes on to tell us is compounded of joy and cupidity, and fear is compounded of cupidity and grief. The function of hope is to have delight in acting and of fear to proceed with circumspection and diligence. He concludes:

But there is a more especial Use of this last Passion, which referreth to Political Matters: For, seeing the greatest part of Men are wicked; scarce any City could stand, if by the Dread of Punishment, they were not kept in aw.[29]

This last must strike us as a very Hobbesian sentiment for one of Hobbes's leading opponents! Although More's definitions do not in an obvious way borrow from Hobbes in their content, the style of presentation, I would submit, is unmistakable.

The English translation of More's work appeared in 1690, the year normally given as the publication date for Locke's *Essay Concerning Human Understanding*. And it is to that work that I now wish to turn, for in it we too, perhaps, may detect the impact of Hobbes's method in ethics. We have already seen that Locke was reluctant to admit the name of Hobbes to his writings, perhaps because he was fearful of being identified as some kind of follower. Yet readers of Locke were soon aware that he had aspirations to produce a demonstrative system of ethics. In the *Essay* he had written that 'morality is capable of demonstration as well as mathematics'.[30] It was a view entirely at one with his

[29] *Virtue*, p. 65.
[30] *Essay*, 3. 11. 16, ed. cit., p. 516.

philosophy and, we may infer from various other sources, one dear to his heart.[31]

We may usefully compare some of Locke's remarks on this topic with Hobbes. We shall discover how remarkably close they were. Expanding on his thesis about the possibility of a demonstrative ethics Locke explained that the case rested on granting the existence of God:

The *Idea* of a supreme Being, infinite in Power, Goodness, and Wisdom, whose Workmanship we are, and on whom we depend; and the *Idea* of our selves, as understanding, rational Beings, being such as are clear in us, would, I suppose, if duly considered, and pursued, afford such Foundations of our Duty and Rules of Action, as might place *Morality amongst the Sciences capable of Demonstration*: wherein I doubt not, but from self-evident Propositions, by necessary Consequences, as incontestable as those in Mathematicks, the measures of right and wrong might be made out, to any one that will apply himself with the same Indifferency and Attention to the one, as he does to the other of these Sciences.[32]

By the time that Locke came to write these words the relevant works of Hobbes had been published over forty years, and we might just on those grounds doubt their relevance. It is worth noting, too, that in the early drafts of the *Essay* of 1671, no concession is made to the possibility of demonstration without quantification.[33] So he could only have come to the idea of a demonstrative system of ethics some time between 1671 and the late 1680s as he completed the first edition of the *Essay*. Yet when we compare Locke's position with that of Hobbes, the similarities are striking.

[31] Locke's friend and admirer in Ireland, Dr William Molyneux, urged Locke from his first letter to him to write '*A Treatise of Morals*, drawn up according to the Hints you frequently give in Your Essay. Of their Being Demonstrable according to the Mathematical Method.' Molyneux to Locke, Aug. 1692, *Correspondence*, iv. 508. Despite Molyneux's continual encouragement Locke was not able to write the work, though there is manuscript evidence that he made attempts to sort his ideas out on the matter for we find among his papers a short piece which attempts to set out some moral axioms. He obviously did not get very far with the project. His remarks on a deductive system of ethics also produced some interest in Holland where Jean Le Clerc raised the matter in a letter to Locke of July 1692. Cf. *Correspondence*, iv. 472.

[32] *Essay*, 4. 3. 18, ed. cit., p. 549.

[33] This is made clear in the second of the 1671 drafts, known as Draft B. Cf. *Drafts of an 'Essay Concerning Human Understanding' and other Philosophical Writings*, ed. P. H. Nidditch and G. A. J. Rogers (Oxford, forthcoming), Draft B. Section 57.

In *Leviathan*, Part 2, chapter 31 'Of the Kingdome of God by Nature', Hobbes argues that subjects owe sovereigns obedience in all things which are not contrary to the laws of God. Whether they know it or not, Hobbes says, men are always subject to the divine power ('men may shake off their Ease but no their Yoke'). But this requires that men can identify the law of God. This they may do by any of three ways: reason, revelation, and prophecy. With all of this Locke was in full agreement. Further, it has been demonstrated by others that Locke would have agreed with a further claim of Hobbes, that the ground of our obedience to God arises not from our having been created by God, 'but from his *Irresistable Power*'.[34] These divine laws or dictates of natural reason are, says Hobbes, the laws of nature which he has already demonstrated. If these are properly applied by the sovereign power then a truly just society can be created. Hobbes, however, is not very optimistic about the likelihood of it ever happening: 'I am at the point of believing', he tells us, 'this my labour, [is] as uselesse, as the Commonwealth of *Plato*'. The problem is that the ideally just state requires sovereigns to be philosophers, and even though they would not need, as Plato believed, to master mathematics, in order to be able to do the required reasoning, no philosopher hitherto 'hath put into order, and sufficiently, or probably proved all the Theoremes of Morall doctrine, that men may learn thereby, both how to govern, and how to obey.'[35] Hobbes's view was a vision of an ideal society, a notion too rarely acknowledged to be part of his objective. Echoes of that vision, I have suggested, may be detected in Locke's aspirations for a demonstrative system of ethics, and further echoes may be discovered, though we shall not seek them here and now, in his wider moral and political theory.

The possibility of a rational and demonstrable system of ethics, a science of morals and politics analogous to the axioms and theorems of geometry, worked deeply into the consciousness of European philosophers in the seventeenth and eighteenth

[34] Cf. Locke's remark that the reason why a Christian believes he should keep his contracts is 'Because God, who has the Power of eternal Life and Death, requires it of us.' There is now very strong evidence from the study of his theological writings that this remark of Locke's should be taken quite literally. As yet unpublished work by young scholars on Locke of which I have had sight argues the case in detail.

[35] *Leviathan*, 2. 31, ed. cit., pp. 407–8.

centuries. It provided a model and an inspiration for the Age of Reason. If what I have said here is anywhere near the truth, then the sad irony is that perhaps springing from that conversation in Arcetri between two of the greatest intellectual figures of the seventeenth century, the aged Galileo and the admiring Thomas Hobbes, there grew a new picture of the possibility of moral knowledge which even today has the ability to cast a spell. We shall let Hobbes have the last word. At the end of the chapter from which I quoted a little earlier he concludes:

> I recover some hope, that one time or other, this writing of mine, may fall into the hands of a Soveraign, who will consider it himselfe (for it is short, and I think clear) without the help of any interested, or envious Interpreter; and by the exercise of entire Soveraignty, in protecting the Publique teaching of it, convert the truth of Speculation, into the Utility of Practice.[36]

We still await such a reader.

[36] Ibid. 408.

INDEX OF NAMES